RHYTHM AND VIGILANCE

Ethnographies of Surveillance and Time

Edited by
Vita Peacock, Mikkel Kenni Bruun,
Claire Elisabeth Dungey, and Matan Shapiro

BRISTOL
UNIVERSITY
PRESS

First published in Great Britain in 2025 by

Bristol University Press
University of Bristol
1–9 Old Park Hill
Bristol
BS2 8BB
UK
t: +44 (0)117 374 6645
e: bup-info@bristol.ac.uk

Details of international sales and distribution partners are available at bristoluniversitypress.co.uk

British Library Cataloguing in Publication Data
A catalogue record for this book is available from the British Library

ISBN 978-1-5292-4652-0 paperback
ISBN 978-1-5292-4653-7 ePub
ISBN 978-1-5292-4654-4 OA PDF

Cover design: Nicky Borowiec
Front cover image: Alamy/Julia Hiebaum
Bristol University Press uses environmentally responsible print partners.
Printed and bound in Great Britain by CPI Group (UK) Ltd, Croydon, CR0 4YY

Contents

List of Figures

Notes on Contributors

Anders Albrechtslund is Professor in Information Studies at Aarhus University and the Director of the Center for Surveillance Studies. The overall aim of his research is to investigate the role and impact of surveillance in society, especially in relation to digital technologies. The focus is on surveillance technologies in individual and organizational contexts, particularly in the areas of everyday social practices, children's lives, and healthcare.

Stinne Aaløkke Ballegaard is a chief research analyst at VIVE – The Danish Center for Social Science Research. Through ethnographic studies, her research focuses on digitalization and the use of technology in care, exploring ethics, patient experiences, self-care, and the transformation of work. Her latest publication, 'Infrastructuring ethical use of surveillance technology in dementia care', focuses on the collaborative efforts to create safe work practices at nursing homes in Denmark: Ballegaard, Meyer, Dindler, and Albrechtslund (2024, e-pub ahead of print), in *CoDesign – International Journal of Cocreation in Design and the Arts*.

Mikkel Kenni Bruun is a social anthropologist and Research Associate at King's College London. His current work on health monitoring in Britain is part of the SAMCOM project funded by the European Research Council (ERC). He holds a PhD in Social Anthropology from the University of Cambridge, where he also teaches anthropology. He is the author of 'Mental Health' in *The Open Encyclopedia of Anthropology* (2023); '"A Factory of Therapy": Accountability and the Monitoring of Psychological Therapy in IAPT' in *Anthropology & Medicine* (2023); and the co-editor of *Towards an Anthropology of Psychology* (Berghahn, forthcoming).

Claire Elisabeth Dungey is a research fellow at the University of Brighton, and was a postdoctoral researcher at King's College London until 2024. She has a PhD in Anthropology from Aarhus University. Claire is part of the ERC SAMCOM project based at King's where she works on childhood, family relations and digital surveillance in Germany. Her research interests include family relations, mobility, and care, as well as children's future aspirations.

She has recently authored an article titled 'A Bird's Eye View: Care, Control, and the Use of Surveillance Apps Among Family Members in Germany' in the Special Issue 'Beyond the Ideal: Surveillance, Control and Complexities of Care', in *Sociológia* (2024).

Sun-ha Hong's work examines forms of uncertainty, doubt, and (dis)belief around artificial intelligence (AI) and data-driven technologies. He is currently a Fellow at the Stanford Humanities Centre, and previously worked at Simon Fraser University and MIT. Sun-ha is the author of *Technologies of Speculation: The Limits of Knowledge in a Data-driven Society* (NYU Press, 2020) and is currently writing *Predictions Without Futures*.

Karolina Kupinska is a PhD candidate in Anthropology at Xiamen University, China. She holds dual degrees in Sociology and Sinology from Warsaw University, Poland. Her research focuses on the dynamics of educational surveillance within Chinese families.

Kalle Kusk is a PhD candidate at the Department of Digital Design and Information Studies, Aarhus University, Denmark. His work ethnographically investigates the emergence of novel work practices, through the notion of algorithmic management. He has published peer-reviewed articles for the ACM international conference on Supporting Group Work (Kusk and Bossen, 2022) and in the Danish journal for Work Life, *Arbejdsliv* (Kusk, Duus, Hansen, and Floros, 2022).

Alice McAlpine-Riddell is a PhD candidate at University College London. Her research interests include digital anthropology, material culture, safety practices, security and surveillance, and urban anthropology. Her previous publications include an article on the intersecting positionalities and unexpected uses of Citizen app in Brooklyn in the journal *Social Inclusion* (2023).

Vita Peacock is Principal Investigator on the ERC SAMCOM project and Research Associate in the Department of Digital Humanities at King's College London. She received her PhD in Social Anthropology from University College London (UCL) in 2014 and is the author of *Digital Initiation Rites: Joining Anonymous in Britain* (Cornell University Press, forthcoming). Vita is an affiliate member of the Minderoo Centre for Technology and Democracy in Cambridge.

Lake Polan is Teaching Fellow in Anthropology and the College at the University of Chicago. He has conducted fieldwork on the techno-politics of privacy since 2014.

Matan Shapiro is a freelance researcher. This chapter was produced in his post as Research Associate on the ERC SAMCOM project based at the Department of Digital Humanities, King's College London. He received his PhD in Social Anthropology from UCL in 2013, and is the editor of *Crypto Crowds: Singularities and Multiplicities on the Blockchain* (Berghahn, 2024).

Andreas Stoiber is a PhD candidate in Anthropology at the University of Amsterdam, as part of the 'Moving Matters: People, Goods, Power and Ideas' research programme, and an Early Career Researcher at the Eur–Asian Border Lab. His research focuses on the socio-material knowledge practices of Space-Eye members and their use of satellite and maritime surveillance to support civil search-and-rescue missions in the Mediterranean. He is interested in EU surveillance infrastructures more broadly, and his work combines approaches from anthropology, science and technology studies (STS), and border studies.

Acknowledgements

The idea for this collection was seeded in the meetings of the Surveillance and Moral Community (SAMCOM) project, supported by the European Research Council (grant no. 947867). Over long lively hours in our office in the Department of Digital Humanities at King's College London and online, we pored over the minutiae of our respective fieldwork. Temporality, it seemed, was key to how new monitoring technologies were being integrated. This prompted an open call for papers for the first workshop of the project, Times of Surveillance, which took place at King's College London in April 2023. All the contributors of the present volume presented at this event, together with Becky Kazansky, Carolina Sanchez Boe, Martin Webb, Martina Eberle, and Sophia Goodfriend. We would like to thank King's College London for hosting the workshop, Kate Davis and Christele Machut for its organization, and all the speakers and audience members for their enriching reflections.

The workshop slowly transformed from one medium into another, from speech onto page, through a steady back-and-forth with all the contributors, and editorial assistance from Floyd Alexander-Hunt. We were then fortunate to land with the dynamic team at Bristol University Press. We would particularly like to thank commissioning editor Paul Stevens for his instant and unfailing enthusiasm for the project, and to Ellen Mitchell and Bahar Muller for their energetic assistance with production and marketing. We would also like to extend sincere thanks to the anonymous reviewers who helped us to see the book from new angles.

Introduction:
Rhythm and Vigilance

Vita Peacock

The delivery driver in his turquoise livery stops at the red light. He is fidgety, knowing he is not being paid to wait, and glances down at his smartphone to double-check the order. The app calculating his journey time says the food is expected by the customer in 18 minutes. 'Not a chance!', he thinks. His company moped travels fast, but this gusty wind along the beach is slowing him down, and he is on his way to that restaurant that always takes longer. A message on his local driver WhatsApp group pops up. It is a photograph of a newborn with the caption 'Celebrate with us!'. He cannot refuse his friend and tells the app to log him off after the order is complete. As soon as the light turns orange he pulls swiftly away, wondering whether he will still make his savings target this week.

*

Two women meet after work. They have a new tradition of going for cocktails once a month, catching up on each other's urban lives. It is dark outside, but warmly lit within as they sip their technicolour drinks. Mid-sip, an alert appears on one of the women's phone. 'Report of Armed Robbery', it reads, beside a glowing yellow square on a black map of streets just a few hundred yards away. 'Not another one!', she jokes. Beneath the levity, though, a familiar worry settles in her chest about the safety of the neighbourhood she has moved to. Once the drinks are finished, she breezily bids goodbye to her friend, but takes a circuitous route home, stopping in a bookstore open late where she pretends to browse. Her phone trembles in her pocket. Another alert has appeared saying the report turned out to be unfounded. She exits the store briskly, chiding herself for her skittishness, and resolves to delete the app altogether.

*

A map of a sea voyage arrives on Signal. The team, spread across the town in coffee shops, libraries, and home offices, receive it simultaneously on their laptops. It is from a civil search-and-rescue vessel crossing the Mediterranean to evacuate boats in distress. This is their cue. They apply their software to scan the satellite images, to see if there are any boats on the route. After an hour, it finds a match. They all peer closely at their screens, separately, but together. Is that mark on the map a refugee boat or something else? The Signal messages stream. They return to check the satellite images, but that part of the sea is obscured by clouds. They may have to wait a whole day for a clearer sky. One of them sends a message back to the ship's crew informing them. Although the team is thousands of miles away, they feel bound to that mark on the screen by a vision of hope and human survival.

*

Digital monitoring technologies are establishing new configurations of space, time, and movement. Global positioning systems, sensors, QR codes, image recognition, automated alarms and alerts, and platformed reporting, among other forms of digitalized vigilance, are redirecting the momentum of social life wherever they are integrated into it. Each of these imagined scenarios, which point to three of the ethnographies within the book, illustrates some of the new interplays between human bodies, mechanical bodies, computation, communication, and climate that are reshaping digitally mediated worlds in different ways.[1]

The central aim of this volume is to gather some of these changes ethnographically, and through this to modulate our understanding of surveillance. The expansion of surveillance technologies across the twentieth and twenty-first centuries has often been represented by the character of Big Brother in George Orwell's *1984* (1990) – the enigmatic figurehead of a totalitarian state. In response, the term has been reworked by scholars of surveillance to emphasize different kinds of relationships. Disassembling power asymmetries into everyday technological encounters, William Staples ventures the existence of 'tiny brothers' (2014, p 2), documenting small-scale action. In her study of surveillance and capitalism, Shoshana Zuboff meanwhile invites the idea of a 'Big Other', to signal a shift away from human intention altogether (2019, p 20). Elsewhere, Pieter Wagenaar and

Kees Boersma employ the term 'Soft Sister' to describe the surveillance enacted in the name of the welfare (2008, p 193). Within this tradition, and condensing the spatio-temporal shifts documented here, we animate another reimagining of Orwell's character – Big Mother.[2]

As a category of surveillant activity, Big Mother was first used to denote the range of technologies developed to monitor children.[3] The application of GPS-tracking on mobile devices, and the use of nannycams and CCTV cameras in nurseries and playgrounds, appeared to signal a broader departure from a historic vision of surveillance as carceral and punitive, towards another as protective and nurturing. The capacity for care potentiated by surveillance had long been recognized by scholars (Lyon, 1994; Albrechtslund and Lauritsen, 2013), but it was arguably only in the wake of the intense public health surveillance surrounding the COVID-19 pandemic that this quality became more widely acknowledged. The intersection of care and control through surveillance is now a lively topic in many fields of scholarship. In this context, the image of Big Mother has been taken up by theorists to describe the feminization of care technologies (Sadowski et al, 2021; Horsley, 2023), with the aim of enrolling users in ever more surveillance. There, it stands for the deliberate simulation of a soothing maternal archetype, while in practice being something more sinister.

Here we seek to retrieve the term from purely sinister connotations, by drawing on another lineage that precedes even Big Brother himself. In 1927, Frederick Britten Austin composed a novel about the 'Big Mother' who made the earth (1970), inspired partly by James Frazer's depictions of pagan mother goddesses (Gibson, 2014).[4] The earth mother concept continued to reverberate throughout the twentieth century into the neo-pagan and eco-feminist movements of the 1970s, and then James Lovelock's now influential figure of Gaia (Lovelock, 2000; Latour, 2017) – an anthropomorphism of the earth as a self-sustaining system. The salient difference with which we seek to connect, is to consider surveillance not as the constant monitoring of activity, but as the *generator* of activity. We animate Big Mother to anthropomorphize the use of monitoring technologies to manage the rhythms of life. In this definition it is predominantly protentive, rather than retentive.[5] Rather than prosecuting or otherwise acting upon the past, it is a modality that constructs human avenues into the future. In lieu of an apparatus of constant observation, imaged by Orwell's chilling posters of Big Brother, with eyes that follow you around the room, observation in the mode of Big Mother may be episodic. Indeed, in its least invasive forms it is not people, but rhythms themselves that are being monitored. I will return to this below.

Before addressing the questions of time and rhythm at greater length, it is important to clarify two other key terms: 'surveillance' and 'vigilance'. In the field of surveillance studies, surveillance has operated as a more or less expressly political concept, involving the use of information to coerce or control, or in more benign terms to manage or supervise (Ball, 2010; Lyon, 2022). It has also been persistently associated with technology, and with the political consequences that technologies have had, particularly from the nineteenth century onwards (Peacock et al, 2023). Vigilance, on the other hand, is a term more associated with human actors and hence with anthropology, though it shares with surveillance the same Latin root *vigilare* – to keep watch. Anthropologist Henrik Vigh has offered a summary definition of vigilance as an awareness and preparedness for negative potentialities (2011), which involves scanning the present for clues. Vigilance is a pose and a practice that has one eye perpetually upon the future, but through this is constitutive of social relations in the present (Ivasiuc et al, 2022). We do not see a pure distinction between the two terms – what surveillance scholars call human or social surveillance, anthropologists may call vigilance. Hence we incorporate both at different points in the text, to speak to these two readerships at once.

Rhythm

Our ethnographic focus is on the temporal effects of surveillance. In this we begin to correct a tilt towards spatiality at the expense of temporality in the study of surveillance, and converge with a rising wave of interest in the temporal effects of mass computing (Kitchin and Fraser, 2020; Volmar and Stine, 2021; Kitchin, 2023). As several of these scholars observe, however, time is a profoundly elusive concept. St Augustine famously declared in the fourth century that he did not know what time was, and the answer remains enigmatic. One clue to this enigma is buried inside the etymology of the word.[6] 'Time', in English, derives from the Latin *tempus*, which also means weather or season. In French and Spanish, the words for time and season are identical. Through this, time is cognate with temperament, temperature, even tempest – phenomena subject to moderate or violent change. A temporal domain, in contrast to a sacred one, is a space of growth and decay. If time at its most rudimentary equals change, then a contradiction arises. Émile Benveniste argued that the paradox of 'chronic time' – the time measured by calendars and clocks – is that it is in fact 'intemporal' (1965, p 5). Efforts to reify time, to hold it somehow steady, are antithetical to its intrinsic character. Rather than allowing the capacity for change, these efforts exist within the realm of human attempts to control.

A second problem stems from the philosophical legacy of Isaac Newton (1971). In the seventeenth century, the growing presence of mechanical clocks in England inspired a cosmological vision which continues to reverberate. Newton pictured the universe as a giant clock moved by divine hands, creating the theological architecture for his scientific theory of absolute space, time, and motion (Snobelen, 2012). Instead of being related and substantial qualities, in the prevailing Aristotelian paradigm, Newton reimagined space and time as abstract and distinct dimensions. Newton's laws were immeasurably productive for the field of mechanics that they instigated, and the myth of his discovery remains more powerful than ever, with tourists picturing themselves holding apples in front of 'his' tree outside Trinity College, Cambridge.[7] Simultaneously however, they set a trap for generations of scholars studying the human experience, by introducing a false dichotomy between space and time that must be repeatedly transcended. Whether space-times or timescapes, synchronizing or unfolding, the temporal concepts employed in what follows assume the inextricability of this relation.

A valuable critique of the dimensionality that is still imposed on time comes from the anthropologist Don Handelman (2021). Rather than thinking of time as something that naturally flows, Handelman views time as a dynamic that is immanent to form. As he says, citing Jorge Luis Borges, 'Time is the substance I am made of. Time is a river which sweeps me along, but I am the river' (Handelman, 2021, p 314). For Handelman, human temporality is the outcome of the intrinsic time trajectories of substantial and related phenomena. In this vein, his most startling insight is to represent the time of organic life – including but not limited to human life – as intrinsically 'curving' (Handelman, 2021, p 313). The difference between inorganic and organic temporality is then not one of linearity and cycles (see Eliade, 1955), but of *volume*. It is the undulations of decay and renewal, deriving from the need for organic life to reproduce itself, which holds the capacity to create experiences that are, what he calls, 'time-full' (Handelman, 2021, p 291). Meanwhile inorganic temporalities, including but not limited to the digital tools we explore, alone endow the human experience of time with minimal volume. What then becomes critical, when examining the temporal consequences of new forms of surveillance, is their interaction. With this in mind, I turn towards the axial time concept.

In his final book, philosopher Henri Lefebvre advocated for the study of rhythm (2009 [1992]). A scholar better known for his work on space (1991), Lefebvre's short treatise *Rhythmanalysis*, asserts the indissolubility of space, time, and movement. 'Everywhere where there is interaction between a place, a time, and an expenditure of energy', he says, 'there is rhythm' (Lefebvre, 2009, p 15). In this he can be considered the anti-Newton, fusing these coordinates back into relation. For Lefebvre, the principal mediator for these relations is the body, 'living or not' (2009, p 1). This encompasses the human body, with its 'garland' of rhythms (Lefebvre, 2009, p 20), as well as the inorganic bodies human beings have produced, with their own mechanical tempos. Besides bodies, critical for rhythm is repetition: whether at exact intervals such as the thud of a metronome, or irregular repetitions such as seasons or tides. Like Gilles Deleuze (1994), repetition for Lefebvre is never simply replication. Though repeated, every repetitive occurrence takes place in conditions of difference, and therefore possesses the potential to reshape subsequent rhythms. From an anthropological perspective, while not necessarily passive, rhythm is to some degree involuntary. 'To grasp a rhythm it is necessary to have been grasped by it', he stresses (Lefebvre, 2009, p 27).

An eccentric text, since it was first published, *Rhythmanalysis* has been considered somewhat niche; however, interest in its applications has been steadily growing across the social sciences (Edensor, 2010; Chen, 2017; Lyon, 2018; Lange, 2019; Walker, 2021). For this collection, three of Lefebvre's analytical terms become particularly salient. The first is *eurhythmia* – a harmony of rhythm that is the body in its 'healthy' state. Eurhythmia is the result of *polyrhythmia* – the multiplicity and diversity of rhythms – which exist within bodies as well as outside of them. Lastly, the antithesis of eurhythmia is *arrhythmia* – the disruption of rhythm – that at worst can yield a 'fatal de-synchronisation' (Lefebvre, 2009, p 68).

Lefebvre takes a trenchant view of technology, for whom it is better at nurturing ideology than everyday life, that is not necessarily shared here. However, if there were a moral-cum-political conclusion that could arise from this collection, it would be to consider the perennial potential for arrhythmia that arises through the increasing incorporation of temporalities that are, as Axel Volmar and Kyle Stine say, 'hardwired' (2021). In the 2020s, the inhabitants of digitally mediated worlds live in the slipstream of several decades of computational rewiring, infrastructuring an acceleration with the capacity to significantly alter temporal environments. This has created, in their view, a yawning discrepancy between the time that is 'lived' by human beings (Volmar and Stine, 2021, p 10) (what Handelman would call 'time-full'), and the times of these technologies. Ethnographically, however, these can only be understood together. The question for us is, rather – what is gained and what is lost, in structural shifts from mother earth to Big Mother? The chapters open this conversation, by collecting a range of human appropriation and response to the use of digital monitoring to manage the rhythms of life.

Before moving on, it is worth earmarking the work of another scholar influenced by the earlier writings of Lefebvre.[8] In 1967, the historian E.P. Thompson published his celebrated essay on temporal changes in the monitoring of work in the wake of the industrial revolution. Transforming pre-industrial entanglements with organic and ecological rhythms, into new spatio-temporal regimes governed by small and large mechanical clocks, Thompson established an ongoing discussion about monitoring, time, and social control, which he theorizes with the language of 'discipline' (Thompson, 1967).[9] Although the essay contains notes of a developmental teleology that is belied by the optics here, it remains an important early contribution to understanding the intersection between surveillance and time.[10] Just ten years later, however, another idea of discipline was conceived, that would shape the study of surveillance for the next quarter-century.

Space and time in surveillance studies

At its moment of inception, surveillance studies was anchored by a spatial image. The panopticon – or more accurately panopticons – were a series of architectural designs produced in the nineteenth-century by English social reformer Jeremy Bentham. The designs proposed building asymmetries of visibility into the spatial configurations of institutions, in order to create behavioural conformity among their occupants, by way of uncertainty about whether they were being surveilled or not. It was in the second significant life of these designs, however, as they were taken up in the work of Michel Foucault (2019), that they exerted their most significant effects on scholarship. This was propelled partly by Foucault's own suggestion that the panopticon be viewed, not simply as an architectural plan, but as a model for a whole imaginary of modern power. While analyses of temporality were present in his work (Lilja, 2018; Portschy, 2020), his move to centre the panopticon prioritized the disciplining effects of space, rather than the transformations in time that had been foregrounded by Thompson. Many of the field's first major works were oriented, implicitly or explicitly, around this image (Gandy, 1993; Lyon, 1994; Mathiesen, 1997).[11] The panopticon travelled particularly well in the context of proliferating CCTV programmes (Norris and Armstrong, 1999). The installation of cameras in public areas from the 1980s onwards rehearsed and remediated these asymmetries, in ways that were consistent with Foucault's proposal.

This characteristic spatiality in the study of surveillance reached an apotheosis around the turn of the millennium. In 2001, the landmark exhibition *Ctrl+Space* went on display in Karlsruhe, Germany, its catalogue published the following year (Levin et al, 2002). A double entendre on the rising control being exerted on certain forms of space, and the role of computing in enabling it, many of its artworks and essays critically examined the effects of camera surveillance on public spatial imaginaries. Because of the indissolubility of space and time, however, they frequently found their way towards attendant shifts in temporality.

Beatriz Colomina's case study in the catalogue is particularly instructive (Colomina, 2002). Colomina describes and theorises the installation 'Glimpses of the USA', at the American National Exhibition in Moscow in 1959. Conceived by art partnership Charles and Ray Eames, the installation consisted of seven 20 ft × 30 ft screens, each showing separate scenes of everyday life in America to their Russian audiences. A reimagination and reversal of the optics of the military control room, the exhibition was among the first to fragment and multiply spatial perspectives through the use of audiovisual reels. While this kind of multiscreen vision has now become commonplace, as users of today's computers and smartphones navigate seamlessly between different windows, in the 1950s this was a radical departure. Yet while it visually fragmented space, it simultaneously fragmented time, as viewers were shown different temporalities as well as different spatialities at once. What then became paramount was flow. As she says, 'Perhaps we can no longer talk about "space", but rather about "structure", or more precisely, about time. Structure for the Eames' is organisation in time' (Colomina, 2002, p 335). The couple were meticulous about the timing of each performance. Each 45-minute showing was minutely choreographed to appear effortless and noise-free. In other words, what came to matter most when space and time were multiplied and pulled apart, was their spatio-temporal reassembly in the bodies of the audience: in Lefebvre's terms, rhythm.

An important exception to this spatial tilt, arrived with William Bogard's *The Simulation of Surveillance* (1996). Bogard argued that even by the 1990s, the historic modality of surveillance was already being superseded. Simulation – in which he includes profiling, gaming, cybernetics, and other kinds of monitoring that rely on modelling – was becoming hegemonic. He argues that where surveillance still maintains a relationship to the real, namely the subject of surveillance, simulation ultimately unhooked itself from subjects, in the final analysis maintaining a relationship only to itself as an imaginary of total control. Bogard sees the difference between surveillance and simulation as temporal. 'Simulation is about the imagination of the "future past", about protecting a future as something already over, ultimately about mastery over time' (Bogard, 1996, p 34). Surveillance in its Foucauldian form was a matter of monitoring the unfolding of life as precondition to political intervention. By contrast, simulation was, 'Full front-end flow control ... simulation instead guarantees to surveillance apparatuses certain flows in advance ... hyper scanned envelopes that wrap around the observer and generate all possible flows' (Bogard, 1996, p 44). Political intervention then becomes a matter of creating certain kinds of flows, while cutting off the potential for others.

Bogard's argument presages the growing role of surveillance as a protentive practice, one that anticipates what is coming next. Many of the forms of digital monitoring explored in this book are artefacts of simulation. We might then ask, does the programmed future, as one which is 'already over', serve to evacuate the time-fullness of those engaging with those forms of digital monitoring? Is it, as Genosko and Thompson argue (2006), that in contracting the temporal horizon they separate their users from understanding, and proliferate fragmented lives? There is certainly ethnographic evidence to support this. As one user of the American live crime app Citizen says, 'I will not go live [to enter a real-time engagement with the app] I want to *live*' (Alice McAlpine-Riddell, Chapter 5, this volume). Living – being in time – and going live – living in the simulated present – are conceived as conflicting. The only way to live is to switch off. This being said, most of the ethnographic subjects take less absolute positions. Either for their convenience, or because they are involuntary mediators of citizenship or labour, many of the engagements documented are framed by what Astrid Meyer, Stinne Aaløkke Ballegaard, and Anders Albrechtslund, following Annemarie Mol, describe as 'tinkering' (Chapter 3, this volume). They consist of human endeavours to make the time trajectories of the technologies work with and towards the rhythms of organic life – to minimize the potential for arrhythmia. I will now identify some of the shared temporalities that are attending the growth of digital monitoring: the extended present, the remembered past, and interruption, before returning to renewal and the role of vigilance over rhythm.

The present

It has been observed by ethnographers and other social scientists, that new monitoring technologies perpetuate a logic of the present. This has been called a 'hyper now' (Barassi, 2020, p 1548), an 'infinite present' (Zuboff, 2019, p 337), or an 'extended present' (Bergroth, 2019, p 199). Yet assessing what the present consists of ethnographically is far from straightforward. For some theorists it is a space of liberation. Exploring the coordinated destruction of clocks in the 1830 July Revolution in Paris, Walter Benjamin introduced the concept of the now-time (*Jetztzeit*) as a moment of revolutionary possibility (1973). Similarly, New Age thinkers consider 'the now' as a time of pure freedom, the ultimate realization of self (Tolle, 2001). On the other hand, those influenced by Karl Marx, particularly Jean Baudrillard, are often critical of concepts of the present, which can be conceived as the ultimate achievement of capitalist time-space compression (Harvey, 1990). In this tradition, Lefebvre considers the present to be entirely distinct from, and moreover antagonistic to, the actual unfolding of 'presence' (2009, p 47). While 'the present simulates presence and introduces simulation (the simulacrum) into social practice ... presence is *here* (and not up there or over there). With presence there is dialogue, the use of time, speech and action' (Lefebvre, 2009, p 47). In other words, while presence is embedded in rhythm, the present imitates this while remaining outside of it.

It is significant to note that the present is a living temporal discourse in Silicon Valley, where many of these technologies are developed. Deep inside a mountain in Texas, a timepiece is currently being constructed called 'The Clock of the Long Now', partly with financial backing from Amazon founder Jeff Bezos. The Clock is several hundred feet tall and designed to measure time accurately for at least ten thousand years, during which it will be powered by solar energy, as well as the movement of those it is intended to attract as a site of pilgrimage. In the vision of those building it, the Long Now is a 20,000-year span of technical evolution beginning with the invention of agriculture and ending with the digital revolution. By contrast, the Now is just three days long: yesterday, today, and tomorrow. At least symbolically, the Clock is continuous with Thompson's examples of the use of clocks as control technologies – the mastery of Time over time – that serves to reinforce and reproduce existing economic asymmetries. In his analysis of the project, Sun-ha Hong argues that through the Clock and its associated ideological schemes, 'We are confronted with the closure of possible worlds and temporalities to the one and only kind of progress' (Hong, 2022, p 374), namely, that of Silicon Valley companies themselves. In its materialization of one kind of temporal imaginary, the Clock of the Long Now is particularly useful at shedding light on the narrow and immobile temporal horizon that many of these technologies call forth. The question for us is – how is this horizon being experienced and negotiated by those using them?

A particularly distributed new form of sociotechnical rhythm is explored by Kalle Kusk (Chapter 4) – platform-mediated food delivery. Platforms such as Deliveroo, Uber Eats, or Bolt operate upon a logic of near-instantaneity, using GPS-monitoring apps installed on employees' smartphones to calculate exact delivery times from the point of order. What Kusk outlines, however, is a general misfit between space-time as simulated by the app – the product of GPS coordinates and algorithmic calculations – and time as experienced by riders themselves. Restaurants may be slow to make the food, there may be traffic or even road closures due to sporting events, all of which must be spontaneously navigated by the riders, who are not paid for their time but on completion of delivery. The result is, Kusk argues, another kind of work that makes this work possible – 'time work' (Flaherty et al, 2020). Time work means not only finding ways of adapting to or outsmarting the app, by cultivating relationships with restaurant workers, or finding ways to entertain themselves while waiting; but also, when necessary, subordinating work to other events in their lives. One pleasant effect reported by some, of the immediacy of employment instigated by logging on, was that they did not need to give notice for absences. Although without the security of an imagined linear future, this kind of time work may hold greater capacity to make space for human life cycle events. One evening in Malta, a number of drivers spontaneously log off their apps to go to a campsite and celebrate the birth of a new son.

Andreas Stoiber and Alice McAlpine-Riddell (Chapters 5 and 6) further complexify the actual temporal dynamics of present-oriented technologies, in different contexts of real-time mapping. Stoiber describes the endeavours of the German non-governmental organization (NGO) Space-Eye, to use satellite imaging of the Mediterranean to support civil sea-rescue missions.

Like Kusk, Stoiber emphasizes the new forms of work that arise in conditions of purported immediacy. The challenge Space-Eye employees face is to synchronize multiple temporal rhythms – which in this case means neural network modelling, satellites and drones, and the organizational temporalities of humanitarian work beyond the state – to locate and assist refugee boats. Stoiber reinforces theories of acceleration (Sharma, 2013), by showing how the politics of speed often structures real-time monitoring in conditions of unequal resourcing. In a different setting, McAlpine-Riddell demonstrates the chimerical quality of the real time among users of the American live crime app Citizen. Citizen combines police information with user reporting to map events potentially harmful to public safety such as fires, shootings, accidents, or even protests. In an illustrative case of simulation as a time out of time, McAlpine-Riddell notes the asynchronous way in which news is transmitted, as she and her interlocutors receive updates at different times, and posts sometimes remain on the map for a month after their occurrence. Faced with repeated disjunctures between real time and the lived space-times of their neighbourhoods, many users simply switch off.

An orientation towards the present can also mean inhabiting a temporality of radical uncertainty. In Chapter 9, Matan Shapiro explores the world of Non-Fungible Token (NFT) collectors in London, and their efforts to identify and exclude dishonest actors. NFTs are based on blockchain technology: the creation of distributed ledgers that produce a total transparency of financial transactions, to obviate monitoring by third parties. The paradox Shapiro uncovers, however, is that when a form of monitoring becomes digitized, in this case the historic monitoring conducted by financial institutions, it may itself necessitate the creation of new forms of vigilance, both in-person and digitally mediated. In this unfolding temporal domain, in which one is never certain whether one is corresponding with an honest actor or a 'scammer', the spaces of exchange where NFT communities gather assumes a heightened importance. These can be online forums such as Reddit threads or Discord channels, where collectors post experience and advice, or simply a shared table in a London pub where members attend to unusual behaviour. Shapiro characterizes this temporality as one of play, in which end results and symbolic meanings are unknown. 'Playtime' is time without the stability of repetition. In Lefebvre's terms, it is thus in some sense outside of, or most likely before, new settlements of social rhythm.

The remembered past

Scholars have shown how the history of monitoring in a given region can influence how new forms of monitoring are received (Samatas, 2005; Frois, 2013; Boersma et al, 2014). How do located memories exert a temporal 'force' (Handelman, 2021, p 306) of the past upon the present, in ways that condition temporalities of citizens or (would-be) users? My ethnography of privacy and data protection advocates in Germany demonstrates the persistent spectre of fascism in framing their political concerns. These mobilizations have, since the 1970s, been critical of making human beings 'machine-readable' – legible to the mechanisms of computing – criticism which involves, directly or indirectly, the role of registration and computing in the Holocaust. Analytically, the chapter traces another historical spectre behind this one, that of the registration systems that attended the making of the modern world. From the eighteenth century onwards, registration of enslaved persons and labourers entailed a 'double fix' – the fixing of identity along biological lines, which accompanied the fixing of labour to land. Through this I introduce a conception of these historic modalities of surveillance (that, is before the Bogardian shift) as 'fixing'. Like other intemporal technologies, colonial and post-colonial registration systems, right up to the mid-twentieth century, operated through reifications that were antagonistic to change. In response, today's German privacy advocates offer a way of thinking about privacy in relation to digital monitoring as 'unfolding' (*Entfaltung*). A word which possesses organic meanings, this discourse and imagery relocates human beings within the natural world of which they are a part (Marx, 1995).

Karolina Kupinska (Chapter 7) demonstrates the indelible mark left by the severe acute respiratory syndrome (SARS) 2003 epidemic in mainland China, which significantly accelerated the response to the first wave of COVID-19. By May 2020, schools were reopening through the use of 'Health Codes' – individual QR codes on users' digital devices that categorized their relative health risk. The health code, as one that delimited a person's movement, produced its own temporalities in numerous ways, such as the clock-based 24/48/72 status, indicating the number of hours since the user's last polymerase chain reaction (PCR) test. Unlike most of the other forms of digital monitoring in this volume, health codes in China were involuntary. Just as the memory of SARS expedited the speed of their introduction, the direct equation between digital monitoring and the Chinese state subsequently introduced a dramatic sear in the temporal fabric two years later. In December 2022, the health code era abruptly ended with the end of the zero-COVID policy. The effect of this centralized rupture, as Kupinska records it, was to open up the temporal horizon for Chinese citizens into spaces of spontaneous navigation.

Interruption

Many of the digital monitoring technologies explored are described by their own creators as disruptive. Meta's chief executive officer Mark Zuckerberg famously declared that the company's early mantra was to 'move fast and break things'. But what precisely was being broken? Martin Holbraad, Bruce Kapferer, and Julia Sauma (2019) argue that the concept of rupture to which disruption is cognate, is an artefact of linear temporality that is specifically Christian. We might think of rupture as linear time's modality of renewal, and thus a subcategory of broader cosmologically specific rhythms that can take different expressions (Kublitz, 2019). 'Ruptures are moments at which value emerges through a break with something', they argue (Holbraad et al, 2019, p 1). In the context of Silicon Valley, this hegemonic value is expressly economic, and arises through breaking apart existing forms of time-fullness to make space for technological need. Lake Polan's ethnography of corporate privacy engineers in San Francisco offers an insight into this dynamic. In a recurring cycle of solicitation, seduction, and betrayal, Polan shows how the makers of these technologies seek self-consciously to get close to users in their initial stages. There is an endeavour by the makers to align 'their respective temporal rhythms', forcing entrepreneurs to feel users' feelings as their own. Whereas in Stoiber's Chapter 6 these efforts towards eurhythmia are framed by the goal of rescuing refugee boats, here rhythm is captured with the ultimate aim of being transformed into shareholder value.

If disruption may be considered not just Meta's temporality, but a meta-temporality of these technology companies, interruption would be its microsocial iteration. The programming of alerts, alarms, and notifications makes microbreaks in the temporalities of users. Sometimes these may be necessary, prompting human beings absorbed in other tasks to respond to physical threat, crisis, or ill health. Citizen app is a tool, nominally to allow Americans to cope with rising violence and other physical dangers in the American public sphere, by placing 'panic buttons' at their fingertips. Similarly in Meyer, Ballegaard and Albrechtslund's Chapter 3, GPS-trackers, motion sensors, and door alarms are integrated into tablet alert systems in Danish nursing homes, to protect the bodies of elderly dementia patients. However – a phenomenon widespread in alert media – the ubiquity of false alarms can desensitize users, and in these settings a 'timely response' may mean ignoring the alarm altogether. In Chapter 1, Mikkel Kenni Bruun illustrates that while often mediated by new forms of self-monitoring, the temporality of interruption need not purely be digital. Ideas of 'checking in' with oneself appear across health-oriented practices in Britain and beyond, where bodies and minds are constituted as objects of continuous self-monitoring and self-reflection. This strikes a pronounced contrast with other kinds of healing practices that are characterized by ritual absorption.

Watching over rhythm

While the spread of digital monitoring has generated new rhythms, and reconfigured those that already exist, human efforts to resocialize these landscapes constitute a form of vigilance *over* rhythm. Rob Kitchin and Alistair Fraser's invitation to slow down computing (2020) is a particularly apt example. Faced with the acceleration of time infrastructured by increasing computational speed, the human experience of time, they argue, echoing scholars above, becomes fragmented and compressed. Drawing on an article which references the slow-living movement from the 1980s onwards (Schneider, 2015), Kitchin and Fraser assemble an array of individual and collective moves that decelerate relationships with digital technology in various ways. Although their abiding metaphor is for slowness as an alternative to acceleration, it is significantly one that recognizes the importance of switching speeds. Echoing Lefebvre's reference to music, there is not only one tempo, they remind us. 'What we are advocating for is a new way of moving', they offer (2020, p 16). There have been a number of prominent efforts to this end. The French 'right to disconnect' policy allows employees to negotiate times in which they are offline, reintroducing modulation into working life. Elsewhere, the microblogging platform Mastodon eschews asynchronous newsfeeds in favour of a chronological timeline. In other words, achieving eurhythmia, a harmony of rhythm, itself requires vigilance.

In Chapter 2, Claire Elisabeth Dungey's ethnography of GPS-monitoring among families in Germany shows how this form of vigilance may be gendered. Mothers in Munich use location-monitoring apps like Life360, Find My iPhone, or Google Family Link to manage the labour of multiple forms of vigilance by watching over rhythms instead. While a dot moving along a simulated map when a child is expected to be walking home from school denotes normality, a dot that stays still for too long in one place may be considered a warning sign and prompt a phone call. Alongside their children's rhythms of travelling to and from school, they may watch over rhythms of media use, or set alerts for themselves to do domestic tasks. In these busy family lives, the smartphone becomes a central tool in the management of polyrhythmia. It is a place where schedules, school timetables, after-school activities, and even their husbands' routines can be brought into relation — and consequently supervision. Dungey also demonstrates how children in these environments are learning to use digital devices the same way. One young girl tracks her exercise routines, her piano playing, and even brushing her teeth, using a 'routine app' to establish and monitor patterns of self-care and self-cultivation.

As Handelman (2021) observes, one of the major differences between organic and inorganic life is that the former must reproduce itself to persist through time. It should not be surprising that one of the most popular and fast-growing sectors of digital monitoring in Europe and the US is FemTech: technology tailored to women's health, of which the highest usage is oriented around reproduction and contraception (Statista, 2024).

New datafications of the so-called Rhythm Method, resituate the cycles that sustain human life across generations within new political economies. Although now taking digital form, FemTech extends the deep history of calendars and other devices to watch over patterned occurrences – whether of seasons, floods, harvests, and so on – that sustain or harm conditions for human life (Peters, 2015). A point of continuity between old and new lies in its visuality. Watching over rhythm requires an image – whether in the mind, on the screen, on paper, or on the walls of a cave – of what that rhythm often looks like. As Bruun's ethnography with fitness and mindfulness practitioners in Britain demonstrates, watching over the vital rhythms of the self entails ideas about what that self consists of, which vary across place and time. Forms of normitivization, such as inherited assumptions about the 28-day menstrual cycle (Clancy, 2023), can also arise when rhythm becomes reified.

In summary, this volume illustrates some of the changes that digital monitoring is ushering into everyday lives, without considering the everyday as a special kind of domain. Rhythmic shifts across multiple materialities and scales, into new polyrhythms of inordinate complexity, emerge as the current time trajectories of the historical encounter between human beings and their creations. Big Mother is not necessarily watching you, but she may be shaping the conditions within which your life unfolds.

Summary of the book

The intersection between surveillance and time is addressed in all of the following chapters. What the substantive chapters likewise share is the use of ethnographic methods – deep and often extensive engagements with human beings – mostly drawing on the field of anthropology but also sibling social sciences. In some chapters, the optic of rhythm comes directly to the fore. In others, it is a background note against which other time concepts are placed. The book is organized into three parts: Care and Wellbeing; Real-Time Monitoring; and Systems Past, Present, and Future; and succeeded by an Afterword. Each of these themes ricochets across the book but is particularly concentrated in the chapters within the relevant part.

Part I, 'Care and Wellbeing' opens with Mikkel Kenni Bruun's study of fitness and mental health advocates in the UK. Bruun shows the increasing importance that monitoring has in the pursuit of physical and mental health, in which, through Fitbits and other devices, basic biological functions and even thought patterns become the object of observation. He historicizes this as the contemporary descendant of ocularcentric logics of medicine and psychology that have become hitched to new forms of self-surveillance and embodied vigilance. Next, Claire Elisabeth Dungey discusses the use of geolocation tools by parents in Munich, Germany, to monitor the movements of their children. Dungey documents the range of attitudes towards these technologies among different family members and emphasizes maternal use. Here Big Mothers, vigilant over temporal patterns, take concrete form. Astrid Meyer, Stinne Aaløkke Ballegaard, and Anders Albrechtslund conclude the section with a study of the gamut of digital monitoring tools being used in nursing homes in Norway and Denmark. They argue that through them, the lives of dementia patients are subsumed within simulated fantasies of total safety, and subsequently, to hopes for optimized futures in Scandinavian welfare systems.

Part II, 'Real-Time Monitoring', starts with Kalle Kusk's ethnography of food delivery workers in Denmark and Malta. Kusk demonstrates the extent to which real-time monitoring is foundational to how new forms of work are being organized. As workers wrestle with algorithms to manage the flow of deliveries, Kusk offers that time itself becomes an object of work that can be managed more or less effectively. Next, Alice McAlpine-Riddell explores real-time monitoring in the use of Citizen by residents of New York City. She takes a trenchant view of what the app in practice delivers. For McAlpine-Riddell, Citizen engenders the hyperreal, replacing space-times with a fractured virtuality that can disrupt and disturb more salubrious rhythms. Then, Andreas Stoiber introduces us to the world of automated satellite surveillance by German NGOs, who seek to support search and rescue missions in the Mediterranean. Stoiber shows the sheer scale and complexity of organic and inorganic temporalities that must be coordinated to make monitoring work. Lastly, Karolina Kupinska documents the use of health codes in Xiamen, China, by middle-class residents during the COVID-19 pandemic. She explores the temporal ruptures instituted by interlocking grids of surveillance in four dramaturgical acts, all while being routinized into everyday living. In China, health monitoring becomes a 'group responsibility' that binds families and strangers together.

In the final part – 'Systems Past, Present, and Future' – and the Afterword, the book drills deeper into some of the structural forces that are inviting new intersections between surveillance and time. In my ethnography with a range of privacy advocacy groups in Germany, I show how privacy is conceived not as something proprietorial, but as a space of indeterminacy, in which what is at stake is the very capacity to grow and change. Matan Shapiro then chronicles meet-ups of NFT traders in London. Shapiro argues that the absence of centralized oversight creates a new labour of hypervigilance in environments saturated with suspicion. Finally, Lake Polan offers context for why anticipation itself has become a site of conflict. Through his work inside Silicon Valley start-ups, he demonstrates the claims upon the future that are intrinsic to their growth trajectories, in which consumers are perpetually betrayed by the infrastructuring of surveillance to the modern internet. Sun-ha Hong closes the volume with a synthetic discussion of the drive for efficiency, one that has sought to make human beings more like the machines they wield. When motivated by capital accumulation, the imposition of linear rhythm can become a form of violence that bends and breaks bodies into contorted shapes. The paradox that Hong presents is that ever more intensive rationalization does not produce greater predictability, but greater volatility. The capacity to reclaim rhythm – to anticipate and to socialize what comes next – thus ultimately emerges as a political task. In the context of growing digital monitoring globally, it is those commanding these tools – whether workers or citizens, consumers, companies, or nation states – who may be more likely to determine the rhythms to come.

The chapters collect ethnography carried out within the current geographic category of the Global North. We should at this point emphasize that this is not to assert that monitoring in the mode of Big Mother is not taking place all across the Global South, and we welcome the development of the argument in these regions. This being said, it is equally important not to project a false evenness onto the production and consumption of digital technologies. Digital divides continue to matter very much, both within the North, but particularly in enduring historically constituted differences between North and South, as remote or less industrialized areas, with only partial access to electricity or the internet, are less likely to be venues for protentive digital monitoring. On the other hand, in the places where digital infrastructures *are* deeply embedded, the studies in this volume offer but a small snapshot of large-scale transformations. Whether these will be the space-times of the future depends, as ever, on the human beings around them.

Notes

[1] Kalle Kusk, Alice McAlpine-Riddell, and Andreas Stoiber advised on the plausibility of these scenarios.

[2] The Big Mother concept was further developed in conversation with the co-editors.

[3] Rouse (2011), Mance (2013), Hanlon (2016). A number of references have also been made by the Big Brother reality television franchise, which bear a direct relation to motherhood. In 2005, the Greek Big Brother series introduced a new format in which contestants appeared with their mothers. An expanded definition of Big Mother has recently been offered by DevX (2023).

[4] This lineage can be extended further back into Johann Bachofen's study of goddess worship (2005), which exerted an influence on Frazer.

[5] See Hui (2021) for a further elaboration of protention and its relation to digital media.

[6] For further detail see Peters (2015, p 244).

[7] The apple tree that stands outside Trinity College, was grafted from a descendant of the tree at his Lincolnshire manor that reportedly inspired Newton to develop his theory of gravity. The original was, elliptically illustrating some of the theoretical statements around change advanced here, blown down by a gale in the nineteenth century.

[8] Thompson cites Lefebvre's *Critique of Everyday Life* (1958), with reference to the difference between cyclical and linear time.

[9] The word 'rhythm' appears at a number of points throughout Thompson's essay, usually to refer to the temporalities distinct from the world of clocks. Indeed, the transition from task-orientation to clock-time that Thompson maps can also be comprehended through

the prism of rhythm. Indeed, from the perspective of labourers themselves, what was at stake was less a categorical transformation – tasks remained enduringly significant – but rather a new rhythm of work in which the mechanical tempos of clocks assumed a more prominent role.

[10] At one point Thompson displays some of his historical biases, expressing confusion that, 'The mother of young children has an imperfect sense of time and attends to other human tides. She has not yet altogether moved out of the conventions of "pre-industrial" society' (1967, p 79). Seeing the time that envelops the earliest forms of human life as 'imperfect' misconstrues one of the most developmentally significant stages of the human life cycle.

[11] For a classic critique of the panoptic model, see Haggerty (2006). Haggerty describes a number of theoretical limitations that have been imposed on the study of surveillance through the panoptic imaginary. Its temporal dimensions can be added to his list; although see Birnhack (2023) for a recent turn in surveillance studies.

References

Albrechtslund, A. and Lauritsen, P. (2013) 'Spaces of Everyday Surveillance: Unfolding an Analytical Concept of Participation', *Geoforum*, 49 (October): 310–16.

Austin, F.B. (1970) *When Mankind was Young*. Freeport, NY: Books for Libraries Press.

Bachofen, J.J. (2005) *An English Translation of Bachofen's Mutterrecht (Mother Right) (1861): A Study of the Religious and Juridical Aspects of Gynecocracy in the Ancient World*. Lewiston, NY: Edwin Mellen Press.

Ball, K. (2010) 'Workplace Surveillance: An Overview', *Labor History*, 51.

Barassi, V. (2020) 'Datafied times: Surveillance capitalism, data technologies and the social construction of time in family life', *New Media & Society*, 22(9): 1545–60.

Benjamin, W. (1973) 'Theses on the Philosophy of History', in H. Zohn (trans.) *Illuminations*. London: Fontana, pp 253–64.

Benveniste, E. (1965) 'Language and Human Experience', *Diogenes*, 13(51), pp 1–12.

Bergroth, H. (2019) '"You can't really control life": dis/assembling self-knowledge with self-tracking technologies', *Distinktion: Journal of Social Theory*, 20(2): 190–206.

Birnhack, M.D. (2023) 'The Temporal Dimension of Surveillance', *Surveillance & Society*, 21(4): 393–408.

Boersma, K., Van Brakel, R.E., Fonio, C., and Wagenaar, P. (eds) (2014) *Histories of State Surveillance in Europe and Beyond*. London: Routledge.

Bogard, W. (1996) *The Simulation of Surveillance: Hypercontrol in Telematic Societies*. Cambridge: Cambridge University Press.

Chen, Y. (2017) *Practising Rhythmanalysis: Theories and Methodologies*. London, England; New York: Rowman & Littlefield International.

Clancy, K. (2023) *Period: The Real Story of Menstruation*. Princeton, NJ: Princeton University Press.

Colomina, B. (2002) 'Enclosed by Images: Architecture in the Post-Sputnik Age', in T.Y. Levin, U. Frohne and P. Weibel (eds) *Ctrl [Space]: Rhetorics of Surveillance from Bentham to Big Brother*. Karlsruhe and London: ZKM, MIT Press, pp 322–37.

Deleuze, G. (1994) *Difference and Repetition*. London: Athlone Press.

DevX (2023) 'Big Mother', DevX. Available from: https://www.devx.com/terms/big-mother/ (Accessed: 26 February 2024).

Edensor, T. (ed) (2010) *Geographies of Rhythm: Nature, Place, Mobilities and Bodies*. Farnham: Ashgate.

Eliade, M. (1955) *The Myth of the Eternal Return*. London: Routledge & Kegan Paul.

Flaherty, M.G., Meinert, L., and Dalsgard, A.L. (eds) (2020) *Time Work: Studies of Temporal Agency*. New York: Berghahn Books.

Frois, C. (2013) *Peripheral Vision: Politics, Technology, and Surveillance*. Oxford and New York: Berghahn Books.

Foucault, M. (2019) *Discipline and Punish: The Birth of the Prison*. Translated by A. Sheridan. London: Penguin Books.

Gandy, O. (1993) *Panoptic Sort: A Political Economy of Personal Information*. London: Routledge.

Genosko, G. and Thompson, S. (2006) 'Tense Theory: The Temporalities of Surveillance', in D. Lyon (ed.) *Theorizing Surveillance: The Panopticon and Beyond*. Cullompton: Willan, pp 97–122.

Gibson, M. (2014) 'Melting the Ice Gods: The Creation and Destruction of Old and New Gods in British Fiction, 1880–1955', *Preternature: Critical and Historical Studies on the Preternatural*, 3(2), pp 339–66.

Haggerty, K.D. (2006) 'Tear Down the Walls: On Demolishing the Panopticon', in D. Lyon (ed.) *Theorizing Surveillance: The Panopticon and Beyond*. Cullompton: Willan, pp 23–45.

Handelman, D. (2021) *Moebius Anthropology: Essays on the Forming of Form*. Edited by M. Shapiro and J. Feldman. New York: Berghahn.

Hanlon, P. (2016) 'Worried About Big Brother? Wait Until You See Big Mother', Forbes. Available from: https://www.forbes.com/sites/patrickhanlon/2016/05/13/worried-about-big-brother-wait-until-you-see-big-mother/ (Accessed: 26 February 2024).

Harvey, D. (1990) *The Condition of Postmodernity: An Enquiry into the Origins of Cultural Change*. Cambridge, MA, and Oxford: Blackwell.

Holbraad, M., Kapferer, B., and Sauma, J.F. (eds) (2019) *Ruptures: Anthropologies of Discontinuity in Times of Turmoil*. London: UCL Press.

Hong, S. (2022) 'Predictions Without Futures', *History and Theory*, 61 (3): 371–90.

Horsley, J. (2023) *Big Mother: The Technological Body of Evil*. London: Aeon Books Ltd.

Hui, Y. (2021) 'Problems of Temporality in the Digital Epoch', in A. Volmar and K. Stine (eds) *Media Infrastructures and the Politics of Digital Time: Essays on Hardwired Temporalities*. Amsterdam: Amsterdam University Press, pp 77–88.

Ivasiuc, A., Dürr, E., and Whittaker, C. (2022) 'Introduction: The Power and Productivity of Vigilance Regimes', *Conflict and Society*, 8(1): 57–72.

Kitchin, R. (2023) *Digital Timescapes: Technology, Temporality and Society*. Cambridge: Polity.

Kitchin, R. and Fraser, A. (2020) *Slow Computing: Why We Need Balanced Digital Lives*. Bristol: Bristol University Press.

Kublitz, A. (2019) 'The Rhythm of Rupture: Attunement among Danish Jihadists', in M. Holbraad, B. Kapferer, and J.F. Sauma (eds) *Ruptures: Anthropologies of Discontinuity in Times of Turmoil*. London: UCL Press, pp 174–92.

Lange, P. (2019) *Thanks for Watching: An Anthropological Study of Video Sharing on YouTube*. Boulder: University Press of Colorado.

Latour, B. (2017) *Facing Gaia: Eight Lectures on the New Climatic Regime*. Translated by C. Porter. Cambridge: Polity.

Lefebvre, H. (1991) *The Production of Space*. Translated by D. Nicholson-Smith. Oxford: Blackwell.

Lefebvre, H. (2009 [1992]) *Rhythmanalysis: Space, Time and Everyday Life*. Translated by S. Elden and G. Moore. London: Continuum.

Lefebvre, H. (2014 [1958]) *Critique of Everyday Life*. Translated by J. Moore and G. Elliott. London: Verso.

Levin, T.Y., Frohne, U., and Weibel, P. (eds) (2002) *Ctrl [Space]: Rhetorics of Surveillance from Bentham to Big Brother*. Karlsruhe: London: ZKM; MIT Press.

Lilja, M. (2018) 'The Politics of Time and Temporality in Foucault's Theorisation of Resistance: Ruptures, Time-lags and Decelerations', *Journal of Political Power*, 11(3): 419–32.

Lovelock, J.E. (2000) *Gaia: A New Look at Life on Earth*. Oxford: Oxford University Press.

Lyon, D. (1994) *The Electronic Eye: The Rise of Surveillance Society*. Cambridge: Polity Press.

Lyon, D. (2022) 'Surveillance', *Internet Policy Review*, 11(4). Available from: https://policyreview.info/concepts/surveillance (Accessed: 6 October 2024).

Lyon, D. (2018) *What is Rhythmanalysis?* London: Bloomsbury Publishing.

Mance, H. (2013) 'Big Mother is Watching You', *Financial Times*, 28 August. Available from: https://www.ft.com/content/0dc2109c-0fbc-11e3-99e0-00144feabdc0 (Accessed: 11 March 2024).

Marx, K. (1995) *Capital: An Abridged Edition*. Oxford: Oxford University Press.

Mathiesen, T. (1997) 'The Viewer Society: Michel Foucault's 'Panopticon' Revisited', *Theoretical Criminology*, 1(2): 215–34.

Newton, I. (1971) *Sir Isaac Newton's Mathematical Principles of Natural Philosophy and His System of the World*. Translated by A. Motte. Berkeley, CA: University of California Press.

Norris, C. and Armstrong, G. (1999) *The Maximum Surveillance Society: The Rise of CCTV as Social Control*. Oxford: Berg.

Orwell, G. (1990) *Nineteen Eighty-four*. Harmondsworth: Penguin Books.

Peacock, V., Bruun, M.K., Dungey, C.E., and Shapiro, M. (2023) 'Surveillance', *The Open Encyclopedia of Anthropology*. Available from: http://doi.org/10.29164/23surveillance (Accessed: 6 October 2024).

Peters, J.D. (2015) *The Marvelous Clouds: Toward a Philosophy of Elemental Media*. Illustrated edition. Chicago, IL: University of Chicago Press.

Portschy, J. (2020) 'Times of Power, Knowledge and Critique in the Work of Foucault', *Time & Society*, 29(2): 392–419.

Rouse, M. (2011) 'Big Mother', *Techopedia*. Available from: https://www.techopedia.com/definition/15390/big-mother (Accessed: 6 October 2024).

Sadowski, J., Strengers, Y., and Kennedy, J. (2021) 'More Work for Big Mother: Revaluing Care and Control in Smart Homes', *Environment and Planning A: Economy and Space*, 56(1), pp 330–45.

Samatas, M. (2005) *Surveillance in Greece: From Anticommunist to Consumer Surveillance*. New York: Pella.

Schneider, N. (2015) 'The Joy of Slow Computing', *The New Republic*, 19 May. Available from: https://newrepublic.com/article/121832/pleasure-do-it-yourself-slow-computing (Accessed: 12 January 2024).

Sharma, S. (2013) *In the Meantime: Temporality and Cultural Politics*. Durham, NC: Duke University Press.

Snobelen, S. (2012) 'The Myth of the Clockwork Universe: Newton, Newtonianism, and the Enlightenment', in C.L. Firestone and N. Jacobs (eds) *The Persistence of the Sacred in Modern Thought*. Notre Dame, IN: University of Notre Dame Press, pp 149–84.

Staples, W.G. (2014) *Everyday Surveillance: Vigilance and Visibility in Postmodern Life*. Second edition. Lanham, MA: Rowman & Littlefield Publishers, Inc.

Statista (2024) 'Global Femtech Market Size 2030'. Available from: https://www.statista.com/statistics/1333181/global-femtech-market-size/ (Accessed: 8 January 2024).

Thompson, E.P. (1967) 'Time, Work-discipline, and Industrial Capitalism', *Past & Present*, 38(1): 56–97.

Tolle, E. (2001) *The Power of Now: A Guide to Spiritual Enlightenment*. London: Yellow Kite.

Vigh, H. (2011) 'Vigilance: On Conflict, Social Invisibility, and Negative Potentiality', *Social Analysis*, 55(3): 93–114.

Volmar, A. and Stine, K. (eds) (2021) *Media Infrastructures and the Politics of Digital Time: Essays on Hardwired Temporalities*. Amsterdam: Amsterdam University Press.

Wagenaar, P. and Boersma, K. (2008) 'Soft Sister and the Rationalization of the World: The Driving Forces Behind Increased Surveillance', *Administrative Theory & Praxis*, 30(2): 184–206.

Walker, G.P. (2021) *Energy and Rhythm: Rhythmanalysis for a Low Carbon Future*. Lanham: Rowman & Littlefield Publishers.

Zuboff, S. (2019) *The Age of Surveillance Capitalism: The Fight for a Human Future at the New Frontier of Power*. New York: PublicAffairs.

PART I

Care and Wellbeing

1

Watching Our Selves: Fitness and Mindfulness as Practices of Self-Monitoring in Britain

Mikkel Kenni Bruun

Introduction: An inverted gaze

> If you could all please check in [referring to the digital screen on the wall]. Now, we are also going to check in with ourselves. We will move in stages through the body, in micro-movements of observation. Scan your body from head to toe. Scan your mind. You are taking a mental note of your body and mind, of yourself: what are your thoughts, feelings, and needs today? Just watch yourself without judgement.
>
> (Mindfulness session, April 2022)

Surveillance can impart an understanding that others are observing and watching. It is a concept enmeshed in ocularcentric ideas: the all-seeing eye, the few observing the many, the state of being seen and inspected. The very notion of surveillance conjures for many an 'Orwellian' world in which one becomes visible before a hostile gaze (Peacock et al, 2023). This chapter explores an inverse scenario of surveillance in which people watch themselves. The short opening vignette of this chapter offers a glimpse of a human capacity to do so, which is now taken for granted in many parts of Europe and elsewhere, where 'health' is actively sought. Everyday acts of observing oneself can be seen to extend quite broadly now in Britain; I refer here to such practices as modes of self-monitoring.

The empirical material on which this chapter draws was gained through anthropological fieldwork in the UK, carried out among mental health and fitness advocates and practitioners.[1] As part of the fieldwork, I attended digital health conferences and mental health workshops that promote monitoring technologies in the form of smartphone apps and wearable devices. I attended yoga classes and mindfulness courses, and became an avid gym-goer. My fieldwork thus involved some mode of 'auto-ethnography'. I wore a self-tracking watch (Fitbit) for over two years, and used several mental health and fitness apps; and I immersed myself as much as possible in 'online communities' on social media that advocate, and form part of, these activities. The details presented in this chapter are considerably condensed from this fieldwork. In the following paragraphs, I highlight two contexts – fitness and mindfulness – where self-monitoring is enacted in the pursuit of health, albeit, as we shall see, in rather different ways. I use these ethnographic contexts to suggest that self-monitoring constitutes 'health' as a particular temporal object, as people are learning to keep 'it' in check under a vigilant gaze. At the same time, particular notions of selfhood come into view.

We might take ethnographic note from the outset that 'vision' features as an ideal central to practices of monitoring. The state of being able to see also figures more broadly as a conceptual language in academic disciplines, influenced by ideas inherited especially from the Enlightenment, with 'light' as a condition for the clear-eyed, scientific vision – what historians of science have called 'epistemologies of the eye' (Daston and Galison, 2007). Much has already been written about the historical, political, and aesthetic preoccupations with spectatorship, sight, and vision in surveillance studies and in anthropological studies of science (see, for example, Lynch and Woolgar, 1990; Goodwin, 1994; Lyon, 1994; Grasseni, 2009; Frois, 2013).

In this chapter, I focus on two interrelated modes of seeing: one that invites an anthropology of surveillance to examine practices of 'watching over ourselves', and one that seeks to hold this very vision of our 'selves' up for ethnographic inspection.[2] In what follows, the surveilling gaze has, in an important sense, been inverted – turned inwards – as we are increasingly encouraged and required to watch our selves.

Health monitoring and the body-self

While efforts to monitor ourselves and others are not historically new, what is novel about present-day practices of monitoring is the highly technoscientific and digital forms they assume. Over the past two decades, digital self-tracking has become increasingly more common as an everyday practice of self-monitoring. Indeed, digital technologies have transformed the very mode of self-monitoring, replacing diaries with digital watches for instance. Scholars in digital humanities and related fields have explored various aspects of digital self-tracking, with a focus especially on the politics of digital culture and data sharing, and the quantification of health and bodies (see, for example, Gregory and Bowker, 2016; Neff and Nafus, 2016; Ajana et al, 2022; Kent, 2023). Although social anthropology has been a relative latecomer to these debates, there are notable ethnographic accounts of self-monitoring in contexts of healthcare and everyday life (see, for example, Lynch and Cohn, 2016; Trnka, 2016; Ruckenstein, 2022; for a review, see Nim, 2019). There have also been calls from within surveillance studies to examine 'how the self is enacted, negotiated and maintained in an environment of increasing and elaborate tracking' (Timan and Albrechtslund, 2018, p 854). While self-tracking has become an established area of research in the social sciences, ethnographic treatment of the 'self' at the centre of monitoring is often absent.

A few general points on the history of monitoring in Britain are important to highlight.[3] Practices of what we might now want to recognize as 'health monitoring', have historically played a key role in constituting not only surveillable spaces and times, but also visible and measurable persons who were ideally reflexive and accountable selves. It is primarily through the development of European medicine (particularly anatomy and epidemiology) and the 'psy' disciplines (psychoanalysis, psychology, and psychiatry) that we have inherited certain salient models of human corporeality and interiority (Danziger, 1997; Robb and Harris, 2013). It was for instance within 'the clinic' in the historiography of madness, as outlined by Foucault (1973, 1988), that the 'inner life' of the person was constituted as an object of observation and intervention.[4] Genealogies of selfhood in Europe (Rose, 1989; Taylor, 1989; Danziger, 1998; Vidal, 2011) have since traced the formation of the psychological subject – the individuated self, comprised of emotions, thoughts, and behaviours, complete with reflective consciousness, intention, and choice – as the constitution of a particular vision of human interiority. Ethnographically, many people now perceive and talk about such an interiority as a matter of 'mental health' (Bruun, 2023b).

In many parts of the world, the category of health is constituted around the twin discourses of mental health and physical health, with disciplinary divisions and specialisms wrought between notions of 'the body' and 'the mind'. The bifurcation of the human into the mental and the physical, the psychological and the physiological, took shape within specific historical circumstances in Europe, influenced by new ideas and regulations of boundaries and bodies in the early modern period, the practice of anatomy from the seventeenth century onwards, and the rise of the psy sciences in the nineteenth and twentieth centuries. With new scientific objectivities (Daston and Galison, 2007) and the formation of the welfare state (Fraser, 1984), bodies were further reified as objects of 'hygiene' and 'health', which could be intervened upon not only medically with drugs or surgical instruments, but also through social and psychological interventions. By the twenty-first century, all the changes in understandings of bodies effected by anatomy and medicine (McDonald, 2014) – with practices of dissection, opening up bodies, cutting and seeing, and a range of attendant biotechnologies – have rendered bodies amenable to observation in particular ways. Concurrently, a range of human interiorities – whether construed as 'the mind', 'the psyche', 'the unconscious', 'personality', or 'subjectivity' – were problematized as observable and measurable, not only in clinical settings but in schools, prisons, the military, and the family, thereby 'inventing our selves' (Rose, 1996). New technologies of introspection (Coon, 1993) were crucial in standardizing and making visible and workable this human subject.

We can note an important connection here between the invention of new observational technologies in the twentieth century, and the development of 'psy' technologies of the same period – both assume an otherwise hidden subject that becomes available for inspection. Psychological practices of inspection and introspection informed a new conceptual and material order of observing and of being observed. And vice versa: technologies of surveillance appeared to confirm assumptions about concealment and opacity intrinsic to human psychology. In the wake of two world wars, health monitoring in Britain was reinforced by the possibility of technological mass observation (Malinowski, 1938) to build a 'strong' and 'healthy' nation and economy – a vision that was key to the foundation of the National Health Service (NHS) in 1948 (Foot, 1975; Busfield, 1998). Through new regulatory structures in public health, disease prevention, healthcare provision, and other innovations owed in part to epidemiological science, the monitoring of 'national health' was constituted more generally as a matter of health *surveillance*. During the twentieth century in Britain, then, the monitoring of publics and populations, and of the private self, emerged as mutually constitutive modalities.

When we leap into the twenty-first century, the proliferation of digital monitoring technologies reflects broader trends in contemporary British public health, which has seen a rapid increase in digitalization of health surveillance. In 2013, for example, NHS Digital was launched as the central regulatory body of the monitoring for public health data in the UK. The effects of the COVID-19 pandemic have further intensified practices of digital health surveillance, as well as offered a moral rationale to justify them. Health monitoring now extends across the NHS in a way that not only involves operational observation through recording and checking but constitutes new practices of 'datafication' that provide and regulate digital services, which in turn produce clinical and economic accountabilities (Ruckenstein and Schüll, 2017; Hoeyer, et al, 2019). The extensive use of health monitoring technologies – in settings ranging from hospitals, clinics, and care homes to gyms, workplaces, and households – has encouraged this vision of digitalization and datafication, and is also a product of it.[5]

Fitness and monitoring: becoming a healthy body

Gyms and fitness classes are important settings in which health and wellbeing are sought through self-monitoring. These are also contexts wherein the body of the gym-goer is shaped by, and aligned with, prevalent understandings of what a healthy body should look and feel like. Becoming a healthy body demands specific proprieties in relation to time, as 'health' emerges as a particular temporal phenomenon that must be kept in check, constantly and vigilantly.

During one conversation with James, a self-tracker I got to know through a running group, he describes how wearing a digital watch allows him to watch himself. He compares health monitoring through his Fitbit watch to a 'second pair of eyes'; one that enables him to observe his progress, not only in the gym and during exercise, but more generally in life. 'I can't sleep without my watch', he says laughing, 'you see, tracking my sleep patterns is essential to how I go about my day and prepare for the next sleeping phase.' He explains how getting just the right amount of sleep – not too little but not too much either, 'about 7–8 hours' – is one of the most important factors, together with a varied diet and exercise, to becoming a healthier, stronger self. 'Not only do we build muscles during sleep, but we also process our stresses and worries, our emotions and thoughts', he explains. 'If you want to look after your body, you have to be good at managing time well.'

On this and other occasions, users of Fitbits and similar devices align the notion of a healthy body and mind with a capacity to monitor time. It is therefore common to talk about health as a matter of routines and habits. One has to cultivate habits of working out, consistently over time, with 'rest days', 'meal prep', and 'sleep' all part of the weekly schedule. Healthy routines are perceived to be a result of a disciplined ability and willingness to make use of time in a particular way. People in turn talk about digital monitoring technologies as a means to facilitate self-discipline. 'My clients often object that they don't have enough time to work out', Erica, a gym instructor and health coach, says. 'But everyone's got time, you've just got to manage your time better.' She explains that this is where wearables like Fitbit come in useful, showing your progress, nudging you to go to bed at consistent times, drink enough water, walk enough steps, and so on. For Erica, it is an important tool of time management.

When using self-monitoring watches like Fitbit, people learn to pay attention in particular ways to what their body-self is made of. Self-tracking devices display a range of colourful diagrams, statistical graphs, and other visual representations, based on the user's 'health data'. Multiple bodies are generated and brought together in the digital interfaces of these technologies, through a broad range of representational features from animated stats, point scoring, and other numerical depictions, to encouraging slogans, emojis, and images. Using smartwatches to monitor health means being able to 'make sense of all the data' that the device generates. 'It takes discipline and time', we are told in the fitness classes. We are invited to understand discipline as 'consistency over time', with the implication that through continuous and consistent practice one cultivates a disciplined relation to one's body and mind which leads to a healthier life. We are learning to develop and maintain 'routines' as an essential component of self-monitoring. 'Health' is thus bound up with notions of time and its enactment. Becoming a healthy body means becoming a timely body.

However, 'becoming a healthier self' is not simply a case of 'applying' technology to an end. Rather, healthy body-selves emerge as constantly in the making. Health is conceived as a distinctly temporal phenomenon. 'Being healthy *is a journey*', James stresses in our workout sessions, 'you are on a fitness journey to become the best version of yourself'. He elaborates: 'Of course, we all have certain health goals – gaining or losing weight, getting stronger, feeling mentally well, etc – but it's really the journey that matters. Keeping ourselves healthy takes continuous effort and time.' Comprehending health as laborious means that the language of 'patience' is not uncommon either as people strive to attune themselves to specific vital rhythms.

In anthropological terms, becoming a healthy body can be understood as a dynamic process of learning to embody, and be affected by, a particular 'environing' world (Toren, 2019). Bodies and their surroundings co-constitute one another. The material training environment of the gym, including all the environing technologies – from the heartbeat-tracking smartwatch to the calorie-tracking app – are shaping, quite literally, the bodies they simulate. The body of the gym-goer must in turn render itself amenable to the corporeal technologies ('gym equipment' for instance) that surround it. Over time, the person acquires a particular body-self shaped by the conceptual and practical engagements with machines, movements, and mirrors; and by wearable devices, fitness apps, protein shakes, weights, meals, and a range of other working objects – all of which become part and parcel of what it means to be healthy.[6] As in other areas of skilled learning (Grasseni, 2009; Latour, 2004; McDonald, 2014), this involves an affective engagement of all environing bodies, both those physically present in the gym, and those digitally and visually mediated by health technologies.

Mindfulness and monitoring: being (in the) present

Practices of watching – whether through digital technologies, exercises or therapeutic techniques – invite people to monitor their selves in particular ways. Self-monitoring necessarily reifies 'the self' as an object of observation. Paying attention on purpose to the workings of 'the body' and 'the mind', is commonly experienced as a caring activity. For those practising 'mindfulness' – and many do – this is already a familiar practice of watching, in which one learns to cultivate a particular 'detached' perspective on thoughts, feelings, and bodily sensations. Mindfulness is offered as a psychological therapy in England through NHS Talking Therapies (Bruun, 2023a), but is also practised in a variety of ways outside clinical contexts (Cook, 2023), in everyday circumstances of self-care for instance, wherein the cultivation of 'mindful awareness' through meditative exercises, breathing techniques, and body scans is considered to have a positive impact on the practitioner's wellbeing. Several mental health apps recommended by NHS England promote mindfulness (mobile apps like Headspace and Be Mindful), and smartphones like the iPhone have inbuilt mindfulness features. Mindfulness-based smartphone apps are typically designed to remind and encourage users to practise mindfulness through guided meditations and reflective breathing exercises – 'mindful minutes' – throughout the day. These apps are often used in tandem with courses and sessions that form part of a person's health routine, as part of yoga classes for instance.

In one mindfulness course, we are invited to participate in 'guided meditations' as one of the central techniques for improving mental health. Mindfulness meditation is also presented in more general terms as a way of learning to 'be more present in your life'. We are assigned various exercises that form part of our homework between sessions. We are told that it is through continuous practice that we can begin to develop 'a healthier relationship with ourselves', through 'cultivating a new way of observing our "thinking mind"'. In the first of eight sessions, we are introduced to the therapists who will lead them. Two instructors are clinical psychologists, and the third is a nurse who recently qualified as a mindfulness therapist. Marie, one of the psychologists, begins: 'Mindfulness is very uncomplicated, you can do it anytime and anywhere. It is a way of thinking and a way of being.' She goes on to describe how mindfulness means paying attention in the present moment, 'attentionally and non-judgmentally'. In this course, as in other mindfulness workshops I attended, the instructors tell us that mindfulness is about realising that 'thoughts are just thoughts: I have thoughts, but I am not my thoughts'.

Drawing on particular strands of East Asian Buddhist philosophy (see McMahan, 2008; Cook, 2023), mindfulness as a mental health practice teaches a notion of selfhood which is not reduced to, or composed of, the 'thoughts' or 'cognitions' that are seen to pass through a 'thinking mind'. Thoughts are described through spatial metaphors as people learn to attend to them like 'clouds in the sky'. Clouds come and go; they are ever-changing. During these sessions, we are gradually introduced to exercises that affirm how, although one might experience the mind as having thoughts, 'it' – the mind – is not its thoughts. Rather, thoughts, like clouds, can be observed. This requires the position of the self as a 'detached observer', we are told; people are encouraged to see their thoughts as merely 'mental events', as opposed to 'a reflection of the self'. Marie continues, 'We can watch our thoughts, acknowledge them compassionately, and then gently let them go'. Through this metaphorical language of watching passing clouds, participants progressively learn to see thoughts, in Marie's words, as 'not really real'.

Negative thoughts are, by contrast, the product of the 'auto-pilot mode' of a mind out of sync: the fearful, insecure, lazy, perfectionist, or self-deprecating parts of a person perceived to have emerged somewhere during one's life course. Being caught up in thoughts is frequently explained as an effect of a 'doing mode' of mind as opposed to a 'being mode'. We are learning then to 'be' with our thoughts, feelings and sensations, rather than 'do' them (for example, reacting to, or acting on, negative thoughts).

Mindfulness practitioners describe negative thoughts as 'internal critics', and it is through learning to practise a decentred perspective, observing intentionally and non-judgementally, that one will eventually be able to recognize thoughts as *just thoughts* – as experientially distinct from a sense of self. As we reach 'the head' in these guided meditations, we are asked to observe our thoughts with 'detached curiosity', to just allow them to be there – 'it is OK: I have thoughts, but *I am not* my thoughts', Marie repeats – watching our negative thoughts pass by like clouds and finally disappear. When participants describe themselves as 'having a thought' in these terms, they are experientially confirming an important model of mind implicit in mindfulness practice: thoughts are distinct from the mind; they are not 'real expressions of who you are'.[7]

In other sessions, they guide us through meditative exercises to 'sense' different body parts through 'mindful breathing' and 'mindful attention', travelling from the feet on the ground to the top of our heads – a technique sometimes referred to as 'the body scan'. As we are 'scanning' each body part, the therapist 'guides' us to distance ourselves from any 'worries' and 'distracting thoughts', by reminding us to constantly bring our attention back to breath: 'Once again, if you notice your attention wandering, just make a mental note of where it's going … and when you do that, just very gently, then, bring your attention back to this moment as you are sitting here.'

The therapists remind us that breathing is with us all the time, even though we may not be aware of it. They instruct us to 'focus on the breath', and if the mind is felt to wander off, 'bring your attention back to it like an anchor'. Marie's colleague adds, 'when our mind is very active or we feel anxious and depressed, we can always bring our attention back to our breath, and thus become aware of ourselves'. A healthier body-self is thus felt to come into view through modes of deliberate and watchful observation ('mindful awareness'). 'Breathing' underlines the inherently temporal dimension of this mode of self-monitoring.

In all of this, through what one of the teachers described as 'micro-movements of observation', we are simultaneously taught to keep the self under control. In the mindfulness sessions, as in the digital spaces of mindfulness apps and online programs where similar practices of self-care are enacted, 'the self' must be kept in check. Those practitioners who go on to progress through these sessions, gradually come to embody new sensibilities of detachment, which some see as the source of a renewed engagement in the 'immediacy of life' (Cook, 2015, p 220). For many people, practising mindfulness, after all, is about learning to be (in the) present. 'Mindful moments' must therefore also be understood, in an important sense, as an embodied practice of watchfulness or vigilance. The self-monitorial ideal that guides mindfulness turns on the possibility of experiencing the rhythm of life itself as a matter of careful observation.

Attuning to vital rhythms

In the training environment of a gym, bodies are shaped by different temporal rhythms through varied practices of self-observation and self-inspection. A broad range of monitorial media are consulted, both 'analogue' and 'digital'. Videos, images, and texts on social media like Instagram and TikTok show users how to live a healthy life: how to manage time, develop good routines, how to exercise, what to eat, when to eat, when to sleep and how much. They show how bodies should move, feel, and look like (or not), and much else besides (see Kent, 2023).

James tells me that I need to rest more in the squat position, 'Drink your morning coffee like this', he says, demonstrating the position. 'Just 10 minutes of squatting a day will do', he suggests. 'You see, it's the natural resting position of the human body.' Others are informed they need more 'natural light', going outside straight after waking up to 'kick-start your natural body-clock'. In a workshop on better sleep and how to boost energy levels, Erica teaches how getting enough natural daylight has a profound impact on our 'Circadian rhythm'. She elaborates, 'Exposure to sunlight in the morning (even on cloudy days as we live in England) helps set your Circadian rhythm for a healthy day'.

People also engage in non-digital modes of self-tracking, using pen and paper for instance, in tandem with digital technologies, plotting food data into calorie-tracking apps while their watches count steps and heartbeats. At the gym, both analogue and digital technologies of recording take the shape of journaling and note-taking to track routines and to write exercises or 'gym sets'. All these technologies – watches, apps, wearables, journals, diaries, and so on – condense their own temporal trajectories. As people move through various contexts of watching over their body-selves, from the gym to the mindfulness class, they are learning to attune themselves to a range of temporal rhythms afforded by these monitoring practices. People often explain how they are learning to 'listen' to their bodies and minds, often in new ways. Colourful displays of physiological and mental states at once reify and make intelligible 'the body' and 'the mind' comprised of structures and functions, patterns, and flows. Sleeping, eating, walking, thinking, and breathing, emerge as quantifiable and visualizable activities through which, by means of careful, day-to-day monitoring, one can adapt to 'the body's natural needs'. People speak about this kind of self-monitoring as inherent to the achievement of a healthier life. Health is, in other words, achieved through ongoing efforts to align oneself with vital rhythms.

'Getting healthy and fit' is a gradual process of not only learning to inhabit the environment of a gym or fitness class, but also becoming attuned to the temporalities of tracking technologies that are seen, in turn, to align with a 'natural' temporality of the human body. Some report how their self-tracking watch aids healthy sleeping patterns, by waking up and going to bed at the same time – consistently, over time. 'It's time to get ready for bed!' is the daily evening reminder from the watch, as it generates sleep patterns based on the data collected during the wearer's sleeping and waking hours. Such prompts, and the general technological assistance with 'self-discipline' that people seek, rely on the user's disciplined and consistent use of the watch, wearing it while sleeping for at least 14 days a month, preferably over several months. A circularity of data and discipline is apparent in these monitorial endeavours, where one must exercise particular temporal proprieties. One must remember to wear the watch daily, charge it regularly, sync it to the app, self-report when prompted, and so on, in order for the technology to collect enough health data which then in turn produce visual representations of the body–self.

Digital health apps require a range of visual, tactile, and often auditory sensorial engagements on the part of the user. Users are therefore learning to be affected by the app's 'environment of expected use' (Bluteau, 2021), as much as they are required to cultivate particular engagements of their own body–self – through walking, rest and sleep, exercise, meditation, and eating. We can speak here, as many scholars of self-tracking have done, about a 'quantified self' (Gregory and Bowker, 2016; Lupton, 2016; Nim, 2019), owed to the technoscientific movement of the same name, and the quantification of bodies in health more generally (Ajana et al, 2022). But there is more going on besides. Apart from quantifying bodies in all sorts of ways, these digital products increasingly offer new ways of *qualifying* the data that the technologies generate. The monitorial watch warrants the reality of a particular model of the body and mind that is already built into the design and operation of the device. This quantification–cum–qualification of our selves involves a deliberate rendering of data into a symbolic and experiential value that is ideally both culturally and morally meaningful to the users. In other words, the watch devises, very literally, people's apprehension of their bodies, of themselves. People simultaneously acquire a particular body–self which experientially confirms the value and validity of the watch and its vital rhythms.

Time and health: objects of control?

The person who strives to live a healthy life is now increasingly encouraged to wear a watch that watches over them. They are encouraged to practise new habits and routines that are seen to make for a healthier life; to eat, exercise, sleep, think, and be in particular ways, attuning to rhythms that promise to transform them for the better. Much of the persuasiveness of digital health monitoring, lies in the technology's promise to optimise the present and future life of its user. Self-tracking watches claim to enable the user to monitor a range of 'bodily' and 'mental' functions. The digital watch, worn around the wrist, capable of monitoring heartbeats and skin surface temperatures, thus underlines a contemporary imperative of everyday vigilance in the pursuit of health goods.

Monitoring technologies must be temporally coordinated with the time cycles of the bodies they assert to watch over. The wearer and the watch are engaged in an ideal act of constant synchronising, which can fail at any time, as body and technology intervene on each other. Thus, bodies are themselves made to cohere with the temporalities of 'human life' presupposed and produced by the device. A technology like Fitbit at once assumes and extends a capacity on the part of the user to 'know' and 'manage' their health. In the process, people's body-selves are constituted as 'always-emergent temporal objects' in which monitoring 'easily develops into a highly systematic and repetitive practice of attaining an empowering experience of control that nevertheless always "'flows away'"' (Bergroth, 2019, p 204).

Yet digital health monitoring may help articulate people's health concerns where these are felt to be muted, offering care for the bodies involved. While not devoid of issues, it is important to highlight that self-monitoring technologies can enable users to achieve epistemic 'certainty', within healthcare contexts where medical uncertainties and inequities prevail. For example, situated within the digital health movement of the Femtech (female technology) industry, menstrual tracking apps have recently become a matter of anthropological enquiry (Ford et al, 2021; Ho, 2023). Sarah Ho has shown how, in what she calls feminist data-imaginaries, personal health data generated by period tracking apps emerge as the solution to medicine's entrenched biases against women in therapeutic encounters. Indeed, the very promise of more Femtech products and the data they will produce are considered to 'free women from "medicine designed for men", improving the state of knowledge of women's health while offering women increasingly personalised care' (Ho, 2023, p 31). Health is also here being sought through disciplined self-monitoring over time, and turns on the possibilities of constituting time itself – the (a)rhythmic periods of a menstruating body – as an object of monitoring.

Despite empirical differences, health-tracking and mindfulness practices have both gained traction as wellbeing-orientated activities within a cultural and conceptual reality that values careful self-observation on the part of the individual person. Health is understood in both contexts as an effect of ongoing, disciplined practice. The traction of mindfulness lies not only in the scientific framework it has established for itself as a psychological therapy and a mental health practice – although not without contention and problems[8] – but in its broader metaphor of life as a matter of being (in the) present. A particular temporality of care emerges here that can be seen to complement the use of digital self-tracking devices, wherein both health and time are construed as objects of control. The person engaged in these modes of self-monitoring is encouraged to cultivate an almost activist approach to health, within a now common discourse of resilience and management that finds ethnographic expression in a language of 'self-care'. In the process, health is constituted temporally through everyday acts of watching over – whether in mindful moments of observing thoughts and body scans, or in the corporeal movements and habits of a body whose full potential lies ever in the future.

A vigilant self and two modes of seeing

We live in a world where body-selves have been historically invented and reinvented through practices of surveillance, and in which new digital monitoring technologies are cementing certain visions of health. Self-monitoring is now part of many people's daily health regimen as everyday activities of eating, sleeping, work, and recreation have become objects of observation, shaped by ambitions to promote personalized forms of health surveillance. In this chapter, I have explored some aspects of contemporary self-monitoring in everyday contexts of care wherein a healthier life is actively sought. The two contexts of care discussed here – fitness and mindfulness – offer an empirical vantage point from which to anthropologically grasp subtler features of a monitorial imperative that many people in Britain and elsewhere now live by. This is not, however, a case simply of Foucauldian governmentality, although biopolitics has not gone away either. Ethnographically, for many people engaged in everyday self-monitoring, what is at stake is a healthier, happier life.

Acquiring a body-self that has learned to practise new rhythms of sleeping, eating, exercising, and being mindful takes discipline and time – and self-monitoring is now at the heart of what it means to be healthy. In anthropological terms, we might understand this kind of self-monitoring as a distributed process of learning to observe. Yet observation is itself an embodied practice that relies on eyes that 'know' how to watch, and 'eyes that are only knowing in the right place' (Candea, 2008, p 209). Watching our selves can thus be understood as a dynamic process of learning to be affected by, and hence 'see', connections between a wide range of data, diagrams, numbers, colours, statements, images, and other visual representations, including the very rhythms they claim to represent, which are only significant to those who have acquired a vigilant gaze.[9] Vigilance comes into being here as the embodiment of self-monitoring.

Part of the appeal that digital health monitoring has for many people lies in the technologies' visual representations of the user's interiority, and their power to explain a range of apparently indiscernible psychological and biological 'functions' that are seen to make up who we are. The persuasiveness of these digital technologies to render a putatively hidden interiority discernible and workable, owes a great deal to the historical developments of a 'scientific vision' and technologies of visualization in science and medicine (Daston and Galison, 2007; Coopmans et al, 2014). There can be a danger in losing sight of other ways of articulating health and wellbeing, however. As we have seen, self-monitoring is inherently reliant on a notion of the human as an individuated, self-contained subject bounded by the skin, comprised of emotions, behaviours and thoughts ready for inspection. This model of the self comes with an assumed human capacity and willingness to observe, and be observed. Put differently, health monitoring hinges on our ability and readiness as humans to make ourselves observable, workable, and recognizable in particular ways in the world we live in and share with others.

In his fictional tale about Nietzsche and Freud, the psychiatrist Irwin Yalom famously noted 'the horror of living an unobserved life' (1992, p 55). He describes the therapeutic virtue of living an observed life, of being watched by an other. Observation takes here the form of psychoanalysis, as a therapeutic practice that brings psychological relief when one becomes a subject of the surveillant gaze. Despite the specifically psychoanalytic significance of (and 'obsession' with) observation that Yalom narrates, an anthropology of surveillance might note a not dissimilar imperative of our present times to live an observed life. Living is, of course, inherently temporal. The monitoring of the rhythms of life is therefore also about the possibilities and promises of constituting time itself as an object of vigilance. Health monitoring emerges here as an entanglement of care and control (Peacock et al, 2023): it can figure as a mechanism of enforcement or self-governance, for instance, yet also offer a life-sustaining, caring practice that can be extended to self and others.

Finally, watching our selves is also an analytical exercise in learning to see twice. An empirically self-aware anthropology of surveillance invites us to examine practices of watching over ourselves, at the same time as we watch our 'selves' emerge as objects of ethnographic inspection. At the heart of self-monitoring lies an elusive self that is always in the making. It is nevertheless a self that must be kept in check under a vigilant gaze. We will, it seems, be watching our selves for some time yet.

Acknowledgements

I owe special thanks to all those who allowed me to observe and participate in their health activities. I would also like to thank Vita Peacock and Claire Elisabeth Dungey for their helpful comments on an earlier version of this chapter. The research on which this paper draws was funded by the European Research Council under the European Union's Horizon 2020 research and innovation programme (grant no. 947867).

Notes

[1]   The main period of full-time fieldwork was carried out between 2022 and 2023 in Cambridgeshire and Greater London. This project received ethical approvals by research ethics committees in the European Research Council (ERC) and King's College London.

[2]   'Holding up for ethnographic inspection' is a phrase owed to Maryon McDonald (1986, p 344).

[3]   In addition to Foucault's often-cited history of panopticism (1991 [1975]), more recent histories of surveillance include Higgs (2004); Ball et al (2014); and Browne (2015). The work of sociologist David Lyon (see, for example, 1994) has been particularly instructive in surveillance studies. For an introduction to the anthropology of surveillance, see Peacock et al (2023).

[4]   It is important to note that Foucault, and many of those cited in this chapter, are dealing mostly with the genealogy of the 'western' subject. There are, of course, other histories and formations (see, for example, Reyes-Foster, 2018, on selfhood and madness in Mexico; Fanon, 1963, on the 'psycho–affective' consequences of colonization in Africa).

[5]   When studying health monitoring in English-speaking societies, 'technology' tends to be understood as an artificial or computational system, machinery or equipment, and it is common for the 'technological' to be seen and comprehended in opposition to a notional 'human' or 'nature'. We should not take this division and related dichotomies for granted. That is to say, the people under study may well hold theories about themselves and the world in which they live that reify and confirm, in discourse and practice, a division of human and technology, nature and culture, body and mind, and so on; such dualities are ethnographically interesting to the anthropologist. At the same time, we can expand the concept of 'technology' analytically, to encompass a range of practices, bodies, and artefacts (Mol et al, 2010; Behrent, 2013) – from the analogue to the digital – and their systematization.

[6]   For ethnographic studies of mobile health (mHealth), see chapters in Hawkins et al (2024); on the 'digital health self' in the context of social media, see Kent (2023).

[7]   The mindfulness therapists I met often discussed a human propensity to conflate thoughts with the self in this way. In my previous research on mindfulness as a psychological therapy practised in the NHS, a separation of thinking from a sense of self was also what patients found most difficult to achieve in practice (see Bruun, 2019). Some psychologists and anthropologists have theorized mindfulness and related practices as a case of 'metacognition' (thinking about thinking) with interesting results (see chapters in Proust and Fortier, 2018; on mindfulness, see Cook, 2023). However, the language of metacognition can also be seen to reify its own moral topography of selfhood (Bruun, 2018).

8   There are important ethical, clinical, and cultural critiques of mindfulness as a mental health practice; see, for example, Ratnayake and Merry (2018); Van Dam et al (2018); Britton and Lindahl (2019); McKay (2022).

9   I am thinking here with a varied anthropological literature on skilled vision (Goodwin, 1994; Grasseni, 2009), distributed cognition (Hutchins, 1995), and bodies that are learning to be affected (Latour, 2004; McDonald, 2014).

References

Ajana, B., Braga, J., and Guidi, S. (eds) (2022) *Quantification of Bodies in Health: Multidisciplinary Perspectives*. Bingley: Emerald Publishing.

Ball, K., Haggerty, K.D. and Lyon, D. (eds) (2014) *Routledge Handbook of Surveillance Studies*. London: Routledge.

Behrent, M.C. (2013) 'Foucault and Technology', *History and Technology*, 29(1): 54–104.

Bergroth, H. (2019) '"You Can't Really Control Life": Dis/Assembling Self-Knowledge with Self-Tracking Technologies', *Distinktion: Journal of Social Theory*, 20(2): 190–206.

Bluteau, J.M. (2021) 'Legitimising Digital Anthropology Through Immersive Cohabitation: Becoming an Observing Participant in a Blended Digital Landscape', *Ethnography*, 22(2): 267–85.

Britton, W.B. and Lindahl, J.R. (2019) '"I Have This Feeling of Not Really Being Here": Buddhist Meditation and Changes in Sense of Self', *Journal of Consciousness Studies*, 26(7–8): 157–83.

Browne, S. (2015) *Dark Matters: On the Surveillance of Blackness*. Durham, NC: Duke University Press.

Bruun, M.K. (2018) 'Studying Psychological Therapies: An Ethnographic Approach to "Metacognition"', presented at ASA 2018: Sociality, Matter, and the Imagination: Re-Creating Anthropology, University of Oxford. Available from: https://nomadit.co.uk/conference/asa2018/paper/45600 (Accessed: 27 January 2025).

Bruun, M.K. (2019) *Scientific Persuasions: Ethnographic Reflections on Evidence-Based Psychological Therapy*. PhD dissertation. University of Cambridge.

Bruun, M.K. (2023a) '"A Factory of Therapy": Accountability and the Monitoring of Psychological Therapy in IAPT', *Anthropology & Medicine*, 30(4): 313–29.

Bruun, M.K. (2023b) 'Mental Health', in H. Nieber (ed) *The Open Encyclopedia of Anthropology*. Available from: https://doi.org/10.29164/23mentalhealth (Accessed: 27 January 2025).

Busfield, J. (1998) 'Restructuring Mental Health Services in Twentieth-Century Britain', in M. Gijswijt-Hofstra and R. Porter (eds) *Cultures of Psychiatry in Post-War Britain and the Netherlands*. Amsterdam: Rodopi.

Candea, M. (2008) 'Fire and Identity as Matters of Concern in Corsica', *Anthropological Theory*, 8(2): 201–16.

Cook, J. (2015) 'Detachment and Engagement in Mindfulness-Based Cognitive Therapy', in T. Yarrow, C. Matei, T. Catherine, and J. Cook (eds) *Detachment: Essays on the Limits of Relational Thinking*. Manchester: Manchester University Press.

Cook, J. (2023) *Making a Mindful Nation: Mental Health and Governance in the Twenty-First Century*. Princeton, NJ, and Oxford: Princeton University Press.

Coon, D.J. (1993) 'Standardizing the Subject: Experimental Psychologists, Introspection, and the Quest for a Technoscientific Ideal', *Technology and Culture*, 34(4): 757–83.

Coopmans, C., Woolgar, S., Vertesi, J., and Lynch, M. (eds) (2014) *Representation in Scientific Practice Revisited*. Cambridge, MA: MIT Press.

Danziger, K. (1997) *Naming the Mind: How Psychology Found Its Language*. London: Sage.

Danziger, K. (1998) *Constructing the Subject: Historical Origins of Psychological Research*. Cambridge: Cambridge University Press.

Daston, L. and Galison, P. (2007) *Objectivity*. New York: Zone Books.

Fanon, F. (1963) *The Wretched of the Earth*. New York: Grove Press.

Foot, M. (1975) *Aneurin Bevan, 1945–1960*. St Albans: Paladin.

Ford, A., De Togni, G., and Miller, L. (2021) 'Hormonal Health: Period Tracking Apps, Wellness, and Self-Management in the Era of Surveillance Capitalism', *Engaging Science, Technology, and Society*, 7(1): 48–66.

Foucault, M. (1973) *The Birth of the Clinic: An Archaeology of Medical Perception*. London: Tavistock.

Foucault, M. (1988) *Madness and Civilization: A History of Insanity in the Age of Reason*. New York: Vintage Books.

Foucault, M. (1991 [1975]) *Discipline and Punish: The Birth of the Prison*. London: Penguin Books.

Fraser, D. (1984) *The Evolution of the British Welfare State: A History of Social Policy Since the Industrial Revolution* (2nd edn). Basingstoke: Macmillan.

Frois, C. (2013) *Peripheral Vision: Politics, Technology, and Surveillance*. Oxford and New York: Berghahn Books.

Goodwin, C. (1994) 'Professional Vision', *American Anthropologist*, 96(3): 606–33.

Grasseni, C. (ed) (2009) *Skilled Visions: Between Apprenticeship and Standards*. Oxford: Berghahn Books.

Gregory, J. and Bowker, G. (2016) 'The Data Citizen, the Quantified Self, and Personal Genomics: Biosensing Technologies in Everyday Life', in D. Nafus (ed) *Quantified: Biosensing Technologies in Everyday Life*. Cambridge, MA: MIT Press.

Hawkins, C., Awondo, P. and Miller, D. (eds) (2024) *An Anthropological Approach to mHealth*. London: UCL Press.

Higgs, E. (2004) *The Information State in England: The Central Collection of Information on Citizens Since 1500*. New York: Palgrave Macmillan.

Ho, S. (2023) *Pursuing Certainty: Exploring Engagements with Menstrual Tracking Amongst Women with Endometriosis and PMDD in the UK*. MPhil dissertation. University of Cambridge.

Hoeyer, K., Bauer, S. and Pickersgill, M. (2019) 'Datafication and Accountability in Public Health: Introduction to a Special Issue', *Social Studies of Science*, 49(4): 459–75.

Hutchins, E. (1995) *Cognition in the Wild*. Cambridge, MA: MIT Press.

Kent, R. (2023) *The Digital Health Self: Wellness, Tracking and Social Media*. Bristol: Bristol University Press.

Latour, B. (2004) 'How to Talk About the Body? The Normative Dimension of Science Studies', *Body & Society*, 10(2–3): 205–29.

Lupton, D. (2016) *The Quantified Self*. Cambridge: Polity Press.

Lynch, M. and Woolgar, S. (eds) (1990) *Representation in Scientific Practice*. Cambridge, MA: MIT Press.

Lynch, R. and Cohn, S. (2016) 'In the Loop: Practices of Self-Monitoring from Accounts by Trial Participants', *Health: An Interdisciplinary Journal for the Social Study of Health, Illness and Medicine*, 20(5): 523–38.

Lyon, D. (1994) *The Electronic Eye: The Rise of Surveillance Society*. Cambridge: Polity Press.

Malinowski, B. (1938) 'A Nation-wide Intelligence Service', in C. Madge and T. Harrison (eds) *First Year's Work 1937–1938 by Mass Observation*. London: Faber and Faber, pp 81–121.

McDonald, M. (1986) 'Celtic Ethnic Kinship and the Problem of Being English', *Current Anthropology*, 27(4): 333–47.

McDonald, M. (2014) 'Bodies and Cadavers', in P. Harvey, E.C. Casella, G. Evans, H. Knox, C. McLean, E.B. Silva, et al (eds) *Objects and Materials: A Routledge Companion*. London and New York: Routledge.

McKay, F. (2022) 'Am I Going Mad? Adverse Meditation Events and the Anthropology of Ethics', *Anthropology Today*, 38(2): 22–6.

McMahan, D.L. (2008) *The Making of Buddhist Modernism*. Oxford and New York: Oxford University Press.

Mol, A., Moser, I., and Pols, J. (eds) (2010) *Care in Practice: On Tinkering in Clinics, Homes and Farms*. Bielefeld: Transcript-Verl.

Neff, G. and Nafus, D. (2016) *Self-Tracking*. Cambridge, MA: MIT Press.

Nim, E. (2019) 'Self-Tracking as a Practice of Quantifying the Body: Conceptual Outlines', *Forum for Anthropology and Culture*, (15), pp 137–52.

Peacock, V., Bruun, M.K., Dungey, C.E., and Shapiro, M. (2023) 'Surveillance', in H. Nieber (ed) *The Open Encyclopedia of Anthropology*. Available from: http://doi.org/10.29164/23surveillance (Accessed: 27 January 2025).

Proust, J. and Fortier, M. (eds) (2018) *Metacognitive Diversity: An Interdisciplinary Approach*. Oxford: Oxford University Press.

Ratnayake, S. and Merry, D. (2018) 'Forgetting Ourselves: Epistemic Costs and Ethical Concerns in Mindfulness Exercises', *Journal of Medical Ethics*, 44(8): 567–74.

Reyes-Foster, B.M. (2018) *Psychiatric Encounters: Madness and Modernity in Yucatan, Mexico*. New Brunswick: Rutgers University Press.

Robb, J. and Harris, O.J.T. (eds) (2013) *The Body in History: Europe from the Palaeolithic to the Future*. Cambridge: Cambridge University Press.

Rose, N. (1989) *Governing the Soul: The Shaping of the Private Self*. London: Free Association Books.

Rose, N. (1996) *Inventing Our Selves: Psychology, Power, and Personhood*. Cambridge: Cambridge University Press.

Ruckenstein, M. (2022) 'Charting the Unknown: Tracking the Self, Experimenting with the Digital: Reflection', in M.H. Bruun, A. Wahlberg, R. Douglas-Jones, C. Hasse, K. Hoeyer, D.B. Kristensen, et al (eds) *The Palgrave Handbook of the Anthropology of Technology*. Singapore: Springer Nature Singapore, pp 253–71.

Ruckenstein, M. and Schüll, N.D. (2017) 'The Datafication of Health', *Annual Review of Anthropology*, 46(1): 261–278.

Taylor, C. (1989) *Sources of the Self: The Making of the Modern Identity*. Cambridge, MA: Harvard University Press.

Timan, T. and Albrechtslund, A. (2018) 'Surveillance, Self and Smartphones: Tracking Practices in the Nightlife', *Science and Engineering Ethics*, 24(3): 853–70.

Toren, C. (2019) 'What Is It to Be Human? A Unified Model Suggests History Will Have the Last Word', in S. Randeria and B. Wittrock (eds) *Social Science at the Crossroads*. Leiden: Brill.

Trnka, S.H. (2016) 'Digital Care: Agency and Temporality in Young People's Use of Health Apps', *Engaging Science, Technology, and Society*, 2: 248–65.

Van Dam, N.T., van Vugt, M.K., Vago, D.R., Schmalzl, L., Saron, C.D., Olendzki, A., et al (2018) 'Mind the Hype: A Critical Evaluation and Prescriptive Agenda for Research on Mindfulness and Meditation', *Perspectives on Psychological Science*, 13(1): 36–61.

Vidal, F. (2011) *The Sciences of the Soul: The Early Modern Origins of Psychology*. Chicago, IL: University of Chicago Press.

Yalom, I.D. (1992) *When Nietzsche Wept: A Novel of Obsession*. New York: HarperPerennial.

2

'I Don't Have Time to Watch Everybody': Location-Based Monitoring, Timescapes, and Family Life in Germany

Claire Elisabeth Dungey

Introduction

'My daughter has just come home', Mariya says as she walks out of a clothes shop in Munich, having bought a handful of colourful dresses. After receiving an app notification around 1 pm, Mariya starts walking quickly to get home to her 14-year-old daughter, while navigating a busy shopping centre. In the morning, during our walk-and-talk interview in a local park, she stopped thoughtfully several times, reflecting on her use of digital apps, and the areas where she would not let her daughter walk alone. Mariya now strides through the park making shortcuts through the wet grass, and we quickly arrive near the car park. After briefly speaking with her husband on the phone, Mariya complains that she cannot understand why her husband has not checked the tracking app Life360,[1] since he could observe her movements by following her on a digital map, so he would know when to pick her up. There was no need to call her, she explains, while still rushing, and she is eventually picked up by her husband in the distance.

This story captures how parents in Germany are increasingly monitoring family members' locations using tracking apps, when managing everyday caring responsibilities.[2] In this chapter, I explore how mothers, in particular, watch over the rhythms of their family members, digitally enabling them to share time with each other, without always being in the same spatial location. Parents often used one app to geolocate their children, and spoke about these practices as *jemanden orten* (tracking/locating someone), seldomly using the term *Überwachung* (surveillance) except when referring to how companies might be extracting data from private users. In Germany, various laws have been implemented to prevent hidden surveillance. In 2017, the Federal Network Agency banned a doll called My Friend Cayla, since it was seen as an illegal espionage device, with a hidden camera and microphone that could record children's voices. Some smartwatches were also banned in 2017 if they contained a concealed microphone.[3] Although none of my respondents spoke about these regulations, all parents who participated in the research asserted that children should not be monitored secretly.

Monitoring has always been a key feature of childhood, and has been used to encourage certain forms of behaviour or for providing safety and managing family logistics (Fotel and Thomsen, 2004; Barron, 2016; Taylor and Rooney, 2016; Mavoa et al, 2023). Scholars are increasingly focusing on the use of data technologies, and how they are influencing everyday routines within families (Marx and Steeves, 2010; Madianou, 2016; Barassi, 2020; Mavoa et al, 2023; Mols et al, 2023). 'Femtech' apps, for instance (see Bruun, Chapter 1, and Peacock, Introduction, this volume), are specifically targeted at women, to allow them to monitor their children at various life stages, from conception to pregnancy, but also after birth, such as monitoring an infant's sleep rhythms, as well as different forms of monitoring once they start at school (Barassi, 2020; Lupton, 2020). Recent technological innovations have enabled the monitoring of young people to reach an unprecedented intensity, and new apps such as Life360 or Google Family Link allow users to monitor each other's geolocations in real time or manage screen time (Taylor and Rooney, 2016; Balmford et al, 2020; Sukk and Siibak, 2021; Widmer and Albrechtslund, 2021; Mavoa et al, 2023).

Studies of gender and surveillance have tended to focus on how technologies privilege typically male, young, white bodies, and have explored relations of inequality, power, and domination (Monahan, 2009; Dubrofsky and Magnet, 2015). Employing the term 'Big Mother' as opposed to 'Big Brother', Peacock (Introduction, this volume) suggests how monitoring can also be motivated by care and protection, rather than a form of monitoring perennially characterized by Orwellian discipline. While relations of power between parents and children may never be equal, it is important to study how monitoring practices can be motivated by love, care, and attentiveness to others, not only oppression (Lupton, 2020; Mols et al, 2023; Dungey, 2024).

Wajcman (2020) discusses how time is organized into daily routines by gendered individuals and suggests that we should pay attention to the rhythms of organizing everyday life, such as coordinating activities in the family. I argue that monitoring is often gendered, as in this study, it is mostly women temporally monitoring their family members. Several of the male participants did not see the need to digitally monitor their children, either due to domestic tasks mainly being carried out by their wives, or because they preferred to take a more relaxed approach to monitoring, and trust that nothing would happen.

In his work *Rhythmanalysis* (Lefebvre, 2004), Lefebvre argues that rhythm is the constellation of time, space, and movement. One of his core concepts, polyrhythmia, he describes as the multiplicity and diversity of rhythms. Here I explore how respondents manage polyrhythmia – such as school timetables, after-school club activities, or the work schedules of their partners. I also draw on Barbara Adam's (2004) concept of a timescape, which has a spatial orientation, and is multifaceted and characterized by power. She traces how clock time became dominant with the industrial revolution in which time was regarded as a commodity. The time–money assumption is now, according to Adam, an unquestioned part of everyday life, and which we talk about in relation to saving or wasting time. Yet time spent by children, the elderly, or unemployed women is often seen as unproductive labour, hence invisible. Adam (2004, 2008) lists various elements of a timescape that are particularly useful here: a timeframe (for example, the beginning of a year), temporality (for example, growing up or ageing), timing (synchronization and coordination), tempo (the speed and intensity of a given activity), duration (for example, temporal distance, or instantaneity), sequence (the order), as well as temporal modalities (past, present, and future imaginaries).

Building on Adam's conceptualization of 'timescapes', Kitchin emphasizes how living in the same household produces shared temporalities around, for instance, mealtimes, leisure, school times, and childcare (Kitchin, 2023). Some may have more temporal power over others, depending on age and gender, for instance, such as children being monitored by their parents. Drawing on Adam (1998, 2004), Kitchin emphasizes that a timescape is a cluster of associated temporal features and relations that collectively reproduce a temporal regime and landscape. Temporalities are embodied and materialized and performed through individual agency, and entangled with the temporalities of others, as well as being structured through institutional arrangements.

Tracking apps and the German context

When exploring the use of tracking apps in Bavaria in relation to children's mobilities, it is important to understand that the city council approach is that children should learn to walk independently to primary school (*Grundschule*) without any mention of app monitoring. Parents are encouraged to support this by, for example, increasing the length of the journey they are walking alone (around the age of six).[4] Over the course of the research, it became apparent that teenagers were monitored more in real time, as well as their media consumption, than their younger siblings under the age of ten. The latter tended to be monitored in analogue ways – for instance by being picked up at various locations – and were often, but not always, trusted to walk a short distance to school, either with their friends or on their own. Whenever the temporal distance to school was short, for example, a five-to ten-minute walk, or a route without complications such as without busy roads, many parents did not see the need to monitor their young children, since the school would provide a *Schulwegshelferin* (a lollipop lady) at least on the way to school, and the school would call parents if their children had not arrived. The institutional structure of changing schools after grade four (around the age of ten) meant that many children had to travel further distances, which made several parents anxious, and for this reason thought it was the right time to buy a phone for their children. Some, however, did not trust the institutional structure of monitoring entirely, and preferred tracking as an extra reassurance.

Several mothers explained that they did not feel comfortable letting their children walk alone, especially if this had not been a practice in their home countries, while those born in Germany emphasized that they had a hard time letting go after having spent all their time with their children. The parents I interacted with tracked their children through phone apps (Life360, Find My iPhone, Google Family Link), smartwatches, or through phone calls and text messages (WhatsApp[5] or traditional phone calls). Few children engaged with tracking apps such as Life360 or Google Family Link, beyond occasionally checking their parents' locations. They were more concerned with seeing where their friends or family members were in other apps with geomonitoring functions such as Snapchat (Snap Map). I now provide some background information on how the apps and devices work, before moving on to the specific case studies and their relationship to timescapes and rhythm.

A smartwatch is often the first choice for parents who want to track their younger children before giving them a phone. A smartwatch such as XPLORA, for instance, allows parents to receive precise information, such as when their children walk out of their 'safe zone' – an area on a digital map determined by parents. The watch enables children and parents to call each other, and it also has an emergency SOS button in case the child wants to call his or her parents. The watch can be set to *Schulmodus* (a school silent mode), which means that the watch will stop working temporarily with limited functionalities.[6]

Life360 is a US tracking app that was originally developed in 2008 following Hurricane Katrina, so that family members could locate each other (Gabriels, 2016). The app is intended for the entire family, which also makes it possible for children to track their parents checking a digital map, and all users must give their consent. The app has an SOS button as well as a notification system that allows users to see each other's battery levels (Gabriels, 2016). The app promotes the idea that parents can protect their children from harm without being physically present, with sufficient intimate user data (Hasinoff, 2017). The free membership of the app allows users a two-day location history, as well as two places with unlimited alerts. There are various paid versions of the app, with the gold version allowing users to get unlimited place alerts and a 30-day location history. This offers users a spatial overview of the month, as well as notifications that can alert them, in case they need to take action, such as driving to a location if their child has not arrived on time. Users can get place alerts without needing to ask family members where they are. The app also has a crash detection function, in both the free and paid version, that can sense collisions and immediately inform family members.[7]

The other oft-cited tracking app is Google Family Link. Family Link was initially released in 2017 by Google, to enable parents to monitor their screen-time use, app usage (such as blocking sites), and to monitor children when moving on a map. The app, which is free, allows parents to receive notifications when their children arrive at destinations. It was originally designed for parents with children under 13 to allow them to have a supervised Google account – however, individual countries have their own restrictions, such as Germany with an age restriction of 16.[8] When a child reaches this age, both parents and children must give their consent before monitoring can start, and the child can opt out which puts the phone into a 24-hour lockdown.[9]

Other families who owned Apple devices used the preinstalled tracking apps on their iPhones. Find My iPhone was released in 2015 by Apple, and included the application 'Find My Friends'. The Find My Friends app was designed with the intention of locating friends or relatives in real time on a map, whereas Find My iPhone was intended to find lost devices, rather than people (Widmer and Albrechtslund, 2021). The research participants referred to it as either Find My iPhone or *'wo ist ...'* ('where is ...'). On Apple's website, it is promoted as a tool to find both lost devices and your friends, if you consent to sharing your location.[10] According to Apple,[11] it is possible to track a device with a low battery level, and even if it has been switched off for 24 hours. With Apple's technology it is possible for family members to share their location, for example, for an hour, a day, or indefinitely.

While parents used the tracking apps previously listed, Snapchat was only used by child respondents. Snapchat is an American app created in 2011. The company defines the app as a camera that is connected to the user's friends (Dunn and Langlais, 2020). The minimum age requirement is 13, but there is no age verification. Snapchat is similar to other social media platforms as users are able to share content and send messages, but has a specific tracking feature that allows users to continuously monitor their friends in real time when users share their live locations (Vanherle et al, 2023). When users of the application send a 'Snap' to each other, which can either be a text, a video or an image, they last for ten seconds, and the only trace of this afterwards is a timestamp (Dunn and Langlais, 2020). Snapchat also has a parental control functionality that allows parents to get a glimpse into who they have messaged within a seven-day timeframe, and an option of limiting sensitive content that is available to their children.[12] Let us at this point turn towards how family members manage busy schedules, either by using tracking apps, or making clear temporal arrangements with their children.

Slowing down and speeding up

Mariya lives in a relatively wealthy part of Munich, surrounded by large houses separated by wooden gates. Most people in this neighbourhood have one or two cars parked in the driveway, as opposed to the neighbourhood area with a park where she likes to go walking on her day off. Near the park you would find mostly identical flats in a continuous line, surrounded by a large shopping centre. Most of my interactions with Mariya are on these walks, and she is one of the few people who checks the app while interacting with me, without being asked about the functionalities. On one of these occasions, she spots a group of young people near the lake, and wishes to know if her daughter is there.

By using Life360, Mariya received notifications when her daughter had arrived at school and checked her daughter's geolocation several times a day. If her daughter was still at school, she would not be in a hurry, and would walk slowly. She explains to me that if her daughter is not moving in the app for ten minutes, for example, she will follow up with a phone call to make sure that nothing is wrong. Often it is simply because her daughter has been chatting with her friends.

After receiving a notification in a department store, I observe how she interrupts her activity, and becomes entirely focused on getting home to ensure that her daughter arrives at home within the expected timeframe and is not alone. In an interview, Mariya explained that she had previously driven her daughter to school, but now she lets her ride her bicycle, since her daughter's current school is a short distance away. Mariya had often been worried when her daughter was on her way, especially due to recent news stories about girls being attacked or abducted. For this reason she paid for the full subscription to Life360. Premium membership allows her to see her family members' geolocations, or receive unlimited alerts about their locations. While Mariya aspires to observe her daughter's movements, she does not have time to check on her husband all the time, for example, how fast her husband was driving in the car, which it is also possible to observe in the app. 'I don't have time to watch everybody', Mariya explains, emphasizing that monitoring family members is a time-consuming and labour-intensive commitment, and she had hence chosen only to monitor her daughter.

When reflecting on Mariya's desire to track her daughter, it is useful to think about Adam's (2004) conceptualization of timescapes. Mariya's time for shopping is bounded by an institutional framing of time, in which she wants to be home at the same time as her daughter finishes her school day. She thus increases the tempo, from having casually gone clothes shopping, to suddenly rushing and walking at a high pace. Her motivation to speed up was further intensified when she coordinated time schedules with her husband, also on the app, to see where her husband and daughter were. In many ways, despite being in three different spatial locations (in the car, walking on the way home from school, and walking away from a shopping centre), the family members were immediately temporally co-present in the app. In this way Mariya manages polyrhythmia. Mariya's daughter is considered old enough to walk on her own, but at the same time too young to travel completely independently. Mariya expects that she will track her until she is 18 years old but might continue after.

Managing cooking times

Karen is a woman in her late 40s, who works part time and uses the free version of Life360. I met Karen frequently, at work-related events that she organized, visiting her family at home, or at regular social events designed for women in a local neighbourhood group. Karen and her family live in a similarly wealthy part of town, slightly outside the city centre, with large multistorey houses and driveways.

Karen says she does not mind using an app to track her family members, since she does not have anything to hide, even if the data is shared. Her youngest daughter (who is nine), does not have a phone with a sim card, which means that Karen spends longer picking her up in the car and bringing her to locations. However, she had found a way to ensure that her daughter travels to school safely. Her neighbour uses a tracking app with her own daughter, and the two children walk together, and Karen receives screenshots of the app when they have arrived safely.

When her daughter was about to change schools in the summer of 2023 (*Grundschule* to *Gymnasium* – a type of secondary school – between grades four and five), her daughter, Mia, got a sim card for her phone so it would no longer only work on a Wi-Fi connection, and she could make a phone call. However, her phone was too old to be linked with Life360.

Karen uses Life360 approximately twice a week to track her husband as well as her teenage daughter who is 15. She explained that having an app saved time and enabled her to look after her family members and plan cooking, although it was not always able to track her daughter, when her phone was in flight mode at school, or whenever there was no phone signal. She would only digitally track her teenage daughter when she had not turned up on time. She seemed to be motivated by the idea of time as a commodity (Adam, 2004), in which she could manage her everyday tasks faster, and therefore free up time. Karen clearly wanted her everyday routines to happen in a particular sequence, and at the right time.

Stefan, her husband, argues, on the other hand, that 'times had changed' in terms of looking after children in Germany. Ideally, he would like his eldest daughter to be able to take public transport to the city, for instance to be able to go to the shops just as he had done already around the age of nine. As a child, he had told his parents when he left the house, and they had an agreed time they had to be home. He suggests that his parents had been more relaxed regarding his upbringing:

> I walked alone to school, what we have is an incredible drama. With a walking bus (*Mit Bus auf Füzen*) walking together to school. They need to be careful. Then there is a main road. I lived by a main road [as a child], there was not a pedestrian crossing. You had to be careful not to be in an accident. Times have changed.

Stefan's complaint about the 'incredible drama' in his household and the 'walking bus to school' (parents and children walking together) is meaningful when reflecting on gendered patterns of monitoring (Wajcman, 2020). Stefan is not particularly interested in the topic of digital tracking, arguing instead that this is a matter that his wife and daughter are much more focused on. He explains that he had been told to 'please install that', suggesting that tracking the children had not been his decision. Moreover, his children are already in the house when he arrives home after work, which means that he did not need to geomonitor their movements. Stefan is often busy in his full-time job, and it is consequently his wife who is mostly busy collecting the children at various locations, and taking care of their everyday routines. Stefan had agreed to use the app but used it minimally – as a family compromise. It is clear that there was a division of labour regarding temporal monitoring, in which his wife is mostly responsible for managing their daughters' routines, as well as her husband's, coordinating multiple rhythms and timetables simultaneously.

Managing screen time and schedules

Some parents in Munich, particularly fathers, are critical of surveillance technologies, and prefer to avoid them altogether, or set up their own private internal systems to track family members. Johann, a father of three in his 40s, is highly critical of digital surveillance as a whole, and had decided to avoid setting up a Google account, instead using an email system that he paid for, arguing that this was more data secure. He explains that he is suspicious of tracking apps downloaded from Google Play Store, since this kind of information is stored on big servers, and he does not know where the information would be stored and for what purpose. Johann instead values telephone calls and making agreements with his children about when they should arrive home, but refuses to use WhatsApp as his wife does. If the children do not turn up on time, there are consequences. For example, they would not be able to go to the park unless they stuck to agreed arrangements. Johann is critical of companies gathering data, but explains that in principle it is possible to set up a private system to track your child in real time. However, he did not think this was necessary, since he 'trusted his children'.

Nevertheless, Johann did not think the same way about his teenage son's (age 14) media consumption. According to Johann, the guidelines for children's media consumption are 14 hours per week,[13] but his son regularly exceeds this. Johann had set up his own internal private server in order to control his son's media time and thought that his son might be mature enough to manage his media consumption by the age of 16. He explains that his son had in fact managed to 'hack' his father's system, in order to circumvent screen-time monitoring.

Daman, who I talk to via a video call while he is cooking, monitors his daughter's media consumption, but also geomonitors her locations using the free version of Google Family Link. He argues that it was hard to manage cooking, going to work, and keeping an eye on his daughter as a single parent. Daman suggested that he would only track her when she was late:

> Let's say she is supposed to be back home by two o'clock but she is not back by three-thirty to four o'clock and she has not told me she will be late, then I check … Mostly coming from school, or a friend's place maybe she tells me that she is going to a friend's place in the evening, and she says she will be back by nine o'clock, and she is not back by nine-thirty to ten. Sometimes I have to check where she is. Sometimes I will call her, but she never picks up the phone, never hears it [he laughs slightly].

Daman uses digital tracking not only to manage cooking time, like Karen, but also when he starts to worry about his daughter being late when it is dark outside. In addition, he wishes to restrict his daughter's time on YouTube, and instead introduce time of 'being bored' since he considers this a healthier approach. Daman has to manage the overlapping rhythms of his work schedule, his daughter's timetables and homecomings, as well as the length of her media consumption. Both Daman and Johann are critical of their data being observed by third parties, but in different ways. Daman had switched off tracking functions in apps on his phone that would track him, only keeping the one that permitted him to track his daughter. He is sceptical of apps with geomonitoring features that children could use, since they could be hacked and observed by external partners. Johann, on the other hand, decided to opt out of free services altogether, and had installed a private system for tracking media time use. In the next section, I explore how a teenage girl monitors her own temporal routines.

The time journal

Alina is 15 years old and lives with her parents and younger sister in Munich. When ranking various apps with her friends, Alina and her friends placed Life360 and Google Family Link at numbers 18 and 19 on the list, in other words some of the least important. On the other hand, calling someone (*anrufen*), and WhatsApp are the most important, even though her parents do monitor her geolocations using these apps.

Alina:	I use it when mummy asks me to check where daddy is. I do it myself, if I want him to come back early because I want us to do something together.
Mother:	It's mainly checking on the dad [the mother laughs].
Alina:	Mummy as well.
Mother:	Do you check on me?
Alina:	I remember once or twice it happened.
Claire:	So you want to know where they are? Or why do you want to check on them?
Alina:	Most of the time to know when they come back home. It's not like I worry about them or anything. I don't think I'm really in a position to. Yeah …
Claire:	Do you ever check in or checkout? [marking in the app when she arrives or leaves]
Alina:	No.
Claire:	You just go to places, right?
Alina:	Yeah. I'm like almost never on this app to be honest.

Alina uses two separate apps to monitor her everyday routines – an app that records her routines, as well as an app that acts like a timer. The difference between the two, is that one of them is giving her instructions (such as telling her to go to bed), while the other one, the time-logging app, records her everyday routine, and shows her how much time she spends on various activities, but does not give particular prompts. Alina lists various examples of daily activities that she records in the routine app, such as brushing her teeth, putting on her clothes, drawing, or playing the piano, and which tells her how many minutes she has spent on each activity.

Alina: I am trying to do my sort of time journal, I just like track what I have been doing … It is pretty much an experiment for me.

Claire: Is this like an app or your own thing?

Alina: I tried doing it on an Excel spread sheet … how many minutes I spend, this one is so much easier so. So here I just track what I have done. Yesterday what I did, try time journals for 13 minutes and 12 seconds. 10.16 to 10.29. After that there was messaging for 30 minutes 54 seconds. 10.29 to 10.42. Then there was a meal for 30 minutes. 10.45 to 11.15. Then I was watching TV with mummy from 10.46 to 11.16 [laughing as she speaks]. Then I was drawing for three hours. 11.24. Then studying, then grocery shopping, then studying.

Here it appears that Alina is endeavouring to control her experience of time by recording every minute of her daily activities, firstly in an Excel spreadsheet but afterwards through the app. My reflection is that Alina is trying to customize her experience of time, both by controlling the frequency of activities, how long they take, as well as ensuring that there is no time wasted (Flaherty, 2011). It may be that this form of self-monitoring or self-cultivation gives her a sense of autonomy over her time, managing it herself rather than being managed by her parents.

Contesting parent perspectives on monitoring

Anna, Katharina, and Paul live in a small town outside Munich. As opposed to Munich's urban bustle, with hundreds of people getting out of public transport, and bicycle riders riding on busy cycle paths, their town seems quiet on a Wednesday afternoon. A mother and a child cycle on the pavement, and two schoolgirls around six or seven, with identical school bags, walk on their own up the quiet street, stopping along the way. I had been given Anna's contact through a local friend who I had met in a so-called *Nachbarschaftstreff* (a neighbourhood socializing group) who thought that Anna would be interesting to talk to due to her use of Alexa[14] and other tracking technologies.

Inside their house, Anna and her daughter Katharina are in the large, combined kitchen/living room waiting to start our conversation and spoke to me at first in German. Anna's son joins us later, after having played video games in his room, and appears more reserved than Katharina, who chats relaxedly for most of the time. Anna's husband is not there. She offers me a cup of tea at the dining table. An Alexa device sits in a corner of the room. It looks like a grey satellite dish, that blends into the other grey colours in the room. The family owns several devices in the home, for example, in the children's bedrooms, as well as a video-recording Alexa in another part of the house. Anna soon switches to English, her mother tongue, perhaps due to her daughter teasing her that she made mistakes in German. Anna uses Find My iPhone to get in touch with her children at a distance. All her family members have Apple products, and it is therefore easy to track each device. When talking to Anna's husband, Elias, while he is eating his breakfast a few days later, after returning from his business trip, he tells me that he never actually checks this information. It is simply a backup for him in case something happens, and they have set their devices to the highest security settings, fearing intrusive surveillance from companies. Anna is anxious about certain apps that performed location-based tracking, such as Snapchat that her daughter used.

Mother (Anna):	I think for this age, I think it's something that worries me that anyone can see where we are at any one time. So they can see, for example, if anyone's home, or maybe not home, if they want to walk in the backyard, walk in the back door, for example. If they could track any of us, if especially kids, for example, they're on the way to school and back at regular times throughout the week. Someone wants to, you know, know where you are then it makes it very easy.
Daughter (Katharina):	It is really, really easy. Because even if you don't have the Snap [Snap Map in Snapchat], I'm not arguing against you. I'm just like, every, like 2,000 kids go to school. At this one point, you can literally wait by the *Sbahn* [train] at a certain time or on the street at a certain time and kidnap somebody
Mother (Anna):	I know. But we don't want to make it too easy for them, right?[15]

Anna, Katharina, and Paul participate in a family discussion about tracking technologies, in which they debate how they use them in their everyday lives. They use Alexa in the house, which means that rather than Anna shouting through the house that the dinner is ready, she speaks into Alexa, to tell them this. In one part of the house, Alexa also had a camera, which Katharina amused herself with, suggesting that her mother was only filming part of her forehead when shouting that dinner was ready. Despite the family being surrounded by digital technologies that could potentially record their voices and faces, Anna had a very cautious approach regarding digital technologies, but still used the tracking app (Find My iPhone) to follow her children.

Anna was concerned about her daughter using the geomonitoring features on Snapchat, and all the potential hackers who could gain access to their data in real time. She wanted this kind of information to be kept within the family. While Anna's son did not say much during the conversation, he clearly stated that he did not use Snap Map since he did not want his friends to know where he was, and he would only call them if he wanted to get hold of them. He used digital technologies to track his exercise routine or background noise, and communicated with his friends on the phone, or by sending messages on the PlayStation.

Anna wanted to make it clear that digital surveillance in Snap Map was risky, due to data about their family members potentially being leaked to others at any given time. Katharina challenged her view on this, by saying that any child could always be kidnapped if someone went to a busy location where children would take public transport, and was not entirely convinced by her mother's concerns. Anna warned her daughter about leaving digital traces on the internet depending on her search history, and kept emphasizing that they were using their own Wi-Fi connection which made digital monitoring safer. Katharina does not seem to be too concerned about leaving digital traces, and suggested instead that this was useful, since she would then receive the kind of adverts that were based on content that she wanted.

Katharina uses a joking style of communication, perhaps as a way of claiming her own viewpoints. For instance, when her mother said that she tracked her 'twice a month', Katharina asserted that this was in fact 'twice a day', and when her mother announces that she used WhatsApp to communicate most of the time, Katharina said this is in fact 'all the time'. When discussing how they would get hold of each other when they were in different locations, Katharina jokes 'I scream into nothingness and sometimes they answer.' Perhaps Katharina wished to say that she did not always feel heard when she 'screams into nothingness', but mentioned later that they use WhatsApp or their Alexa device as a 'walkie-talkie' to communicate with each other in real time in the same house.

Anna is more concerned about how the app does not offer precise information and gives the example of how the app had shown that Katharina was at the airport, around 40 kilometres from their location, even though this had not been the case. She thus raises the topic of children's independent mobilities outside the house. Anna is concerned about whether her daughter's battery had gone flat. Katharina clearly contests her mother's view, arguing that she had sent a photo of where she was (after being requested to do this), which indicated that her phone had battery and had hence been temporally co-present at least.

Katharina is keen to monitor her friends in Snap Map, but said that although she did not actually want to share her own location, she would always know when her friends would leave a location in real time. She said that this was useful in terms of determining whether friends or their potential lovers were being truthful, as anyone could always see where they had been. While her mother contests this, suggesting that any relationship should rely on trust, Katharina asserts an approach to technology that is characterized by being together in time, and datasets that she trusted, arguing that people could be lying.

Our conversation is soon interrupted by an alarm that Anna had set, since she wanted her daughter to pick up her bicycle at the train station. Her mother has set several alarms and reminders, for instance to empty the washing machine, or alarms for her daughter to go to after-school activities, which clearly impacts the temporal rhythms of the household. Although Katharina asks whether she can stay at home, her mother decides on her behalf that she should not miss her after-school activity.

Anna is present throughout, and hence shaped her children's views, seeming to steer them towards what she sees as appropriate use of digital media. Katharina, on the other hand, communicates in a joking style to assert her own autonomy and capacity to influence the direction of the conversation. In her view, digital tracking in Snap Map is a useful tool to manage her relationships with friends, by tracking them in real time.

Conclusion

This chapter has focused on the everyday temporal rhythms that families engage in when using monitoring technologies. Barassi (2020) discusses the time regime of surveillance capitalism in which corporations have come to govern people through time. Examples of these include apps to increase productivity, exercise, or tracking apps to track children's everyday movements, and media activities in which data is extracted for profit. Barassi argues that immediacy has come to define a way of life in data-driven economies and particularly within families, who stay connected in real time and organize everyday rhythms through technologies. Co-surveillance in family life is largely structured by the design of data technologies, which in the case of my research was characterized by children checking their friends' location in real time in Snap Map, or parents checking where their children were in Life360 or other tracking apps and devices.

It is clear that parents and children in Germany are reflexive about the pros and cons of using digital tracking technologies, and how they were being used for profit. Several parents warned their children about this and preferred that they only tracked each other as a family unit, without introducing external watchers or hackers. Tracking technologies carried an ambivalence that was two-fold. On the one hand, many parents explained that it was helpful in managing family logistics and the temporal organization of family life, for example, picking up children at various locations, or knowing when someone would come home in the family to plan activities. Yet on the other hand, many were concerned about digital surveillance since it prejudiced children's privacy and autonomy, as well as trusting relations between parents and children. Some therefore considered it important to emphasize that tracking children should not be carried out all the time, but occasionally instead. The children I engaged with were less sceptical of digital surveillance technologies than their parents, and often showed little interest in using the apps themselves, beyond occasionally checking their parents' locations in real time, especially when being asked to do this. Both Paul and Katharina do not want to show their own locations in real time, perhaps due to their parents' warnings about data safety, but Katharina is keen on being able to 'watch' others as a way of being co-present with her friends. Alina, on the other hand, monitors her own activities down to minutes and hours, an expression of temporal autonomy.

The chapter has shown how parents are keen to track their children's temporal routines to provide protection from bad actors, but also to offer convenience in managing the everyday durations and timings of various activities. As Lefebvre (2004) suggests, organic and inorganic rhythms were continually interacting. Parents would speed up or slow down after checking the information provided by their apps, or they would check app information as a way of determining how long their children had been away, and when they thought they should return. In this context, monitoring appears highly gendered. It is often mothers who carry out the care work of digital monitoring, which in some cases involves convincing reluctant husbands to engage with these technologies.

Acknowledgements

I would like to thank all research participants who participated in this study in Germany, who generously invited me to their homes or met me in a location of their choice and spoke about their own or other family members in relation to digital technologies and monitoring. I would also like to thank those who recommended relevant research participants. A special thanks to the other co-editors, as well as the participants at the King's College London workshop 'Times of Surveillance' who provided useful comments and suggestions. I would like to thank the European Research Council for funding this project (grant no. 947868).

Notes

[1]   Life360 is explained in the next section.
[2]   This chapter is based on nine months of ethnographic fieldwork in Munich between 2022 and 2023 with parents and children in various settings, such as neighbourhood group meetups, in private homes, or in public venues. This included participation in public or private events, as well as formal or informal interviews/conversations with parents and

children about digital monitoring. Some participants were born in Germany, whereas others had settled in southern Germany after living in other countries: in Africa, in Asia, elsewhere in Europe, in Australia or in the US. For anonymity reasons the specificities of these details have been left out. A core part of the approach has been shifting between different roles, such as playing and interacting with children between eight and 17 in informal ways after their parents consented to this, but also listening to adult perspectives and viewpoints. All names are pseudonyms. This project has received ethical approval from the European Research Council and the ethics committee at King's College London.

[3] Bundesnetzagentur (2024): https://www.bundesnetzagentur.de/SharedDocs/Pressemitte ilungen/DE/2018/20180405_GPStracker.html (Accessed: 29 February 2024).

[4] München Unterwegs (2023): https://muenchenunterwegs.de/angebote/schulweg-darum-lohnt-sich-der-weg-zu-fuss (Accessed: 28 September 2023).

[5] Whatsapp is a messaging service owned by Meta/Facebook that allows users to send messages, videos, and photos. Whatsapp (2024): https://www.whatsapp.com/ (Accessed: 29 September 2024).

[6] XPLORA (2024): https://myxplora.de/ (Accessed: 28 February 2024).

[7] Life360 (2024): https://www.life360.com/uk/ (Accessed: 28 February 2024).

[8] Google account help (2024): https://support.google.com/accounts/answer/1350409?hl= en#zippy=%2Ceurope (Accessed: 29 February 2024).

[9] The Verge (2024): https://www.theverge.com/2018/9/18/17855746/google-assistant-family-link-parental-controls (Accessed: 29 February 2024).

[10] Apple (2024): https://support.apple.com/de-de/102648 (Accessed: 29 February 2024).

[11] Apple (2024): https://www.apple.com/uk/icloud/find-my/ (Accessed: 26 February 2024).

[12] Snapchat (2024): https://www.snapchat.com/ (Accessed: 29 February 2024).

[13] Johann does not mention specific guidelines, but similar recommendations can be found on Klicksafe (2020): https://www.klicksafe.de/bildschirm-und-medienzeit-was-ist-fuer-kinder-in-ordnung/bildschirmzeiten-bei-kindern-von-12-16-jahren (Accessed: 22 October 2024).

[14] Alexa is a virtual assistant technology owned by Amazon with voice AI that allows users to ask questions, and receive answers from the virtual assistant, as well as play music. When users have multiple devices, they can use them to communicate with each other in a household. Alexa can be taught the voices of the household members. Amazon (2024): https://www.amazon.com/alexa-for-kids/b?ie=UTF8&node=21474972 011&ref=pe_alxhub_aucc_en_us_IC_HP_9_HUB_KID (Accessed: 29 February 2024).

[15] Excerpt from a group discussion with Anna (mother) Katharina (daughter, 13), and Paul (son, 15) conducted in English, July 2023.

References

Adam, B. (1998) *Timescapes of Modernity: The Environment and Invisible Hazards*. London and New York: Routledge.

Adam, B. (2004) *Time*. Cambridge: Polity Press.

Adam, B. (2008) 'The Timescapes Challenge: Engagement with the Invisible Temporal', in B. Adam, J. Hockey, P. Thompson, and R. Edwards (eds) *Researching Lives Through Time: Time, Generation and Life Stories*. Leeds: University of Leeds, pp 7–12.

Balmford, W., Hjorth, L., and Richardson, I. (2020) 'Intimate Surveillance and Children's Mobile Media Usage', in L. Green, D. Holloway, K. Stevenson, T. Leaver, and L. Haddon (eds), *The Routledge Companion to Digital Media and Children*. New York and London: Routledge, pp 393–402.

Barassi, V. (2020) 'Datafied Times: Surveillance Capitalism, Data Technologies and the Social Construction of Time in Family Life', *New Media & Society*, 22(9): 1545–60.

Barron, C. (2016) ' "Where Are You, Who Are You With, What Are You Doing?": Children's Strategies of Negotiation and Resistance to Parental Monitoring and Surveillance via Mobile Phones', in E. Taylor and T. Rooney (eds) *Surveillance Futures: Social and Ethical Implications of New Technologies for Children and Young People*. London and New York: Routledge, pp 110–21.

Dubrofsky, R.E. and Magnet, S.A. (2015) 'Introduction: Feminist Surveillance Studies: Critical Interventions', in R.E. Dubrofsky and S.A. Magnet (eds) *Feminist Surveillance Studies*. Durham, NC, and London: Duke University Press, pp 1–17.

Dungey, C.E. (2024) 'A Bird's Eye View: Care, Control, and the Use of Surveillance Apps Among Family Members in Germany', *Sociológia – Slovak Sociological Review*, 56(4): 325–45.

Dunn, T.R. and Langlais, M.R. (2020) ' "Oh, Snap!": A Mixed-Methods Approach to Analyzing the Dark Side of Snapchat', *The Journal of Social Media in Society*, 9(2): 69–104.

Flaherty, M.G. (2011) *The Textures of Time: Agency and Temporal Experience*. Philadelphia: Temple University Press.

Fotel, T. and Thomsen, T.U. (2004) 'The Surveillance of Children's Mobility.', *Surveillance & Society*, 1(4): 535–54.

Gabriels, K. (2016) ' "I Keep a Close Watch on this Child of Mine": A Moral Critique of Other-Tracking Apps', *Ethics and Information Technology*, 18(3): 175–84.

Hasinoff, A.A. (2017) 'Where Are You? Location Tracking and the Promise of Child Safety', *Television & New Media*, 18(6): 496–512.

Kitchin, R. (2023) *Digital Timescapes: Technology, Temporality and Society*. Cambridge and Hoboken: Polity Press.

Lefebvre, H. (2004) *Rhythmanalysis: Space, Time and Everyday LifeI*. Translated by Stuart Elden and Gerald Moore. London and New York: Continuum.

Lupton, D. (2020) 'Caring Dataveillance: Women's Use of Apps To Monitor Pregnancy And Children', in L. Green, D. Holloway, K. Stevenson, T. Leaver, and L. Haddon (eds), *The Routledge Companion to Digital Media and Children*. New York and London: Routledge, pp 393–402.

Madianou, M. (2016) 'Ambient Co-Presence: Transnational Family Practices in Polymedia Environments', *Global Networks*, 16(2): 183–201.

Marx, G. and Steeves, V. (2010) 'From the Beginning: Children as Subjects and Agents of Surveillance', *Surveillance & Society*, 7(3/4): 192–230.

Mavoa, J., Coghlan, S., and Nansen, B. (2023) ' "It's About Safety Not Snooping": Parental Attitudes to Child Tracking Technologies and Geolocation Data', *Surveillance & Society*, 21(1): 45–60.

Mols, A., Campos, J.P., and Pridmore, J. (2023) 'Family Surveillance: Understanding Parental Monitoring, Reciprocal Practices, and Digital Resilience', *Surveillance & Society*, 21(4): 469–84.

Monahan, T. (2009) 'Dreams of Control at a Distance: Gender, Surveillance, and Social Control', *Cultural Studies ↔ Critical Methodologies*, 9(2): 286–305.

Sukk, M. and Siibak, A. (2021) 'Caring Dataveillance and the Construction of "Good Parenting": Estonian Parents' and Pre-Teens' Reflections on the Use of Tracking Technologies', *Communications*, 46(3): 446–67.

Taylor, E. and Rooney, T. (2016) *Surveillance Futures: Social and Ethical Implications of New Technologies for Children and Young People*. Oxford and New York: Routledge.

Vanherle, R., Trekels, J., Hermans, S., Vranken, P., and Beullens, K. (2023) 'How It Feels to Be "Left on Read": Social Surveillance on Snapchat and Young Individuals' Mental Health', *Cyberpsychology: Journal of Psychosocial Research on Cyberspace*, 17(5): 1–25.

Wajcman, J. (2020) *Pressed For Time: The Acceleration of Life in Digital Capitalism*. Chicago, IL: University of Chicago Press.

Widmer, S. and Albrechtslund, A. (2021) 'The Ambiguities of Surveillance as Care and Control: Struggles in the Domestication of Location-Tracking Applications by Danish Parents', *Nordicom Review*, 42(s4): 79–93.

3

Tinkering with Time and Technologies in Dementia Care

Astrid Meyer, Stinne Aaløkke Ballegaard, and Anders Albrechtslund

Introduction

In Scandinavia, many technologies have been adopted as so-called 'welfare technologies' since the late 2000s (Kamp et al, 2019). These technologies are linked to the idea of securing and improving welfare. The term encompasses technologies used 'to maintain or increase security, activity, participation or independence for people with a disability or the elderly' (Nordic Welfare Centre, 2024), and includes automatic toilets, Global Positioning System (GPS) trackers, eating robots, tele-care solutions and other devices (Kamp et al, 2019). While there are differences across the Scandinavian countries, for example, in how fast various welfare technologies are implemented (Kamp et al, 2019), all three Scandinavian countries have established national platforms to support knowledge sharing and implementation (Helsedirektoratet, 2024; RISE, 2024; Videnscenter for digitalisering og teknologi, 2025).

Welfare technologies are embedded in a discourse of a *better future* in different ways (Kamp et al, 2019; Peine and Neven, 2019; KL Local Government Denmark, 2021). Some focus on supporting people with disabilities and frail older people in living lives without depending on carers, while others aim to support and enhance care work itself. This chapter focuses on the second type, which aims to facilitate care. More specifically, we look at the use of video-based check-ins, GPS tracking, door alarms, and motion sensors in dementia care. These technologies aim to detect the needs of vulnerable people who have difficulties articulating when they need support or help. In this sense, they are shaped around the idea of triggering an alarm when it is time to react. This helps care workers who are alerted through the technology. For instance, when someone like John, who needs a supportive hand because he forgets his walker, gets up at night, he triggers a motion sensor; or when someone like Elsa, who enjoys walks but gets lost easily, leaves the premises, she triggers an alarm through her wearable GPS tracker.

Watching over, detecting needs, and monitoring have always been part of care work, but using new technologies drastically changes the scope and method used (Kamp et al, 2023). The technologies we look at do not merely monitor. They monitor to modulate the time of response and intervention as part of care practice. For this reason, we understand them as surveillance technologies, and will refer to them as such throughout the chapter.

We base this understanding on Peacock et al's modification of Lyon's influential definition of surveillance, in which surveillance is understood as 'watching over through human and/or non-human technologies for an intended purpose' (2023, p 2). These technologies arrive with a strong, normative sense of purpose, in terms of supporting certain care responses to obtain a specific understanding of welfare. By referring to these technologies as surveillance technologies, we wish to bring their aims of enhanced care through technologically mediated vigilance to the foreground. Through ethnographic examples of various technologies that aim to modulate the response time, we explore what happens when aims for a timely response meet everyday care practices at three Scandinavian nursing homes.

Surveillance, time, and care work

Surveillance is often understood through a dystopian imaginary, where it is an Orwellian tool enforcing discipline. However, more recent studies conceptualize surveillance in a much more nuanced way. Lyon (2001) describes surveillance as two-faced as it involves both care and control, which are sometimes impossible to separate. This volume challenges the idea of surveillance as an Orwellian force of discipline, by stressing the caring and protective (Dungey, Chapter 2, this volume) and self-care (Bruun, Chapter 1, this volume) features of surveillance. Furthermore, this approach to surveillance also highlights the importance of considering surveillance as a *practice* rather than a pre-given, non-negotiable force. Surveillance technologies are rarely adopted at face value, but adapted and made malleable to fit the situation (Schwennesen, 2019; Kamp et al, 2023).

Stressing the value of looking at practices and adaptations is also fundamental within Science and Technology Studies (STS). Especially within STS studies of care technologies, scholars have highlighted the importance of *tinkering* (Law, 2010; Mol et al, 2010; Pols and Willems, 2011; Molterer et al, 2020; Jansky, 2024; Kamp et al, 2023). Tinkering is used to characterize how people 'adapt their tools to a specific situation while adapting the situation to the tools, on and on, endless tinkering' (Mol et al, 2010, p 15). It is a term that helps articulate the attentive experimentation with technologies and practices to make them run more smoothly. As explained in the Introduction (Peacock, this volume), tinkering can be understood to make time trajectories of technologies work in harmony with the rhythms of lived life. Drawing on *Rhythmanalysis* (Lefebvre, 2009), tinkering is thus an attempt to avoid *arrhythmia* (disruption of rhythms) by attending to the *polyrhythmia* of everyday life where many different rhythmic demands exist simultaneously.

Following these lines of thought, we are particularly interested in how care workers tinker with time, and navigate polyrhythmia, when using surveillance technologies. Other studies have engaged with tinkering (Kamp et al, 2023) and temporality (Kamp, 2021) in a Danish nursing home context. Meanwhile, Løvschal-Nielsen et al (2022) have used tinkering to characterize how children with cancer navigate and negotiate situations in hospitals. While our use of the term similarly recognizes how time is adjustable through unplanned, socio-material actions, we use the idea of tinkering with time primarily to characterize the relationships between care workers, time, and technologies. In our approach, we draw on Grosen and Hansen (2021) and their concept of 'responsive care' (Grosen and Hansen, 2021, p 263). The study points to how care workers do not necessarily follow the temporal demands of the technologies, as they continue to walk rounds even though the technology is meant to guide their attention (Grosen and Hansen, 2021, p 269). Thus, there appears to be some tension between temporality enacted by the technologies, and the way time is enacted and experienced at nursing homes. There is a fine line between rejecting technological determinism and recognizing the consequences of using technologies in care work. In this chapter, we walk the same theoretical line, while closely examining surveillance technologies in dementia care and temporality at nursing homes.

One way to conceptualize some of the consequences of using surveillance technologies in care work, is through Bogard's concept of simulation (1996). Bogard uses the idea of simulation to draw attention to the seductive imaginaries of surveillance technologies. Bogard argues that 'to understand what the technology of surveillance is and the effects it aims for today, increasingly we have to appreciate the fantasy that drives it' (Bogard, 1996, pp 8–9). We recognize the powerful and seductive character of a simulation, in the Scandinavian, and especially Danish, context of using alarms and surveillance technologies in dementia care. Municipal administration, tech companies, and the media have great hopes for the technologies, and expect them to support timely care and prevent people with dementia from getting hurt (See KL Local Government Denmark, 2021; Nyvang Burmeister, 2022).

Focusing specifically on temporality and rhythms in care work, and how they are reconfigured, intertwined with, and occasionally clash with the temporal demands ingrained in care technologies, we explore *how care workers negotiate and balance temporality when working with surveillance technologies.* Surveillance practices are used differently during the day and at night. To accommodate this, we look at alarms, monitoring technologies, and timely responses, first during night, and then during day shifts. In the last part of the chapter, we draw on Bogard's work of surveillance as simulation, to further articulate how the technologies understood as surveillance play a role in simulating ideals for a timely response in dementia care.

Context and method: surveillance technologies at three nursing homes

Our analysis is based on ethnographic fieldwork at three nursing homes that use different surveillance technologies. The first nursing home, Lakeside[1] in Denmark, uses technologies focused on tracking or detecting movements, such as motion sensors, door sensors, and GPS trackers (see Figures 3.1, 3.2, and 3.3). A legal framework[2] in Denmark was developed for increased use of these technologies. Previously, nursing homes had to apply to the municipality for permission to use these technologies. Now, the head of

Figure 3.1: A motion sensor

Source: Photo by Astrid Meyer

Figure 3.2: A door sensor

Source: Photo by Astrid Meyer

the nursing home can make the decision autonomously (as long as the resident or relatives do not object). The legislative revision reflects a change in how the technologies are perceived. Previously, the technologies were associated with an invasion of privacy and a use of force. In contrast, now they are framed as 'safety-enhancing welfare technologies', which alert care workers when potentially dangerous situations occur, enabling them to take preventive actions immediately. Thus, motion sensors alert care workers whenever a resident who is at risk of falling leaves the bed, while door sensors alert care workers when a resident with dementia, who needs companionship to stay safe outside the nursing home, leaves the apartment

Figure 3.3: GPS trackers

Source: Photo by Astrid Meyer

or unit. GPS tracking is used in two ways. Firstly, it is used to support the care of residents who enjoy walks. In this case, the intention of the GPS tracker is to make it safer for them to continue walking alone, as they are easy to find if they get lost. Secondly, the GPS tracker is used to prevent residents from leaving the nursing home alone if they are deemed unable, for instance, to navigate safely in traffic. In such cases, the GPS tracker is typically linked to a geo-fence, which triggers an alarm when the resident leaves the premises. Through the GPS coordinates, carers can quickly find and accompany the person back.

The two other nursing homes, Norwegian Glenview and Danish Evergreen, have expanded surveillance further by using technologies that display live images of residents' apartments. At Glenview, the images are modified, making it impossible to recognize the displayed person, but possible to see whether a resident is out of bed or has fallen over (see Figure 3.4). Meanwhile, Evergreen uses unmodified live images (see Figure 3.5). In both nursing homes, the care workers make use of the live images with residents who are disturbed by a physical check. In these cases, this type of video check-in technology is considered to be less intrusive than a physical check, where care workers risk waking residents.

Ethnographic fieldwork was carried out to study the use of the technologies. Extensive fieldwork took place at Lakeside between April 2021 and September 2022 as part of a large, collaborative research project where the nursing home, the municipality, and researchers explored the use of surveillance in care work together, and the ethical issues that emerged when using these technologies.[3] Two researchers, AM and SAB, shadowed and interviewed care workers (Czarniawska-Joerges, 2007), and residents, and observed daily life at the nursing home. Meanwhile, the fieldwork by SAB at Glenview and Evergreen was less extensive, consisting of six to nine interviews and observations at each place. The fieldwork at Glenview took place in August 2022, and was part of a research project investigating international experiences of using surveillance technologies. Between 2017 and 2022, the fieldwork at Evergreen explored the implications of a trial, in which the Danish Ministry of the Interior had granted seven municipalities permission to use video check-ins in care for nursing home residents with dementia, after they or their relatives approved its use[4] (Ballegaard and Andersen, 2023).

The legislation in Denmark and Norway is similar, as both allow for certain surveillance technologies to be used to enhance safety for people

Figure 3.4: A live image depicted by the sensors used at Glenview

Source: Sensio, used with permission

Figure 3.5: A sensor in a resident's apartment at Glenview

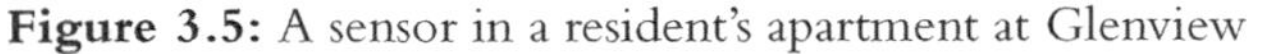

Source: Photo by Stinne Aaløkke Ballegaard

with dementia who are at risk of being harmed. The usage presupposes that surveillance technology is the least intrusive means of taking care of residents with dementia.[5] While both countries agree that GPS tracking and sensor technologies may be the least intrusive ways of monitoring movement, they did not agree on the use of video during our fieldwork. In Norway, the use of video was, and still is, seen as less intrusive than a physical visit (Eide and Barken, 2021), while additions to the Danish Social Services Act[6] explicitly mentioned that video cannot be used to monitor residents.[7] Thus, in Denmark, video check-ins could, during our fieldwork, only be used in the trial cited earlier, where special permission was granted.

Night

Surveillance and timely responses

We start by looking at the use of surveillance technologies during the night. At all three nursing homes, care workers used technologies aiming to support timely care, while avoiding waking or disturbing residents. A noteworthy example took place at Evergreen, where Linda, the night watch, explains how she used technologies in two ways to help the resident John. Firstly, the motion sensor alerted her if John left the bed. He struggled with his balance and needed either a supportive hand or a walker to get to the bathroom safely, but suffering from dementia, he would often forget this. Secondly, Linda used the video check-in during the morning to see if John was awake. Using video-based check-ins provided valuable information on his morning state, and helped her decide on the right time to enter his apartment. Linda explains that she must not enter too early, as this would agitate him since he needed time to wake up, but not too late either, as this entailed a risk of him falling, or becoming confused and frustrated by the effort of trying to put his own clothes on.

This example points to how surveillance technologies support care workers in aligning care work to the resident's rhythm, and consequently achieving timely responses. At the same time, it also points to how a timely response has multiple levels. Based on studies of controller systems such as air traffic control and crisis responses, Johansson and Lundberg (2017) suggest that a timely response is characterized by three basic notions: firstly, *temporal expectancies* linked to the particular environment help regulate activities. They relate to expectations of 'how processes will develop over time, on the times and timings of change, and on the times and timings of required corrective actions' (Johansson and Lundberg, 2017, p 116). Secondly, they argue for the idea of *time scales* when understanding timely responses. Here, the points of *perception, decision,* and *action* are differentiated, to understand more complex situations where expectations alone are insufficient for a timely response. This framework is centred around the idea of a controller who can perceive a task, decide what to do, and act on it (see Figure 3.6 for a visualization). Thirdly, the framework highlights the importance of *recovery intervals.* Drawing on Woods (2010), Lundberg and Johansson use the term recovery interval to consider a timely response as acting within the window where actions can be taken to avoid (negative) consequences.

As Linda describes her use of the motion sensor, it appears to follow the trajectory of perception leading to decision leading to action, laid out by Johansson and Lundberg. The care worker is alerted by the technology, decides what to do in the situation, and acts on the decision. However, in the case of video check-ins, the idea of a timely response appears to be more complex. Linda's temporal expectations are involved from the onset

Figure 3.6: A visualization of Lundberg and Johansson's time scales for a timely response

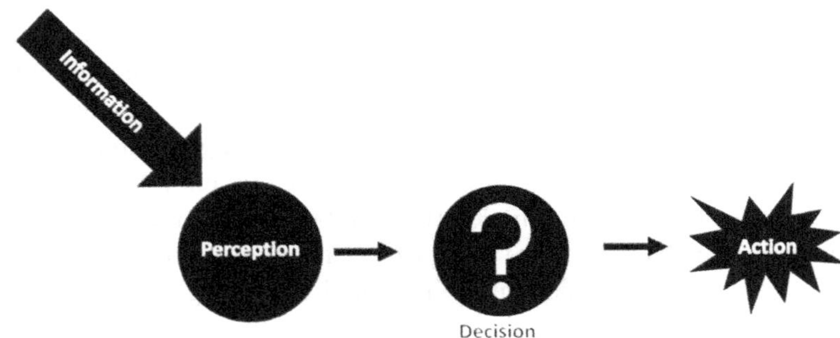

Source: Modified from Johansson and Lundberg (2017)

as she, rather than being alerted, must check in on John when she expects him to be awake. Furthermore, her temporal expectations also matter, when she waits a little while to enter at the right time. This idea of entering at the right time is equally interesting in terms of the recovery interval, as a component of a timely response. It points to how there is a window of time when entering may prevent John from falling, getting confused, or getting frustrated. At the same time, this observation also points to an additional aspect of the recovery interval: namely, that acting too early may disrupt a timely response. In this way, Linda's temporal expectations are key to finding the right time to act. In other words, surveillance technologies can support care workers in achieving timely responses, but Johansson and Lundberg's framework helps to articulate how this is by no means something the technology achieves alone. Rather, the timely responses potentiated by the surveillance technologies hinge on the care worker's existing knowledge and expectations. It shows how surveillance technologies can play a role in tinkering with time, as they provide information, which fits into the experimental effort to be at the right place at the right time. Care workers hence use surveillance technologies to avoid or reduce everyday arrhythmia, as they balance the complex polyrhythmic demands of institutional care work.

Supplementing the technology

During our fieldwork, we also saw examples of care workers who encountered challenges when using surveillance technologies during the night, and who actively tried to bridge these challenges. At Lakeside, the night watch, Sandra, would sneak in and adjust every motion sensor at the beginning of her shift to ensure it faced the right direction, and then trigger the alarm to check that it worked. She would then rush out again and close the door, before the alarm sounded on her tablet. Sandra would do all this while being highly conscious not to wake the resident. When asked why she went through all the trouble of adjusting, she explains that the sensor could have been moved ever so slightly, making it unlikely to register relevant movement. Checking the sensors in person was the only way for her to make sure she could trust the alarms throughout the night. This is an example of a care worker who actively engages with surveillance technologies and wants to depend on them in her work. However, she first needed to tinker with the technologies, to ensure they did what she expected. This type of tinkering could be conceptualized as repair work (Schwennesen, 2021), as Sandra actively engages with the technology to make it meet established safety expectations.

While Sandra tries to bridge the challenges of using surveillance technology in care work by adjusting it to fit her own and the residents' needs, we witness other types of adjustments unfold at the Norwegian nursing home. At Glenview, the night watch is instructed to perform digital video check-ins three times during the night. However, they explain that there are limits to what can be observed digitally, specifically breathing or the lack thereof. Therefore, some night watches continue to perform physical checks in the morning, to ensure that all residents are alive and well. A unit manager explains that this had been a key issue when introducing the video check-in, as some care workers felt they failed to do their job properly if a resident passed away during their shift without their knowledge. Not noticing straightaway that someone has died conflicts immensely with a sense of moral responsibility and duty of care. To deal with this, some of the care workers take it upon themselves to take on additional work, by checking in person without being encouraged or instructed to do so.

Both these cases involve care workers who work with surveillance technologies and encounter challenges in trusting the system completely. They see gaps and work to fill these gaps in different ways. At Lakeside, this happens by tinkering with, and repairing, the set-up of the technology to make it more likely to give alarms. In this way, Sandra made sure the technology worked according to her expectations. However, at Glenview, the care workers supplement the technology by checking up on residents physically when they encounter gaps. This points to a reversal of how technologies are envisioned as being aids or supplements to human systems,[8] as the system comes to depend on care workers who deal with the system's blind spots. These ethnographic examples show surveillance as motivated by, but also depending on, care, as the technologies need care workers who complement and supplement them. As a result, surveillance technologies in nursing homes are by no means able to totalize care, they depend on continual tinkering.

Day

Timing use

Surveillance technologies are, in some cases, meant to indicate needs. When the residents cannot convey their needs themselves, the technologies may help facilitate timely responses. This is the case at night, where using the technologies is typically characterized by switching them on and leaving them on for the whole night. During the day, however, it is necessary to time when alarms are needed. Residents often spend their days on activities such as going for walks, getting visitors, napping, or watching TV. Throughout the day, there are activities where tracking technologies make sense, and situations where they are redundant or even a nuisance – such as when care workers may trigger alarms themselves by walking in front of a motion sensor while helping a resident. As a result, a particular type of time-specific work is associated with switching the technologies on and off. To find the right timing for using the technologies, the nursing home primarily relied on establishing routines and daily rhythms for using technologies adapted to each resident. This would be based on professional assessments, and annotated in the day-protocol[9] for each resident, which, for instance, reminded care workers to turn the motion sensor off first thing in the morning, to avoid triggering alarms while helping a resident get up.

Timing the use of technologies did, however, also often rely on the residents themselves accepting these technologies. This acceptance played a role in terms of respecting the residents, but in some situations, they also relied on the residents' acceptance and participation in terms of timing the use of the technologies. AM saw an example of this when she met Elsa. Elsa was a Lakeside resident who enjoyed walking to the nearby lake. Elsa got lost during such a walk before we started our fieldwork, and as a result, the nursing home asked her to wear a GPS tracker when going for a walk. Subsequently, Elsa could continue her walks, and it would be easy to find her if she got lost again. During an informal interview, Elsa extends an invitation for AM to go on a walk with her down to the lake. Upon leaving, Elsa first drops by the staff office to say she is going for a walk and asks for 'one'. By 'one', Elsa means a GPS tracker. The nursing home staff had made an agreement with Elsa to pick up a GPS tracker and let them know she was leaving. In this way, she did not need to wear a tracker the whole time, but only while walking. On the way out of the nursing home, AM asks Elsa about what she thought about wearing a GPS tracker. Elsa replies that she knew it told them where she was, and that was good. This shows how Elsa played an active role in finding the right time to wear a technology like GPS tracking. Social factors and communication between residents and staff thus also play an important role in establishing routines for the technologies. However, as dementia is a condition that changes over time, these routines must be adapted constantly to fit the current situation. This was also the case for Elsa, who, towards the end of our fieldwork, no longer remembered to ask for a GPS tracker before leaving. As a result, the nursing home ordered a GPS watch for her to wear constantly. Understanding this type of continuous follow-ups as tinkering makes it possible to highlight the ongoing problem-solving adapted to the concrete situation and the technologies used.

Tinkering towards a careful response

During the day, care work is characterized by being hands-on and socially present. Care tasks like helping someone get dressed, serving a meal, assisting with personal hygiene, and providing medication depend on tuning in and responding to the person needing help. Furthermore, documentation, coordination, and discussion on the course of treatment and care are important aspects of care due to daily developments in residents' situations and health. As a result, many different needs often coincide during the day, and care workers must juggle overlapping tasks. A care assistant at Lakeside summarizes this when she says: 'You never *just* do something at a nursing home' (italics added). She emphasizes that even just walking down the hallway to attend to a resident can involve multiple interruptions, as other care workers and residents call for her attention.

Surveillance technologies also play a role in constituting Lakeside's many interruptions, as the motion sensors, door alarms, and GPS trackers all trigger tablet alarms, which the care workers are always expected to carry. The tablets allow the care workers to read the residents' journals, write observations, and respond to alarms. They make a loud sound that many care workers describe as 'annoying'. The alarms are meant to interrupt as they indicate something is happening, which the care workers should react to. While observing at Lakeside, we encounter two problems with the tablet alarms. Firstly, at a very material level, the tablets are too big to fit in most pockets, which means they are put down often, usually on the trolleys care workers push around in the hallways when attending to residents (see Meyer et al, forthcoming). Secondly, some residents react strongly to the tablets when an alarm is triggered. Caroline, a care assistant, elaborates on this as AM shadows her:

> She explained that there are some residents, like Kaj, a man with severe dementia, who just cannot take hearing the sound of the alarm. When care workers attend to these residents, they typically leave the tablets outside. Then, alarms may go off without anyone around to attend to them. (Extract from AM's fieldnotes)

This way of dealing with alarms in certain care situations, points to an aspect of surveillance technologies raised by Wajcman (2015), on the relation between time and technology. Based on long-term studies in an office environment focusing on interruptions from calls, emails, and voice messages, Wajcman argues against a mechanistic approach to technologies as something constituting an environment of interruptions. Rather, she shows how employees are rarely in situations where their 'only response is to attend to the call for their attention' (2015, p 98). Wajcman argues for a socio-material understanding of time and temporality, entailing that both technologies and humans shape practices. This appears to be the case after the adoption of tablets with alarms at Lakeside. As articulated, the alarms make it possible for care workers to be at the right place at the right time. In some situations, care workers find it impossible to reconcile the alarms with their other work, and as a result, they bypass the alarms by leaving them out of hearing range. When care workers leave their tablets outside in the hallway and physically remove themselves from the alarms, they tinker with time in a different way. They tinker with how surveillance technologies facilitate time. By leaving the tablets behind, care workers weigh two rhythmic demands up against each other. On the one hand, there is the timely response facilitated by the tablets. This depends on responsive and alert care workers, who can be trusted to repeatedly hear and react to the alarm. On the other hand, there is the value of being present, to care for the person in front of them. This implies approaching care in ways that emphasize reoccurring, relational qualities and meaningful interpersonal connectedness (Tronto, 2015; Molterer et al, 2020). Receiving loud alarms in a setting where residents react badly to the alarm indicates a tension between the two. Care workers address this tension by altering between carrying the tablet around with them and leaving it behind. This is not a complete rejection of the technology, because they pick it up again. Rather, it is a tactic to decide when to value the uninterrupted care for, and wellbeing of, certain residents higher than timely responses to the needs of other residents as determined by the technology.

Tensions creating more tensions

On many occasions, care workers tell us about how they think there are too many alarms, that the alarms contribute to a stressful work environment, and that the alarms keep ringing in their heads after they go home. At Lakeside, we observe how care workers distancing themselves from the tablets affects the number of alarms. The fact that care workers often leave their tablets in the hallway when attending to residents, means that the unanswered alarms pass from one tablet to the next. Consequently, the same event can trigger multiple alarms. Thus, tinkering sometimes multiplies the alarms to an extent where care workers experience too many alarms during the workday to take all of them seriously.

The term *alarm fatigue* is often used to describe situations where alarms are considered a 'nuisance', and where people, as a consequence, may 'disable, silence or ignore the warning that is intended to make the environment safe' (Cvach, 2012, p 269). In such situations, the nuisance alarms create encourages desensitization rather than making the environment safer. We argue that surveillance technology depends on the care workers who tinker with it, and how they integrate it with their existing knowledge. However, care workers tinker with the technology in ways that often prioritize the person in front of them, rather than the system at large. Care workers are placed in difficult situations without any obvious solutions. If they refrain from tinkering with the surveillance technology and alarms, this may affect the quality of care. If, on the other hand, they continue to tinker as they have done, they can end up with an unhelpful and even desensitizing number of alarms.

Surveillance perceived as a solution

Policy makers, municipal administration, tech companies, and the media point to increased use of technological solutions to the challenges associated with dementia care (KL Local Government Denmark, 2021; Nyvang Burmeister, 2022; Stella Care, 2023). Here, welfare technologies are often linked to saving time and optimizing care (Kamp et al, 2019). We saw a drastic increase in the use of surveillance technologies, while spending time at the nursing homes. For example, the number of GPS trackers at Lakeside went up from ten to just over twenty during the year and a half of our fieldwork.

Care workers often talk about the limitations of the technologies and how they come up short in many situations. At the same time, they often stress the technologies' importance and use terms like 'huge help' and 'a source of safety' when discussing them. While witnessing this combination of conflict and appreciation, we are left with questions about how nursing homes dealt with the care challenges addressed by video check-ins, GPS tracking, door alarms, and motion sensors before the technologies were available. We ask Marianne, an experienced care worker at Lakeside with 35 years of experience in Danish nursing homes, about this. She tells us how, when she first started working, she would receive calls about people with dementia who had left the nursing homes she worked at and would have to find a solution, usually involving a taxi, to get them back. She does, however, also underline that the premise had changed dramatically, as the residents today are older, sicker, and in need of more care:

> The category of residents is getting heavier and heavier and more and more difficult, and they do so both physically, psychologically, and

socially. The ones who come here, they always bring a lot of baggage and problems with them. (Interview with Marianne)

Marianne partially attributes this development to the Danish policy of allowing people to age in their own homes for as long as possible (see also Kamp and Hvid, 2012). As a result, the residents moving into a nursing home like Lakeside are older, frailer, and more ill than residents were when she started working. She sees the new technologies as troublesome and often unpredictable, but also as a resource. Several other care workers and nursing home management similarly stressed that surveillance technologies figured as a resource to tap into. This points to a complex picture of care work and technologies as experienced by care workers. They are dealing with emerging and ever-moving care challenges, and see the technologies as a part of this moving picture.

William Bogard's *The Simulation of Surveillance* (1996) helps to understand the profound disparity between the surface-level portrayal of events at nursing homes and the intricate realities of care work. In Bogard's view, surveillance does not go behind or penetrate the surface of things to make everything transparent and available. Instead, it carries with it a fantasy of a manageable world that transcends the limits of physical presence and provides the illusion of omnipresence. Systems like video check-ins, GPS tracking, door alarms, and motion sensors are positioned in ways where they at once represent the challenges and offer a solution to them. They offer a fantasy of a system where care workers are made aware of problems in time for them to react and prevent them. Bogard characterizes this as hypercontrol, a concept that steps beyond being efficient and instead is 'prefficient' as it 'eliminates problems before they emerge' (Bogard, 2005, p 60). As we have shown, this logic of hypercontrol does not last long in everyday care situations. The alarms meant to facilitate timely responses require interpretations and judgement, and may not always reach the busy care worker. Care workers deal with the ambiguity between alarms indicating that they ought to be alert and how they tinker with the system daily. As reflected by Marianne and the other care workers, this ambiguity is exacerbated by perceiving surveillance technologies as a solution to many care challenges at nursing homes, while constantly struggling when working with them. While surveillance systems may offer the fantasy that hypercontrol is within reach, it does not take many hours at a nursing home to establish that this remains a simulation, and impossible to realize in practice.

Recognizing tinkering

It is important to recognize that care workers often tinker, while also interacting with the surveillance system through tablets. The surveillance system does not register how care workers adjust the technology continuously, and it does not see the logic when they refrain from responding to certain alarms. This poses a potential issue if policy makers, tech companies, and administrative staff follow the traces left in the system and continue to push the technologies based on the simulation in the system. Peter, who works administratively at the municipality and helps in person at nursing homes when they experience technical difficulties, told us more about this. He was fully aware of the challenge of looking at the surveillance system alone. He shares a story in which he accidentally witnessed a resident leaving unaccompanied, and later was able to observe the same resident through the system:

> I drove past a man who evidently was confused and upset. There was a car from the municipality, and two care workers who tried to calm him down and help him. I could guess what the scenario was, and after a quick glance at the [surveillance] system's dashboard I could see that no one had handled the geofence alarm. It was handled 85 minutes later. This is a good illustration of how the data only is 'half the truth'. Care workers had responded to the alarm immediately. … The resident was very fast and got far through a network of paths … but the care workers were with him within 15–20 minutes. Here, the data might show we don't do enough, but in this scenario, the reality is different – the care workers had heard the alarm, and in the 'heat of the battle', they had not handled the alarm [in the app], but everyone knew what to do. (Extract from email correspondence with Peter)

This shows how surveillance data does not necessarily reflect care workers' timely responses. Had Peter only looked at the surveillance system, it would have seemed like a situation in which the care workers had failed to *do enough* or had acted too late, while, in fact, they responded promptly when the resident left the nursing home. This is work which bypasses the system without leaving accurate data behind.

The flip side of this story, where emergencies develop, which the simulation cannot see, is also worth considering. These are incidents such as when the resident Kurt left Lakeside and went missing for eight hours. He wore a GPS tracker, but one day, a substitute care worker forgot to charge it, and the tracker ran out of battery. Later that same day, Kurt went out on a long walk alone, wearing shorts in the brisk autumn weather; he took a bus to the other side of town and finding him again involved a long, stressful search. Luckily, he was unharmed, but this tale shows that there are situations where people get lost, and the GPS tracker cannot register it. In tandem with Peter's story, it points to how a simulation involves reducing the inherent complexity of care work into an easily digestible overview, yet the reduction loses much of the richness and nuance that goes into the subtleties and intricacies of care work.

Given the strong push for technologies in care work, the implications of surveillance as simulation are concerning. The simulation of surveillance creates a sense of order and control which can be reassuring from the perspective of administrators and policy makers, but without recognizing tinkering there is a risk that simulation produces the illusion of control. This underlines the importance of people who, like Peter, know of the limitations when looking at information from the surveillance system alone. A surveillance system is not necessarily able to surveil or regulate itself, as it is blind to the many ways people adjust the technology. This tension between simulation and lived reality is important, and we maintain that there is a need to recognize tinkering as essential to making care work at nursing homes. As a result, it is crucial to keep looking at situated practices with surveillance technologies when making regulatory decisions about them.

Conclusion

In this chapter, we have focused on those forms of surveillance motivated by an attempt to improve care. We have explored how timely responses and surveillance technologies, such as GPS tracking, motion sensors, door alarms, and video check-ins, intertwine and sometimes clash with dementia care. Drawing on ethnographic fieldwork from three nursing homes in Scandinavia, we looked at how care workers negotiate and balance temporality when working with technologies. In this context, we employed the idea of tinkering as an experimental approach to care and technology.

We find that surveillance technologies, especially at night, depend on care workers who tinker when they combine their existing knowledge with the technologies to support timely responses, and align themselves with residents' rhythms. At the same time, the technologies also depend on ongoing tinkering, as care workers adjust and supplement them. During the day, the relationship between timely responses and alarms is more intricate. It requires care workers who engage actively in negotiating and balancing temporalities – in ways that sometimes involve minimizing or even blinding their surveillance gazes, when care workers physically distance themselves from the tablets to avoid unwelcome interruptions. Consequently, working with surveillance technologies is a complex process involving weighing up values, and balancing responsibilities through various timely responses. We argue that care workers tinker with the technology to find ways to address the complex tensions that arise when introducing alarm-intensive technologies into nursing homes.

Care workers tinkering with the system may address problems and moral dilemmas in concrete situations, but not at a larger scale. Because care workers tinker with the surveillance in ways that run parallel to the system, much of their tinkering is unregistered, or recorded in misleading ways by the technologies. Drawing on Bogard's concept of surveillance as a simulation helps us to highlight how a system can render tinkering invisible, while simultaneously offering a fantasy of a manageable world. This serves as a reminder that the problems and dilemmas care workers tinker with are also rendered invisible through this very process. Given the push for increased use of welfare technology, such as surveillance technology, in care work, it is important to know how surveillance may simulate a reality that is blind to many problems and solutions of everyday care work. When making decisions about surveillance in care work, it is crucial to be aware of these limitations, to avoid decisions based on a fantasy.

Acknowledgements

We would like to thank all the research participants who invited us into their homes and workplaces and shared their experiences with us. We also want to thank the editors for all their work towards realizing this volume, and especially Claire Elisabeth Dungey for her helpful comments and suggestions, as well as the participants at the King's College London workshop 'Times of Surveillance' for their insightful discussions and comments. Lastly, we want to thank our funders – the VELUX Foundation.

Notes

[1]   Throughout the chapter, we use pseudonyms for people and place names.

[2]   Bekendtgørelse om Tryghedsskabende velfærdsteknologiske løsninger i relation til afsnit VII I lov om social service, BEK nr. 1412 (Danish Order).

[3]   Through this, we gained access to the fieldwork opportunity at the nursing home collaborating with the project. The fieldwork was approved by The Danish Centre for Social Science research's ethical review board.

[4]   Bekendtgørelse af lov om frikommunenetværk. LBK nr 831 (Danish Act).

[5]   Lov om pasient- og brukerrettigheter, nr 30 (Norwegian Act), and Bekendtgørelse af lov om social service LBK nr 170 (Danish Act).

[6]   Lovforslag nr. L 156, fremsat d. 6.2.2019, Forslag til Lov om ændring af lov om social service, lov om almene boliger m.v., lov om leje af almene boliger og forskellige andre love, afsnit 2.6.3.

[7]   This addition was revoked in 2024 after our fieldwork, where legal changes allowed nursing homes to use live images in specific situations. See: Lov om ændring af lov om social service, lov om voksenansvar for anbragte børn og unge, lov om retssikkerhed og administration på det sociale område og lov om opkrævning af underholdsbidrag LOV nr 680 (Danish Act).

[8]   An example of this is how welfare technologies are described, by the Nordic Welfare Centre (2024), as 'an important tool for, among other things, enabling the Nordic region's around 1,200 municipalities to handle the pressure and to continue to provide high-quality social welfare.'

[9]   Each resident has a so-called 'visiting plan' (*besøgsplan*) which is a detailed daily care plan.

References

Ballegaard, S.A. and Andersen, D.B. (2023) Teknologi til støtte og omsorg: undersøgelse af forlængede frikommuneforsøg med teknologi til borgere med demens eller kognitiv funktionsnedsættelse. *VIVE*. Available from: https://www.vive.dk/media/pure/4vlroovj/18706400

Bogard, W. (1996) *The Simulation of Surveillance*. Cambridge: Cambridge University Press.

Bogard, W. (2005) 'Welcome to the Society of Control: The Simulation of Surveillance Revisited', in K. Haggerty and R. Ericson (eds) *The New Politics of Surveillance and Visibility*. Toronto: University of Toronto Press, pp 55–78.

Cvach, M. (2012) 'Monitor Alarm Fatigue: An Integrative Review', *Biomedical Instrumentation & Technology*, 46(4): 268–77.

Czarniawska-Joerges, B. (2007) *Shadowing: And Other Techniques for Doing Fieldwork in Modern Societies*. Malmö, Sweden: Herndon, VA: Oslo: Liber; Copenhagen Business School Press; Universitetsforlaget.

Eide, T. and Barken, T. (2021) Etikk, lovverk, informasjons- sikkerhet og personvern. Helsedirektoratet. Available from: https://www.ks.no/globa lassets/fagomrader/helse-og-omsorg/velferdsteknologiens-abc/Velferdst eknologiens-ABC-Emne-C-F41-web.pdf

Grosen, S.L. and Hansen, A.M. (2021) 'Sensor-floors: Changing Work and Values in Care for Frail Older Persons', *Science, Technology, & Human Values*, 46(2): 254–74.

Helsedirektoratet (2024) Digital hjemmeoppfølging, hjemmesykehus og velferdsteknologi. Available from: https://www.helsedirektoratet.no/ tema/digital-hjemmeoppfolging-hjemmesykehus-og-velferdsteknologi (Accessed: 28 February 2024).

Jansky, B. (2024) 'Digitized Patients: Elaborative Tinkering and Knowledge Practices in the Open-source Type 1 Diabetes "Looper Community"', *Science, Technology, & Human Values*, 49(1): 53–77.

Johansson, B.J. and Lundberg, J. (2017) 'Resilience and the Temporal Dimension – The Chimera of Timely Response', *Theoretical Issues in Ergonomics Science*, 18(2): 110–27.

Kamp, A. (2021) 'Temporalities of Digital Eldercare', in H. Hirvonen, M. Tammelin, R. Hänninen, and E.J.M. Wouters (eds) *Digital Transformations in Care for Older People*. London: Routledge, pp 93–110.

Kamp, A. and Hvid, H. (2012) *Elderly Care in Transition: Management, Meaning and Identity at Work*. Copenhagen: Copenhagen Business School Press. Available from: https://tidsskrift.dk/njwls/article/view/26760 (Accessed: 8 February 2024).

Kamp, A., Grosen, S.L., and Hansen, A.M. (2023) 'Tinkering with (In)visibilities: Caring for Older People with Surveillance Technologies', *Sociology of Health & Illness*, 45(3): 605–22.

Kamp, A., Obstfelder, A., and Andersson, K. (2019) 'Welfare Technologies in Care Work', *Nordic Journal of Working Life Studies*, 9(S5): 1–12.

KL Local Government Denmark (2021) Fælles erklæring om velfærdsteknologi. Available from: https://videncenter.kl.dk/media/27695/kl_faelles-erklaer ing-om-velfaerdsteknologi.pdf (Accessed: 12 March 2023).

Law, J. (2010) 'Tensions in Veterinary Practice', in Mol, A., Moser, I., and Pols, J. (eds) *Care in Practice: On Tinkering in Clinics, Homes and Farms*. Bielefeld: Transcript-Verlag, pp 57–72.

Lefebvre, H. (2009) *Rhythmanalysis: Space, Time and Everyday Life*. Translated by S. Elden and G. Moore. Continuum.

Lyon, D. (2001) *Surveillance Society: Monitoring Everyday Life*. Buckingham [England]; Philadelphia: Open University Press (Issues in Society).

Løvschal-Nielsen, P., Andersen, R.S., and Meinert, L. (2022) 'Tinkering with Time versus Being under the Spell of Time', *Medical Anthropology*, 41(2): 215–227.

Meyer, A., Ballegaard, S.A., and Albrechtslund, A. (forthcoming) 'Hard-Earned Glimpses: Using GPS Tracking in Dementia Care'.

Mol, A., Moser, I., and Pols, J. (eds) (2010) *Care in Practice: On Tinkering in Clinics, Homes and Farms*. Bielefeld: Transcript Verlag.

Molterer, K., Hoyer, P., and Steyaert, C. (2020) 'A Practical Ethics of Care: Tinkering with Different "Goods" in Residential Nursing Homes', *Journal of Business Ethics*, 165(1): 95–111.

Nordic Welfare Centre (2024) Welfare Technologies. Available from: https://nordicwelfare.org/en/welfare-policy/welfare-technology/ (Accessed: 28 February 2024).

Nyvang Burmeister, L. (2022) '260 GPS'er er i brug til 4.000 demente: »Svært at vurdere, om det er det rigtige leje', Lokalavisen Aarhus, 19 March. Available from: https://aarhus.lokalavisen.dk/samfund/ECE13802647/260-gpser-er-i-brug-til-4000-demente-svaert-at-vurdere-om-det-er-det-rigtige-leje/ (Accessed: 28 February 2024).

Peacock, V., Bruun, M.K., Dungey, C.E., and Shapiro, M. (2023) 'Surveillance', in H. Nieber (ed) *The Open Encyclopedia of Anthropology*. http://doi.org/10.29164/23surveillance (Accessed: 28 February 2024).

Peine, A. and Neven, L. (2019) 'From Intervention to Co-constitution: New Directions in Theorizing about Aging and Technology', *The Gerontologist*, 59(1): 15–21.

Pols, J. and Willems, D. (2011) 'Innovation and Evaluation: Taming and Unleashing Telecare Technology', *Sociology of Health & Illness*, 33(3): 484–98.

RISE (2024) Digital Vård och Omsorg. Available from: https://www.digitalvardochomsorg.se/om/ (Accessed: 28 February 2024).

Schwennesen, N. (2019) 'Surveillance Entanglements: Digital Data Flows and Ageing Bodies in Motion in the Danish Welfare State', *Anthropology & Aging,* 40(2): 10–22.

Schwennesen, N. (2021) 'Between Repair and Bricolage: Digital Entanglements and Fragile Connections in Dementia Care Work in Denmark', in A. Peine, B. Marshall, W. Martin, and L. Neven (eds) *Socio-Gerontechnology: Interdisciplinary Critical Studies of Ageing and Technology*. London: Routledge, pp 175–88.

Stella Care (2023) The Best GPS Devices for People with Dementia. Available from: https://stellacare.dk/en/ (Accessed: 23 February 2023).

Tronto, J.C. (2015) *Moral Boundaries: A Political Argument for an Ethic of Care* (1st edn). New York: Routledge.

Videncenter for digitalisering og teknologi (2025) Sundhed og ældre. Available from: https://videncenter.kl.dk/fagomraader/sundhed-og-aeldre (Accessed: 19 February 2025).

Wajcman, J. (2015) *Pressed for Time: The Acceleration of Life in Digital Capitalism.* Chicago, IL: University of Chicago Press.

Woods, D.D. (ed) (2010) *Behind Human Error* (2nd edn). Farnham; Burlington, VT: Ashgate.

PART II

Real-Time Monitoring

4

Divergent Temporal Dynamics and Time Work Among Delivery Workers in Denmark and Malta

Kalle Kusk

Introduction

'Did you watch this one?'
'We've seen all of them, three, four times.'
I was browsing through Bollywood movies in the YouTube app on the centrepiece 65" TV. We settled on a drama after a bit of discussion.

While this discussion is taking place, the smartphone locations of the delivery drivers are shared with their employers every few seconds in real time. They do not have to, nor do they, pay much attention to this unceasing tracking, and instead their conversation centres around whether this or that movie features a famous Hollywood monkey. These delivery workers, my interlocutors, are waiting for orders to be assigned to them in the northern part of Malta, a small island country in the Mediterranean Sea.[1]

I never had to wait long enough to watch movies during my stint as a delivery worker in Aarhus, Denmark. Here, my fellow workers and I received orders constantly, and applied optimization strategies: efforts that meant we were always moving. However, the workers in Malta, as well as my colleagues in Aarhus, wore the same fluorescent company jackets and delivery bags, just as we interacted with the same app on our phones to receive the work. In this chapter, I illustrate the divergent temporal dynamics of platform-mediated delivery work, where real-time tracking is fundamental to the surveillance through which work is organized. I begin with my fieldwork in Aarhus, where I worked as a delivery worker for six months, and then describe work practices in Malta, where, during three months of ethnographic fieldwork,

85

I met a group of workers who invited me in to watch movies with them while they were logged into the app.[2]

This chapter illustrates how temporal dynamics, or, in Lefebvrian terms, 'rhythms', are not only the product of specific technologies, as in this case of real-time monitoring, but instead formed in extended socio-material assemblages where both local conditions and workers' efforts to manipulate time play central roles. Here, I build on Judy Wajcman's (2014) argument that 'objects only take on their significance by way of our recurrent use of them' (Wajcman, 2014, p 34). In the context of platform-mediated work, surveillance sits inconspicuously at the core, as platforms use so-called 'data doubles' to algorithmically manage a fleet of loosely connected workers (Lee et al, 2015; Haggerty and Ericson, 2000; Duus et al, 2023). I use the concept of 'time work' offered by Michael Flaherty (2003) to analyse how people, in this case, food delivery workers, vigilantly customize their experience of time in various ways. In other words, this chapter aims to illustrate the extreme range of rhythms possible in platform-mediated work practices, contingent not just on contextual and technological factors, but also on vigilance from individuals and groups of workers.

This chapter's temporal focus pushes other pertinent aspects into the background, such as the economic disparity between the two settings, and the general living conditions of this precariously positioned class of migrant workers, whose families in their home countries often depend on their earnings (Floros and Jørgensen, 2022). These disparities are central to discussions of the platform economy, and many scholars are examining them, as they address the working conditions at single locations, and establish international collaborations to rate working conditions (Fairwork Foundation, 2024). However, in keeping with this volume, through a focus on temporality I show – through ethnographic detail – how real-time monitoring is the foundation of the everyday lives of platform workers, and how differences, and in particular disparities, in this type of platform-based delivery job, are contingent on factors outside both their and the platforms' control.

Delivering in real time

Platform-mediated food delivery work revolves around a smartphone app, typically installed on the workers' phones (Veen et al, 2020). This app dispatches orders to workers based on their current GPS location. The inner workings of this system are mostly opaque from the workers' perspective, but the platforms present it as the app offering a given order to the worker who is most optimally located, based on the restaurant's, customer's, and courier's locations, thus minimizing the distance to be travelled (see, for example, Wolt, 2024). After receiving an order from the app, workers pick up the food at the restaurant and deliver it to the customer, confirming that they have completed each step in the app. For the system to work, workers' locations in real time are constantly monitored, and the time taken to complete each step may be recorded and potentially commodified (van Doorn and Badger, 2020).

The platform I studied remunerated delivery workers on a piece-rate basis, meaning they received a fee per delivery. Piece-rate remuneration is common in food delivery, in particular, and in the gig economy, more generally (see, for example, Alkhatib et al, 2017), and rewards workers for completing as many tasks as possible in the shortest amount of time. This system, complemented by the often quite short delivery times required to deliver food before it is spoiled, means that the pace of work is often high. Julie Chen and Ping Sun take this up as they study the intersection of time and platform-mediated delivery work in China (Chen and Sun, 2020). They show how the dominant temporal order among Chinese food couriers leads to 'increasingly frenetic and fragmented manner[s]' (p 1563), with workers often rushing from one order to the next, neglecting traffic rules and safety to satisfy customers' 'expectations of immediate services' (p 1576). According to Duus et al (2023), this speed is connected to the attempt by platforms to create an image of aspatial information and communication technology (ICT) time, where time is compressed, and duration replaced by instantaneity.

Both the Chinese setting and Duus et al's setting in Belgium resonate with my experience in Aarhus, where the working speed was high. Soon after I started fieldwork, following the advice of an experienced worker, I upgraded my bike to one with an electric motor to move faster, and (once again following a colleague's advice) I tracked how many orders I could deliver in an hour. When working, I would pick up my bike in the basement under my apartment around 17:30, register as being online on my phone, and often while I was pulling my bike up the stairs, 10 to 15 seconds later, I would receive my first order. This frequently continued, with orders coming one after the other (or more than one at once, as I discuss later). My workday ended either when the number of orders slowed down, in which case I would sign off myself in the app, or when I had other things to attend to, in which case I would contact the human support team and request to go offline (Kusk and Bossen, 2022). Occasionally there were small breaks with no incoming orders, where I would, once again following a strategy shared with me by a colleague, bike around to change my location, so the platform would provide me with more orders. A recurring issue was that restaurants would be behind schedule, and a continuous source of frustration was that workers felt slowed down. One worker, Mathias, tells me about a negative interaction he had with a restaurant employee:

> Perhaps she was provoked when I asked her if they could prepare the food faster. ... She saw it as me telling them to hurry up and get their act together. ... But what I meant was that – just politely asking if they

could have the food ready a bit sooner, so I didn't have to wait for that long. Perhaps it was a misunderstanding, I don't know …

As this 'misunderstanding' demonstrates, interactions in this context are framed by the expectation that things will move quickly. Speed is the drivers' principal goal, as they are paid only for the orders delivered.

Owing to this relatively high pace, I would be quite lightly dressed, and expect to spend most of my working time either picking up or dropping off orders, and talking to other couriers only while waiting in restaurants. This pace meant that I would typically deliver between three and six orders per hour, depending on whether the restaurants were on time, and the distances I had to cover. Importantly, the workers are not harried in the sense that the company penalizes them for being late, as they would be in China (Chen and Sun, 2020).[3] Instead, they are motivated by the piece-rate remuneration to optimize their hourly earnings. Thus, they take advantage of this temporal order, and although they do face risks, they also reap some of the rewards of this speed by having generous flexibility, and report hourly earnings that are higher than what they would earn in other jobs with similar prerequisites.

A different p(l)ace

The frequency with which workers receive orders in Malta is much lower than in Aarhus.[4] When I travelled to Malta, I was a bit worried about whether and how I would find workers to interview, as I would not be undertaking work myself. However, finding workers with time to talk proved relatively straightforward. The workers are present on most centrally located street corners, and if I wanted to find a large group, I simply went to a fast-food restaurant, where they would be waiting in the dozens, leaving large clusters of motorbikes around (see Figure 4.1).

Figure 4.1: A cluster of motorbikes used by delivery workers in Malta

Photo: Kalle Kusk

Because of the long waits between orders, the average number of orders they deliver per hour is much lower than in Aarhus. Even during the busiest hours, workers end up waiting upwards of half an hour for an order. Just like the workers in Aarhus, the workers in Malta are paid per delivery, and the slow pace of work means that their income is very low, compared with the income from similar jobs in Malta. I spent time at various locations, and although there were exceptions, a typical character emerged – a young migrant man from South Asia who had migrated to Malta to work as a delivery worker. This worker struggles to make ends meet, and responds by working a greater number of hours at a lower intensity (and much lower pay) than before coming to Malta.

After moving between locations for a month, I settled in a square where I came to know a group of Nepali workers. They told me their stories of how they had come to Malta, how long they were in Malta, about their families, their favourite teams in the football World Cup, all between getting orders. As I am talking to a group of workers in the square, one of the workers I had spoken with several times, Rahim, comes over to chat. He tells me that he has not received an order for 45 minutes, so will be staying online all night. He is off to get some food in preparation.

After spending almost every day for two weeks in the square, I am invited to the nearby apartment where Rahim is living with his fellow workers. As I sit on the balcony, I see how the workers I got to know in the square drop in and out as they deliver orders. This apartment becomes my primary location when I return five months later.

The experience of the six workers who live in this four-bedroom apartment is vastly different from that of their counterparts in Aarhus. They wake up in the early morning and go online in the courier app, typically while still in bed. If an order is dispatched to them, they leave, then return to the apartment, cooking breakfast between orders. Starting around 10 in the morning, the group in the apartment gradually expands as more workers join. All these visiting workers, who are also Nepali, live in other apartments across the town, and either head directly to the apartment after waking up or go there after delivering their first order of the day. As these workers arrive, the workday gradually commences – often, each of the workers has been online (which is to say at work) for several hours already.

Movies, often Bollywood ones, run constantly on the apartment's TV, and their vibrant soundscape fills the atmosphere. Feature films, characterized by sketches, form an ideal background to the 'ding ding dings' that chime intermittently from the delivery apps, summoning the drivers to pick up delivery orders. As we wait, the workers and I sit on a leather couch. Each of them has two phones, one for work and one for leisure. In the afternoon, Rahim might be playing *Clash of Clans* on my left, while Sajit is scrolling through Instagram, then TikTok, then Facebook, on my right, beginning again in a continuous loop. Others look up news and sports results, which then become the subject of discussion. Video-calling family and friends is also a recurring daily event for everyone in the apartment and, often, calls would also be going on either side of me. The number of incoming orders takes on a rhythm throughout the day. The day starts with very few orders in the morning, then the pace picks up around noon for lunch, slows in the afternoon, with another peak around dinnertime, before slowing down for the night. Eventually, this pattern becomes so predictable that I too begin to scroll social media, play games, and stay updated on all kinds of recent events.

As in Aarhus, the workers in Malta are not penalized for failing to meet deadlines. However, the low number of orders dispatched per worker has implications. The fast pace that characterized my experience of working in Aarhus is not there. So, whereas I would be lightly dressed and remain seated on my bike between orders, the workers in Malta would arrive at the apartment and remove several layers of clothing between orders, unable to reap the rewards from the performance-based piece-rate model that the workers in Aarhus do.

Manipulating temporal experience

The difference in the number of orders between the two locations was an underlying condition that significantly altered the temporal dynamics of working through the platform, but the workers were also active in shaping the temporal dynamics of their work. Flaherty's concept of time work describes the various efforts humans make to 'promote or suppress a particular temporal experience' (Flaherty, 2003, p 19). Duus et al (2023) present two ways in which food delivery workers in Brussels engage in time work. Firstly, the workers use the scheduling flexibility afforded by the platform to 'exercise the kind of flexibility that allowed them to prioritize other activities, their studies for instance, as well as enabling them to avoid any commitment to a longer employment horizon' (Duus et al, 2023, p 203), thus they use the job to 'make' time for activities that are unrelated to the job, by exercising control over how their time is allocated and restricted. This means that the workers in Duus et al's study are not fitting life around work, but 'fitting work around life' (Duus et al, 2023, pp 203–5). Secondly, the riders manipulate the duration of parts of the work as they engage in 'different tactics for reducing unwanted time in the app' (Duus et al, 2023, pp 205–6). The workers in Brussels attempt to outsmart the app by identifying workarounds to control and optimize their interactions with the app, urging the restaurant staff to speed things up, and making waiting time more pleasant by finding ways to entertain themselves. These two types of time work – allocation and duration – provide a useful starting point for identifying differences between the workers in Aarhus, and those in Malta.

In Aarhus, as in Brussels, workers are generally able to fit work around life. They develop strategies for optimizing their schedules around outside activities, following customer demand on the platform (Kusk and Bossen, 2022). This includes flexibility in day-to-day scheduling, where workers will take other activities into account. For instance, one worker bases his work hours on his girlfriend's ever-changing schedule at a local cafe. Also, the contract the workers sign with the platform does not demand a minimum number of hours, as exemplified by one worker who took an 18-month break from work while remaining registered with the platform: 'It was probably a year and a half or so break, something like that', he says.

This worker simply found himself a bit short of money, and explains that he used his earnings from food delivery to supplement the student aid he received from the government. As Duus et al (2023) also observe of workers in Brussels, this flexibility is one of the main aspects that draws workers to start working through the delivery platform, and many of them remained cold at the prospect of a fixed-hours contract offered by a rival platform. Even more than in Brussels, where the workers had to sign up for shifts, the workers in Aarhus could simply slide online, and start delivering whenever they had time. There were no guaranteed earnings, and they were remunerated only for the orders they delivered.

On a day-to-day basis, the workers in Malta enjoy similar scheduling flexibility to those in Aarhus – there are no set times when they have to work and have no fixed earnings. As one says,

> The food delivery job is like a freedom job, I think. Because it's like you don't have like starting time or ending time, you know. You can start whenever you want ... and you end whenever you want. ... If you want to work like 18 hours, 20 hours per day, you can go online. ... If I don't want to work today or I don't want to work now, go offline. So, it's not like that in our contract.

This means that workers can take time off whenever they wish. One Thursday evening, when I visit the apartment, I expect everyone to be working. Instead, I am presented with an invitation: 'Let's go to a nearby campsite and party'. We ride off in two cars, celebrating the fact that one of the workers' wives had given birth the night before. The workers do not tell anyone that they were taking this – comparatively busy – evening off. Instead, all the other workers in the town deliver more orders, and thus, as in Aarhus, and more so than in Brussels, the workers possess the temporal agency to allocate time to work on a day-to-day basis.

A key difference between Aarhus and Malta lay in the fact that, before arriving, the workers in Malta had allocated an extended period of their lives to the primary goal of earning money. Thus, unlike the workers in Aarhus and Brussels, who go through only a brief onboarding process, the workers who arrived in Malta had already allocated a significant amount of time, work, and financial investment. As one worker explains one day in the apartment:

> '*How did you get your visa? How long did the process take?*'
> 'It takes almost nine months. … it's expensive. It's almost like €7,000, maybe more than that. Right.'
> '*And how did you pay? Loans?*'
> 'Yes, I take loans from the banks. From relatives.'

To make their effort and financial investment pay off, the workers in Malta allocate several years to earning money for themselves and their families, in which applying for visas in Malta itself becomes a form of time work. On top of the significant upfront investment, upon arriving in Malta, workers will often set up work visas and contracts for at least a year into the future, and many of them planned to stay in Europe for at least a few more years. This commitment to being in Malta primarily to work meant that they were typically also online outside of the busiest hours. This becomes evident one evening in the apartment, when Rahim offers me a spare bed, and I jot down as I walk home: 'Rahim's roommate is currently sleeping on the couch because he's online around the clock. There was a blanket.'

Rahim's roommate is just one of several delivery workers who planned to work around the clock. More commonly, however, the workers told me they worked between 14 and 16 hours per day, six to seven days a week, significantly more than they had been working before coming to Malta.

This difference, between allocating time over the short and over the long term, to some degree tracks the difference between those who were dependent or non-dependent on platform-mediated work (Schor et al, 2020). Yet the circumstances in Brussels, and those in Aarhus, feature workers who are dependent on their earnings from platform-mediated work as their sole income, without having allocated a period of their lives to work. Meanwhile, some part-time workers in Malta had another income, and thus, although not dependent on the work, performed it on the side to increase their income, often only working in hours with high demand.

Duus et al (2023) show how delivery workers in Brussels manipulated the perceived and actual duration of events, as they removed various forms of unwanted time through workarounds, and optimized interactions with the platform. Workers in Aarhus and Malta similarly identified workarounds and optimized their interaction with the platform to improve their earnings.

Elsewhere I have called such efforts 'on-the-road strategies' (Kusk and Bossen, 2022). These include waiting at certain steps of the process to pick up more than one order at a time, thus allowing them to get 'bundle orders', where they carry more than one order from a given restaurant to several customers at the same time. This is then complemented by routine interactions with restaurant staff, customers, and tech support, to reduce waiting time (Kusk et al, 2022).

An equally important part of optimizing efforts occurs when deciding which orders to accept. In Aarhus,[5] this is often up to the individual courier. However, given the slower pace in Malta, workers often have time to confer when an order comes in. This became particularly apparent in one conversation with someone new to the job. As I jot in my fieldnotes:

> After a while, he gets an order that he accepts. Then three guys gather around him, and I can just see the interface as they go through the various menus in the Bolt app. They're helping him with each step of unassigning the order. And they help him to accept the next one he gets, as well, and tell him to change his status to 'bicycle' in the app.

Thus, the workers do not do their time work in isolation but as a group.

The second aspect of manipulating duration is to shorten the perceived time. In Aarhus, this is hardly a problem: time passes quickly, as I am continuously delivering orders. The constant influx of new destinations, combined with a mindset of reducing unwanted time, is only occasionally disturbed by a slow restaurant. One evening I try to add some entertainment by listening to a podcast while working, but soon discover that the speed of activity is generally too high for me to pay proper attention to its content while working. Instead, I decide to settle on music. This is in contrast to Malta, where the apartment always has an ambience of Bollywood movies, which the workers watched while playing smartphone games, scrolling social media, making video calls, cooking, or talking with one another about life in Malta during the long waits between orders.

End of an era

During my weeks in the apartment in Malta, it becomes clear that the domestic setting is significantly shaping their work practices. It offers the workers ample opportunity to manipulate their temporal experience of working, at the same time as forming a social arena where they can communicate. However, this contingent setup did not last long.

One Sunday afternoon I am sitting on the balcony of the apartment and remark that in many ways, this apartment is perfect. The worker next to me nods in agreement, and then goes on to say what a shame it is that they have to move out the coming Wednesday: their lease is not going to be extended, and so they have found a new place to live through Facebook Marketplace.

The following Thursday morning, I walk around town, looking for members of the group. After looking for a few hours, I text one of them and am given the address of what appears to be a hotel on the other side of town. I walk to the location: 'It's up here, we'll come get you', a worker yells from a window above. Upon entering, I am greeted by an antiquated aparthotel. Their new apartment is noticeably smaller than their old one, and does not have the same amenities: the recliner couch is replaced by worn-down hotel chairs, the kitchen only has two old burners, and the smart TV is replaced by a broken 12" TV.

In addition to the material downgrade, this apartment is not situated in the restaurant district that surrounds the old one. The distance to the restaurant district, and the inconvenient third-floor location, means that the workers are less likely to receive orders there, and also that it takes longer to get to the restaurants once they do get an order. This means that in the days following the move, their daily work habits change drastically. There is no more sitting back and watching movies while waiting for work, now they have to stay out on the roads.

The loss of the apartment illustrates how contingent the work practice was upon a socio-material assemblage that, in Malta, included the apartment. A good waiting location was crucial for the workers in Malta, where the apartment allowed for both social interactions and individual expressions of temporal agency. Notably, neither the workers nor the platform had full control over this aspect, yet, from the workers' perspective, it was central to shaping their work, all of which happened outside of the real-time tracking. In other words, it was disconnected from their 'data double' (Haggerty and Ericson, 2000). Thus, the workers went back to their old way of working outside. However, they did not go back to the square where I first met them; instead, the group started to meet in the street below the apartment where they previously lived. No change had been implemented by the platform, yet over this time the work practice for these workers had significantly changed. The community, fostered by the apartment as a collective space, could no longer watch movies together, now belonging to an informally organized group with ties to the apartment.

A temporal twist

Fluctuations in customer demand are an everyday aspect of working through a food delivery platform, and knowing the nature of these swings helps workers decide when to work. However, these swings in demand occur not only on a day-to-day basis, but also depend on longer-term temporalities, such as seasons. In Aarhus, workers commonly accept that during the summer, the work is slower, whereas in winter, customers are more likely to order, and workers less likely to make themselves available. In Malta, these seasonal trends are reversed, as the customers were often tourists who mostly visit Malta in the summer months. In Aarhus, I worked from the autumn until early spring, whereas in Malta, I was with the workers in both winter and early summer. Both sets of seasonal conditions explain part of the difference in the relative number of orders in each setting. This means that although I am comparing the temporal dynamics of platform-mediated food delivery work in two different places – Malta and Aarhus – the full story must take into account the seasonality in both.

Even more important are the effects of the COVID-19 pandemic. When I was conducting my fieldwork in Aarhus, Denmark was under strict lockdown, and customers were not allowed to eat in restaurants. As a consequence, many food delivery platforms more than doubled their revenue, compared to the previous year. Although I never heard of two-hour waits in Denmark, some of the workers who had worked before the pandemic reported that they were seeing more orders during it.

In contrast, most of the workers I interviewed and interacted with in Malta, including all the workers in the apartment, did not work in Malta during the COVID-19 lockdown. Most of the workers in the apartment had arrived in September 2022, when most restaurants had reopened in Malta. However, when I was there, I occasionally met workers who had worked in Malta through the platform during the pandemic. They were not happy about the current situation: 'It's a big s*** now. Write that. … Last summer we earned more than €200 per day.'

This Eastern European worker, and two colleagues who wait with him outside of a centrally located McDonald's, are frustrated that it is impossible to earn as much as they did during and right after the COVID-19 pandemic. They initially blamed this on the fact that customers now went to restaurants to eat, and therefore ordered less. However, as the discussion continues, they go on to complain that more and more workers were arriving from South Asian countries, although there is not enough work to go round to start with.

The slowdown after the pandemic was not only due to a smaller number of orders, but also a greater influx of delivery workers. This was confirmed by two Nepali workers in the square. They tell me that their visa process had been going on for three years: 'We booked three appointments to go … Before the COVID my permit was accepted. Then COVID … and my permit is expired.' Because of the pandemic, the Maltese government put all visa applications from countries like Nepal on hold or rejected them. This in turn entailed increased earnings for the delivery workers who are already in Malta, or from an EU country and thus not required to obtain a visa.

The difference in number of orders per worker between the countries and, consequently, the pace of work should not be regarded as products of the differences between Denmark and Malta. Instead, they should be considered in terms of temporal dynamics, and as an illustration of the extreme variation in rhythm that is possible when working through these platforms. The number of workers, the number of orders, and local policies all have an impact on these dynamics.

Conclusion

For these food delivery workers, real-time monitoring is a quotidian precondition for working through a platform. Workers share their location continuously, which is then picked up by an opaque and centralized system that then dispatches their orders. In some settings, this real-time monitoring has an accelerating effect, as workers are continually pressed with orders that they deliver to customers to avoid penalties (as in China), or to increase their earnings (as in Aarhus).

The circumstances in Malta, however, demonstrate that real-time monitoring does not necessarily end in acceleration. As the workers waited between orders, this much slower pace of work resulted in low earnings and low productivity. Alongside the significant investment made by the predominantly non-European migrants to get a working visa in Malta, a vicious cycle was created. They continuously worked longer hours but with less work: a spiral that decelerated the flow, altering the rhythm of their day-to-day activities, to the point where they were waiting hours between orders. Although these external circumstances shaped their work, the workers in both Malta and Aarhus also shaped their own experience of working through the platform by engaging in time work, as they manipulated the allocation of time, and the duration of how long events would take and feel. This suggests that while the slowdown was involuntary, it did not produce passive workers. The domestic setting of the apartment in Malta played a central role, particularly in the latter form of time work, as it enabled the workers to spend time off the streets, socializing and watching movies. Because of this much slower pace, this domestic setting possessed a central role that only became apparent when their lease expired, and the workers had to resume working from the streets.

Documenting the perspectives of platform-mediated delivery workers offers ways to think about how working conditions at the local scale might be improved. For example, one way to do this might be to ensure comfortable waiting areas, which facilitate contact with other workers, as well as ensuring that the number of workers is commensurate with the work available. To some extent, the responsibility for such initiatives lies with the platforms. Yet, this ethnography shows the extent to which work practices are shaped beyond the platforms' control. It could be that assuming such responsibilities would entail even more intensive surveillance, which may not favour the workers. Consequently, although political directives help to establish better labour conditions, there are still locally contingent factors better addressed at a smaller scale. Moreover, the fact that the platforms still attempt to portray themselves as 'technology companies' rather than employers (Gillespie, 2010), in the many legal cases around worker classification in the platform economy at large, makes them even less willing to accommodate these workers through local material initiatives. This makes it even more important to call for locally based initiatives to improve the lives of platform workers.

Besides proposing local alternatives to large-scale initiatives, this chapter, to some extent, also problematizes some of the tacit assumptions that lie beneath, for example, the Fairwork Principles introduced by the Fairwork Foundation (2024). These principles include uncontroversial ideas such as 'a fair wage', where the platforms are rated as fairer when they have a 'mechanism to ensure workers earned above the minimum wage' (Fairwork Indonesia, 2023). The ethnographic work I offer here, however, brings out some of the nuances, showing how workers in Aarhus and Malta actually appreciate the temporal flexibility offered by the absence of set shifts, which is hard to reckon with guaranteed hourly earnings. Thus, a seemingly indisputably just principle envisions a way of working that is at some distance from how work is currently being done through the platforms, and potentially even at odds with some of the workers' own interests in 'shaping work around life'. Staying attuned to delivery drivers' own testimonies and experiences, and the forms of time work they undertake, will be key to ensuring that these principles support workers in the future.

Notes

[1]   In fact, Malta is so small that, in food delivery terms, it is only one delivery area, meaning that the same workers could work in the entire country. This justifies the comparison between Aarhus (a city, one delivery area) and Malta (a country, one delivery area) in this chapter.

[2]   Between the two periods of fieldwork in Aarhus and Malta, I also spent three months researching food delivery practices in Helsinki, Finland. These three months inevitably also shaped my view of the practice. However, for the sake of clarity here, I focus on examples from the contrasting experiences in Aarhus and Malta.

[3]   The lack of penalties also forms the basis of our argument elsewhere (Kusk and Bossen, 2022) that, in our case, the algorithmic management was more 'lenient' than what had been observed in other places.

[4]   Malta was chosen as a field-study location for following the same platform (Wolt) in a different setting than its native Nordic region, but one which was still inside the European Union. For this chapter, the two settings mainly perform the function of contrasting with each other, in terms of their temporal dynamics.

[5]   The centrality of these efforts was made clear to me during my field study in Helsinki (Kusk and Bossen, 2022).

References

Alkhatib, A., Bernstein, M.S., and Levi, M. (2017) 'Examining Crowd Work and Gig Work Through the Historical Lens of Piecework', *Proceedings of the 2017 CHI Conference on Human Factors in Computing Systems*, pp 4599–616.

Chen, J.Y. and Sun, P. (2020) 'Temporal Arbitrage, Fragmented Rush, and Opportunistic Behaviors: The Labor Politics of Time in the Platform Economy', *New Media & Society*, 22(9): 1561–79.

Duus, K., Bruun, M.H., and Dalsgård, A.L. (2023) 'Riders in App Time: Exploring the Temporal Experiences of Food Delivery Platform Work', *Time & Society*, 32(2): 190–209.

Fairwork Foundation (2024) *Fairwork Ratings*. Available from: https://fair.work/en/fw/ratings/ (Accessed: 20 October 2024).

Fairwork Indonesia (2023) 'Indonesia Ratings'. *SS*.

Flaherty, M.G. (2003) 'Time Work: Customizing Temporal Experience', *Social Psychology Quarterly*, 66(1): 17–33.

Floros, K. and Jørgensen, M.B. (2022) ' "Danish is Never a Requirement for these Jobs": Platform Housecleaning in Denmark through a Migration Lens', *Glocalism: Journal of Culture, Politics and Innovation*, 3. Available from: https://doi.org/10.12893/gjcpi.2022.3.5 (Accessed: 20 October 2024).

Gillespie, T. (2010) 'The Politics of "Platforms"', *New Media & Society*, 12(3): 347–64.

Haggerty, K.D. and Ericson, R.V. (2000) The Surveillant Assemblage. *The British Journal of Sociology*, 51(4): 605–22.

Kusk, K. and Bossen, C. (2022) 'Working with Wolt: An Ethnographic Study of Lenient Algorithmic Management on a Food Delivery Platform', *Proceedings of the ACM on Human-Computer Interaction*, 6(4): 1–4.

Kusk, K., Duus, K., Scott-Hansen, S., and Floros, K. (2022) 'Det usynlige menneske i platformsarbejde – en kvalitativ undersøgelse af algoritmisk ledelse', *Tidsskrift for Arbejdsliv*, 24(3): 28–42.

Lee, M.K., Kusbit, D., Metsky, E., and Dabbish, L. (2015) 'Working with Machines: The Impact of Algorithmic and Data-Driven Management on Human Workers', *Proceedings of the 33rd Annual ACM Conference on Human Factors in Computing Systems – CHI '15*, pp 1603–12.

Schor, J.B., Attwood-Charles, W., Cansoy, M., Ladegaard, I., and Wengronowitz, R. (2020) 'Dependence and Precarity in the Platform Economy', *Theory and Society*, 49: 833–61.

van Doorn, N., and Badger, A. (2020) 'Platform Capitalism's Hidden Abode: Producing Data Assets in the Gig Economy', *Antipode*, 52(5): 1475–95.

Veen, A., Barratt, T., and Goods, C. (2020) 'Platform-Capital's "App-etite" for Control: A Labour Process Analysis of Food-Delivery Work in Australia', *Work, Employment and Society*, 34(3): 388–406.

Wajcman, J. (2014) *Pressed for Time: The Acceleration of Life in Digital Capitalism*. Chicago, IL: University of Chicago Press.

Wolt (2024). *Wolt for couriers – Wolt*. Available from: https://wolt.com/en/couriers (Accessed: 20 October 2024).

5

Uncertain Times:
Citizen App and Temporalities
of Personalized Security
in New York City

Alice McAlpine-Riddell

Introduction

I am sitting in a Twin Peaks themed coffee shop in Bushwick, Brooklyn (NY) at eight thirty on a Monday morning, getting coffee with Tina and Kim before they start work. The shop serves beverages like lavender lattes and peppermint red eyes, the coffee cup sleeves adorned with quotes from the show, 'This is − excuse me − a damn fine cup of coffee'. It is raining heavily outside, the streets flowing rivers of dirty water from litter-blocked drains. Both Tina and Kim are White women in their mid-thirties who work remotely from their respective apartments a few blocks away. They are both slightly jaded after spending Sunday at the Renaissance Faire in Pennsylvania, a re-enactment entertainment extravaganza, combining a hodge-podge of bygone eras. As they discuss the corsets they wore, the sword swallowing they witnessed, and the cider donuts they ate, Tina receives a notification from Citizen, interrupting the conversation. 'Man slashed, two in custody', she reads out loud. Kim exclaims, 'It is eight in the morning, people!', while Tina continues this thought, 'I see them [notifications] when I wake up at night, and sometimes they are useful like information about a fire, but other times its missing children or a shooting. It's a lot and its constant.' She counts the notifications, 'two, four, six, eight, ten, ten from yesterday'.

Tina scrolls through all her Citizen notifications from the past week, which are saved on her iPhone notification centre. The list keeps rolling, ostensibly endless, against the backdrop of her home screen − a photo of her rescue dog Cookies. Alerts include 'Electrical Fire'; 'Missing 14-year-old'; 'Police mobilization'; 'Armed shoplifting at Walmart'; 'Search for robbery suspects'; 'Possible gunshot detected'; 'triple shooting'. Often the text trails off, 'person barricaded with …', 'White BMW fled from pol …', due to the condensed nature of notifications, prompting the user to click and swipe open to gain a fuller picture. Kim is quiet. She also has Citizen on her phone but has chosen to turn off notifications because she does not want to feel fearful in her neighbourhood. 'I know the dangers', she tells me on another occasion, 'I don't have to have it in my face.' Once the coffee is finished, I too receive the 'man slashed' notification, some 30 minutes after Tina.

This moment condenses the complex temporal and rhythmic entanglements of Citizen app and its users. Citizen is a live crime-and-safety tracking app operating in 60 US cities, with over nine million users across the country (Citizen, 2024). Citizen proclaims to be a 'personal safety network', providing access to 'real-time 911 alerts', scraped from police scanners that are relevant to 'public safety', such as fires, shootings, accidents, and protests. It also offers 'magic moments', reporting on local news like the return of a missing cat or on humorous events, such as 'rooster making noise in apartment'. The app sends out alerts, to users based on their location, whilst also pinning the incidents, represented as yellow and red squares, to an ever-updating dark-mode map of the city. Citizen also allows users to self-report incidents, and utilizes user-recorded footage, as users near an ongoing incident are prompted to 'go live' and film the situation as it unfolds. Functioning like a form of social media, users can also comment and post expressive emojis of anger, shock, and hope, that bubble across the screen. In 2020, Citizen topped the Apple charts for the most downloaded 'news app', ahead of *The New York Times*, Twitter, and *Fox News* (Bertoni, 2020). Its rule-breaking founder and Chief Executive Officer (CEO), Andrew Frame, was once arrested as a teenager for hacking into the National Aeronautics and Space Administration (NASA), before going on to make millions investing in early Facebook (Bertoni, 2020). So far, over ten billion alerts have reportedly been sent to users across the US (Citizen, 2024).

Citizen is a digital technology for community monitoring, as it encourages users to watch and report on one another. It is a form of 'digitalized vigilance' (Peacock, Introduction, this volume), as illustrated by its original name. When the app launched in 2016 it was called 'Vigilante', before being pulled from the Apple app store for violating the guidelines on user-generated content apps that risk physical safety. A few months later, the app rebranded and relaunched as Citizen, although many of the affordances remained the same. Vigilante's #CrimeNoMore, was replaced by Citizen's #ProtectTheWorld. The term 'Citizen' evokes a nationalistic mythology of the patriotic hero, in the form of the law-abiding citizen. It is both a personal call to action, and an inclusion in a broader community of like-minded concerned citizens. This deviation from the crime fighting of Vigilante, to Citizen's imperative towards safety, reflects a shift towards 'Big Mother' surveillance in general (Peacock, Introduction, this volume). It draws on the increasingly femininized language of empowerment, and treads a delicate balance between care and control. I have discussed this ambivalence and tension elsewhere (Riddell, 2023).

This chapter presents the ways in which Citizen app impacts the temporality of its users, through the immediacy of the 'go live' function and real-time crime mapping, and the interruption of notifications. It does so from the perspective of two bordering neighbourhoods of Brooklyn, New York: Bushwick and Bedford-Stuyvesant (Bed-Stuy).[1] In these neighbourhoods, there is a tension between the temporal modalities of Citizen, and the space-time experienced by its users. Following the Bogardian shift of surveillance towards simulation outlined in the volume's introduction, and how it effects social rhythm, this chapter explores the hyperreality of Citizen app and the production of disruption and arrythmia among its users. Through ethnography with users, I conceptualize Citizen as a simulation in which crime is instant and constant, as Citizen notifications become a jarring interruption into the everyday, creating an isolated present at odds with the rhythm of the neighbourhoods. In practice, Citizen often fails to provide updates in real time, sending out notifications at different times to users in the same location, or failing to remove historic crimes that haunt the homepage map. This creeping arrythmia creates uncertainty and alienation in users, which can develop into resistance and nonchalance, as some users switch off notifications, refuse to 'go live', and practise indifference. Others engage cyclically with the app, demonstrating a different kind of response. As I will show, the concept of 'affordances-in-practice' can offer insights (Costa 2018). Through it we can see technological affordances as more than mere architectural features of a platform, but rather, culturally informed artefacts, used in a variety of specific ways, in localized situations and social contexts.

Real-time crime, all the time

As Rob Kitchin argues, 'digital technologies are reconfiguring everyday temporalities' (2023). Smartphones are the constant companions of urbanites, sustaining a life that is 'always on' (boyd, 2012), characterized by an 'ubiquitous connectivity' (Madianou, 2016). A plethora of services available at one's fingertips, from goods to be delivered, rooms to be reserved, or cars to be ordered, all seemingly in an instant and on-demand, furnishes the impression of 'time compressed to zero degree' (Stine and Volmar, 2021, p 10). Citizen app exists within this landscape as one form of emergency media. From 911 calls and Facebook's safety check feature, to national and regional emergency alert systems about weather warnings, missing children, or even incoming missiles,[2] emergency media is versatile and ever evolving. As Elizabeth Ellcessor argues, 'the speed, interconnection, and everydayness of digital mobile media have created virtual "panic buttons" at our fingertips' (2022, p 3). From social media like X, to apps like Citizen, there is a proliferation of participatory engagement with emergency media, and 'crime in real-time', enabled by the promised immediacy of technology, creating 'uncensored, unsanitized, unfiltered versions of crime events' (Powel et al, 2018, p 69).

Citizen describes itself as enabling access to these crime events, providing 'real-time 911 alerts' and 'instant help' (Citizen 2024), cultivating a 'real-time awareness of nearby events' (Chordia et al, 2023, p 7). These real-time alerts are frequent and intense. A hallmark of simulation is how it professes reality, such as real-time or reality TV. It does not oppose the real but is rather a means of verisimilitude (Der Derian, 1990), in which virtual processes replace the actual (Bogard, 1996). Not only does Citizen purport to provide a map of crime in real time, but it simultaneously creates an atmosphere in which there is, to appropriate a headline, 'All the Crime, All the Time' (Herrman, 2019). This is Jenny's experience, who has lived in the city for most of her life. She expresses concerns about Citizen, and the skewed perspective of her neighbourhood it gives:

> The app makes it seem like we live in like a very crime riddled neighbourhood. I'll have a notification that 3 miles away, someone was stabbed. And then we walk the dog and see nothing is wrong out here. It makes it seem a lot worse than it seems to me just being around the neighbourhood.

While, for Bogard, 'surveillance always looks *through or behind* something; simulation is a projection *onto* something (a screen)' (Bogard, 1996, p 21, emphasis in original). Bogard's argument is that surveillance has shifted in the televisual age to being a simulation, a hyperreal illusion of control. He gives examples of simulations such as cybernetics, gaming, and police profiling, which work to transform the subject of the simulation's sense of rhythm (Lefebvre, 2013). I use the term 'rhythm' following Lefebvre's expansion of spacetime to encompass energy, as, 'everywhere where there is interaction between a place, a time and an expenditure of energy, there is rhythm', (2013, p 25), which includes repetition, and linear and cyclical processes. The everyday is fundamentally an experience of and in rhythm. There are multiplicitous rhythms of the everyday and the body, which Lefebvre refers to as 'polyrhythmia', and when internal rhythms are in accord there exists a state of 'eurhythmia'. The inverse, 'the discordance of rhythms', results in the 'fatal disorder' of 'arrhythmia' (2013, p 25). Regarding temporality, Lefebvre aligns 'presence', a being in rhythm with oneself, others, and the polyrhythms of one's neighbourhood, with eurhythmia, and the 'present', the immediate and real time, conversely with arrhythmia. Thus, for Jenny, Citizen projects an image onto her neighbourhood via her phone screen, an image that is 'very crime riddled', and at odds with her lived experience of the polyrhythms of her neighbourhood. This is not to say that Citizen is a-rhythmic but rather that its rhythms are in discord with Jenny's experiences of her neighbourhood, producing a sense of arrythmia. Moreover, when users speak of this dissonance, the hyperreality of Citizen is revealed, in which the perception of crime, as happening all the time, replaces the reality of decreasing crime rates (Akinnibi and Wahid, 2022; Fetterman et al, 2023) and the relative safety of Brooklyn neighbourhoods.

The hyperreal is a simulation of reality that appears more real than reality itself. The term was first coined in 1975 by Umberto Eco (1990), a reference to the North American imagination for the real fake, citing Disneyland and Las Vegas as the original sites of simulation. Jean Baudrillard similarly framed the US as hyperreal, as 'a giant hologram … a three-dimensional dream' (2010, p 29). For Baudrillard, hyperreality is a simulation, where the distinction between reality and its representations dissolves (1994). I am using the concept of hyperreal as a filter through which to analyse Citizen app. It is important to note that Baudrillard has been critiqued for a lack of evidence to support his theoretical claims (Cole, 2010). My application of hyperreality comes from my fieldwork, in which Citizen is frequently framed as representing a neighbourhood at odds with my interlocutors' concrete experiences of their neighbourhoods. This is not to say that it is unreal, but rather that it creates a hyperreality within a multiplicity of subjective realities that co-exist and overlap as competing rhythms within the city. New York, 'the shining and perishable dream itself', (Didion, 2008, p 231), also has an air of hyperreality, in the sense that it is place continually recreated and recast by its representations, through the filmic imagination of Hollywood. Picturing New York City as Gotham, a crime-filled city in need of cleaning up by a vigilante hero, is an image Citizen has latched onto. Calls of 'Gotham needs Batman' fill comments sections, and the ominous dark mode map further encourages such links.[3]

The hyperreal is sustained by the image. Images represent a surreal enterprise, and to quote Susan Sontag, are a 'creation of a duplicate world, of a reality in second degree, narrower but more dramatic than the one perceived by natural vision' (2019a). This is exemplified by the photos and clips posted on Citizen, which are often sensational: flames exploding out of buildings and rows of emergency vehicles with flashing red and blue lights. The frame is specific, withholding context, focusing on the most evocative and theatrical moments of the scene. This is amplified in the isolated, contracted present of the real time, which 'engulfs the subject with indescribable vividness, a materiality of perception properly overwhelming, which effectively dramatizes the power of the material' (Jameson, 1991, p 27). For example, Drew, a 28-year-old musician and grad student living in

Bushwick, is a somewhat reluctant Citizen user. He uses the app until it 'becomes too depressing', or evokes feelings of unsafety, and then deletes it, only to re-download it weeks or months later when an event piques his interest on Instagram or in the neighbourhood. Drew then deletes Citizen again when these feelings of uncertainty and insecurity creep back in. When I ask him the reason for his most recent re-download, his answer is dramatic:

> A car had blown up like a block down and the first thing that came to mind, actually I called 911 first and said 'Hey, there is a car on fire do something', and then I saw people gathering around the car and I thought ok I'm going to check Citizen and lo and behold I now have thirty angles of this car that is actively exploding. … It's interesting because it's so dystopian, this multi-cam of crime that nosy people want to check out.

Such vivid images resulting from this 'multi-cam of crime' are seen as dystopian because they are '*copies conforming to a standard*, parodies of presence' (Lefebvre, 2013, p 33). Lefebvre expands further:

> you attend the incessant fêtes or massacres, you see the dead bodies, you contemplate the explosions; missiles are fired before your eyes. You are there! … but no, you are not there; your present is composed of simulacra; the image before you simulates the real, drives it out, it is not there. (Lefebvre, 2013, p 41)

The real time simulates the real, through the image, making the experience feel immediate, as Drew says, he now has 30 angles of the car actively exploding, generating the illusion of presence. Citizen as a simulation creates '*unmediated immediacy* of remote places and times' (Bogard, 1996, p 49, emphasis in original), through the representational strategy of transparency, which attempts to obscures the medium (Bolter and Grusin, 2000) as a technology for the cultural (re)production of the real.

Drew engages with Citizen cyclically, deleting and re-downloading the app around ten times over the course of two years.[4] He explains, 'in my neighborhood, I felt more paranoid and on guard when I was using it, normally I am pretty trusting of my surroundings, but with Citizen I'm constantly thinking, "what's that guy doing over there?"' Once again, there is a divergence between Citizen's real-time crime and the lived everyday of walking around one's neighbourhood: creating dissonance, misplaced suspicion, and uncertainty. To obviate this arrythmia, Drew deletes Citizen; however, the enticing nature of the simulation as a technology of vigilance draws him back in, as the desire to stay connected results in continuous patterns of redownloading, reflecting an urge to stay in the loop, and avoid a fear of missing out (FOMO). In this way Citizen can function like a trap, a technology that enchants and beguiles (Gell, 1999). Considering it through the lens of traps further implies the dissolution of the 'dichotomy between the voluntary and the coerced' (Seaver, 2019, p 424), as agency circulates between the technology of entrapment and the trapped. As Lefebvre argues, 'if you have the ability to take the flows and streams (TV, the press, etc) as *rhythms* among others, you avoid the trap of the *present* that gives itself as presence' (2013, p 32, emphasis in original). Drew experiences Citizen itself rhythmically,[5] through the act of deleting and re-downloading, engaging with the app in an oscillating manner to avoid entropy, offset arrhythmia and mediate the feelings of uncertainty that arise. Such a cycle of delete/re-download reflects the tension between presence (deleting) and the present (re-downloading the simulation).

Often such feelings of uncertainty arise from the illusion of the real time, in a two-fold way. Firstly, this is because the real time is simulated and therefore chimerical, and secondly, because Citizen often fails to provide real-time reporting, as it claims to. As with Tina and Kim, alerts from the same location may arrive at different times to different users. Such hypermodulation fails to create synchrony between users (Pettman, 2015), further fuelling experiences of uncertainty, arrhythmia, and this sense of 'time out of joint' (Derrida, 1994; Fisher, 2012).[6] Additionally, rather than consistently providing information that is relevant to the 'here and now', some incidents remain on the map up to a month after they happened. Often these 'there and then' incidents that remain are highly emotive, such as shootings. Yet there is no way to tell when they took place without clicking onto the incidence on the map, and even then, the information, 'live on the scene 14 days ago', is unobvious and in small print. These past crimes remain spectral to the simulation. Mark Fisher says that hauntings happen, 'when a place is stained by time, or when a particular place becomes the site for an encounter with broken time' (2012, p 19), like the fracturing real time of Citizen.

Lizzie, a queer events coordinator and political strategist, describes the app as 'spooky', going on to describe lingering past events which were weeks or even months old. Her word choice emphasizes this spectrality, being not of this time, and the creation of 'temporal disunity, shining with an eerie glossiness' (Genosko and Thompson, 2006, p 127). When I remark that I had just seen a woman's stabbing stay on the map for weeks, she responds surprisingly offhandedly, 'Yeah, that's not helping me now, okay, a bird s*** in the spot an hour ago. Like, I don't think it's coming back here to s*** again.' Here she shifts quickly from spooked to flippant, trivializing a serious event. I contend that this 'blasé attitude' (Simmel, 2012, p 14) is typical of and heightened in New Yorkers, where indifference becomes a defence mechanism. I now turn to the affordance of real-time notifications, and how they interrupt my interlocutors' everyday rhythmicity.

Notifications and interruption

> I'm confronted with somebody else's humanity. And it's in this bite-sized little notification just on the top of my screen. And I'm just trying to take a photo of a dog or something and then there are three stabbings and my heart is like … [trailing off]. (Sammy, 28-year-old graduate student living in Bed–Stuy)

Push notifications are smartphone pop-up alerts which appear at the top of the screen and are generated by closed apps to indicate something of interest to the user, prompting them to click on the notification and open the app. Push notifications are mundane and prosaic occurrences that simultaneously punctuate and disrupt the flow of the everyday. They are both everyday, and an interruption to the everyday. Notifications are thus inherently temporal and, in the case of Citizen, can jarringly disrupt the day without warning. Wherever you happen to be, be it at work, on the subway, or at home in your bedroom, the app blurs the boundaries between public and private.

The lives of city dwellers are deeply mediated by technology, and specifically by smartphone apps. Digital interruptions from smartphone notifications are part of the undulations of the everyday and are as commonplace as catching up with friends over coffee − if not more so. Yet there is arguably a meaningful difference between a notification of an iMessage from a friend, or an Instagram like, and the highly emotive and confronting nature of Citizen notifications, which can evoke anxiety, uncertainty and, in Sammy's case, a confrontation with humanity. This is not to say that there is such a time as uninterrupted time, or that digital media necessarily creates more disruption, but rather that the content, consistency, and intensity of Citizen notifications, which purport to inform one's sense of safety and security (based on geolocation awareness and physical proximity), function at a different affective register that may produce an interruption with greater impact. For example, Sammy's tone shifts from saccharine cheerfulness (when mentioning a photograph of a dog) to alarm and despondency that results in her sentence ending prematurely, stymied by competing emotions. Sammy, in a later conversation, states, 'I feel a lot depending on notification. But consistently I feel interrupted (I stop what I'm doing to read it).' It is important to ponder on Sammy's use of words, 'I feel interrupted'. Here interruption itself has become an affect, something to be felt and experienced.

Citizen's real-time notifications puncture the everyday, disjointing time and throwing off harmonies. Its present disrupts and consumes presence (Lefebvre, 2013), as, for example, when Sammy's act of photographing a dog (presence) is interrupted by a real-time notification of three stabbings (present). The name 'push notification' is telling, one that *pushes* the present and consequently an incremental arrhythmia into daily life. In the context of security, Ellcessor places emergency in an extended, intensified, present tense, due to its 'nowness', its 'disruption', as emergency is 'defined by it's *happening*' (2022, p 12, emphasis in original). Anjali Nath describes Metadata+, an app that sends out notifications when a US drone strike is reported, as an interactive practice that reimagines users' concept of temporal and geographic orientation in a 'present-continuous tense' (2016, p 325). Metadata+, like Citizen, is predicated upon 'a future unfolding in real time' (p 326) and, thus, a future unfolding out of time. This is because the real-time 'causes a condensation of the past and future in a strange durationless' (Genosko and Thompson, 2006, p 129), a compressed and isolated present that feels dislodged from everyday rhythms. With these supposedly real-time notifications there is an intrusion of the simulated present, 'a time all of its own' (Bogard, 1996, p 52), into presence, and the rhythms of everyday life, which are informed by experiences of the past and expectations of the future. For users, Citizen can feel out of time, because it does not correspond with past experiences, and future anticipations of one's neighbourhood being safe.

However, these notifications are 'consensual disruptions', (Nath, 2016, p 325) which are curated, most often pushing in from other apps that users have chosen to download.[7] That choice can be extended to turning off notifications on certain apps, a choice made by many of my interlocutors. Indeed, the choice to keep notifications on, would often be met with a wonderous, 'Oh wow, so you have notifications *on*!' Lisa Stevenson has described interruption as, 'a moment of disorientation, of terror, of boredom, of uncertainty' (Hölsgens, 2020). These undulations are representative of experiences of Citizen, in particular those of uncertainty. Such confusion also arises due to the frequency of notifications declaring incidences to be 'unconfirmed', 'unfounded', or 'false'. Often this uncertainty prompted my interlocutors to turn off notifications, refusing these jarring interruptions. Lizzie switched off notifications because she didn't want to hear, 'about robberies every five seconds', hence rejecting the simulation's seemingly constant encroachment into her everyday life, the exaggerated framing, 'every five seconds', evoking this sense of constancy. Meanwhile, Cyrus, a nightlife entertainer in their late twenties, describes turning off notifications because: 'I want to live in the real world, and I don't want to get caught up in this metaverse of crime.' Here Cyrus distinguishes between the actuality of 'living in the real world', and the virtuality of being 'caught up in the metaverse of crime'. Their choice of words is significant. 'Caught up' alludes to the trap-like nature of Citizen articulated earlier, and the 'metaverse of crime' not only references Citizen as a simulation, but speaks to its gamification.

Brayne et al (2023) write about the ways in which surveillance is deputized by the state, via private tech companies, onto the individual citizen. They argue that one of the tactics of such deputization is gamification (see also

Shapiro, Chapter 9, this volume). They cite Fourcade and Johns (2020), who argue that 'platforms employ psycho-social strategies and campaigns to draw people in and form habits by drumming up reciprocity and participation through notifications and rewards' (Brayne et al, 2013, p 473). Citizen employs similar tactics and gamified affordances – press the big red button to record, as text bubbles of 'the community needs you' appear against the dark mode map. This gamification, strangely paired with such moralizing language as 'the community needs you', builds affective attachment to offset the often fallible nature of such vigilant technology (see Sun-ha Hong, Afterword, this volume).

In 2023, the gamification of the 'go live' affordance escalated to include a cash incentive and a chance to 'win $500!' Citizen's promotional videos further entrench this gaming atmosphere, with dramatic clips of searches for missing persons, using language such as, 'watch my back' and 'agents standing by', the background music evocative of video games or Hollywood action movies. This gamification strategy also reinforces the hyperreal nature of Citizen, as games are another example of simulation (Der Derian, 1990; Bogard, 1996) that try to entice users with rewards and 'videoludic' (Vanolo, 2018, p 320) infotainment. However, many simply refuse to play the game, as I will now describe.

'Go live, go *live*, go eat a donut!'

> [Simulations] hyperrealize our experiences of time, space, agency, and society itself. Push a button, enter a code, and go anywhere. (Bogard, 1996)

Sammy is a self-described woman of colour and active Citizen user. She describes herself as an 'information seeker', originally downloading the app during the 2020 Black Lives Matter protests, to monitor narratives about protestors, and the behaviour of the police. Sammy recalls a particularly intense interaction with the app. She was walking from her apartment to go roller-skating in her local park when she heard gunshots. Within minutes she received a notification: 'reports of shots fired 900 Feet away'. 'The community needs you!', the message read, above a cylindrical red button with a camera icon and the words, 'I'm on it', encouraging her to 'go live' and film the unfolding situation with a touch of her screen. She continued around the block, away from the incident and towards the park, when she received a follow-up notification, 'Shots Fired in Bed-Stuy: Police located shell casings on the scene. Use caution in this area. This is an ongoing investigation.' At this point Sammy realized she had left her skates at home and turned back. She debated whether she should still skate, but felt she still needed to 'decompress' so she turned back. At that point she realized that the incident had been a lot closer to her than the alert showed, as she had been briskly walking away from that location at the time. Fifteen minutes after the shooting follow-up notification, Sammy received another separate notification, 'report of person brandished knife'. When I ask how these numerous notifications made her feel, she responds, 'Girl, I was heavily activated!', before adding, 'but I'm staying safe lol'. She speculates that because there was such an abundance of gun violence recently around her area, it could be gang related. Sammy observes that Citizen is a unique tool to map these kinds of incidents over time, while also acknowledging — 'I just know racist vigilantes[8] foam at the mouth for it.'

As discussed, the hyperreal obscures the distinction between the real and its representations. It is therefore not contradictory to speak of Citizen as a simulation, while also acknowledging the actual reality of *some*[9] of the incidences reported there, which at times do correspond to experiences of one's neighbourhood, as, for instance, in Sammy's case, when she heard the gunshots that were being reported. Rather, it is through the uncertainty and blurring of what is and is not 'real', namely what is either confirmed or unfounded on the app, that the hyperreal emerges. It therefore abounds in paradox. Sammy describes the 'go live' prompt, in particular, as, 'truly unreal. Absolutely not,' is her rejoinder, 'I will not go live, I want to *live*'. Other scholars have similarly questioned how the 'go live' feature can be reconciled with the app's purported mission of user safety (Chordia et al, 2023). Sammy's utterance, 'to live' can also be understood as a desire to remain alive. I am, however, more interested in Sammy's refusal to alter her everyday rhythm and succumb to the encroaching real time of digital monitoring, as she instead went to the park to roller-skate as planned. Sammy's choice of words is pertinent, calling the prompt to 'go live', as 'truly unreal'. It references both the unbelievability, as well as the simulated nature of the real time. By saying that she wants to live, Sammy, like Cyrus, emphasizes the fragmentation Citizen can create, encapsulating the potentially alienating nature of real-time recording, which would place her outside of her ordinary rhythms and into a state of arrhythmia.

Sammy's refusal to 'go live' is further compounded by her nonchalant comment, 'but I'm staying safe lol'. I encountered this kind of irreverence often in the field, exhibited too by Lizzie's flippancy noted earlier. In fact, this was an aspect of the fieldwork from the very beginning. On a Saturday in March 2022, I went thrifting with a group of women in East Williamsburg, bordering Bushwick. We had decided to take a break and get a rose donut from a small Iranian bakery. Upon sitting down to eat, I received a Citizen notification which I dutifully opened. 'Report of Man Armed with Gun', it read, just metres away, our blue location circle adjacent to the glowing yellow square alert. It was broad daylight on a very busy semi-commercial street. Because of its potential gravity, I shared this news with the group.

Some were slightly concerned, but mostly it was donut-absorbed 'oh s***'s that murmured around the table. Looking at the screen over my shoulder, Marysol read out, 'It was reported 21 minutes ago', while another responded, 'It's probably fine now.' Z exclaimed 'why, Citizen!', almost irritated that I had brought it up. We all gazed around at each other once more, a cursory glance with a nonchalance that, for me, felt at odds with the incident. We finished our donuts, walked out of the bakery, and the episode was never mentioned again.

Insistent yet uncertain rhythms of (in)security pulsate in the everyday, threatening to impact time spent with friends, eating donuts and roller-skating. As I have shown, such encroachment is often resisted, by turning off notifications or by refusing the insistence to 'go live'. However, there is in addition a more subtle refusal, an emotional disengagement taking place, in which nonchalance is employed to create a further emotional firewall into Citizen's intrusive simulation of the city. 'The ordinary is a shifting assemblage of practices and practical knowledges, a scene of both liveness and exhaustion', Kathleen Stewart argues (2007, p 1). This conceptualization of the everyday is apt for city life: excitement and stimulation exist on a knife-edge, alongside indifference and weariness. This 'blasé spirit' is indicative of the attitude of New Yorkers, or even of those who have lived in the city for a few years. In the early twentieth century Georg Simmel described the inhabitants of metropoles as 'indifferent', as exhibiting a 'blasé metropolitan attitude'. He contended that this was due to the visual oversaturation of 'violent stimuli' in the city so much so that 'the metropolitan type … creates a protective organ for itself against the profound disruption with which the fluctuations and discontinuities of the external milieu threaten it' (2012, p 12). Such violent visual stimuli of the city are amplified through digital monitoring media like Citizen, where the image is prioritized and sensationalized. A blasé spirit is harnessed to block disruptions to spatiotemporal experiences of one's neighbourhood. It is important to emphasize that, as Simmel contends, the city itself is a place of intensity. Yet I further argue that Citizen brings its incidents of violence into focus, creating a hyperreality of crime as immediate and constant. This is something my interlocutors well recognized, as Kim, earlier, says, 'I know the dangers, I don't have to have it in my face'.

While Simmel was writing more generally about the city, his description is equally apt for my interlocutors and their experiences of New York City (NYC). As Vanessa, a born-and-bred New Yorker who grew up there, observes, 'the stereotype of New York is kind of true and people heard the stereotype of being hardy New Yorkers always seeing s*** and then moving on, and then they move here and perpetuate the stereotype by being like omg crazy s*** but whatever its just NYC'. Indeed, often stories regaling shocking or concerning incidents witnessed by my 'transplant'[10] interlocutors were often concluded with the utterance, 'you're not a New Yorker until you've seen … [insert shocking or concerning incident]'. Thus, for many of my interlocutors the blasé attitude is two-fold: it is an expression of resistance to the arrhythmic real time presented by Citizen app, and an adopted or perceived spirit of being a New Yorker. There is a pervasive attitude of 'only in New York', a prideful shrug at all the weird and wonderful inhabitants and happenings in the city, in which indifference and a fear of missing out intermingle in complex ways. Moreover, feelings and perceptions of fear and (in)security are culturally informed and socially situated. This may explain why I found the nonchalance misfitting at the bakery, because I mapped my own security imagination (Schwell, 2015, p 104) of London onto Brooklyn. What constitutes a threat, as well as the modality of response, depends on specific localized contexts.

This also exemplifies the tension between how my interlocutors talk about Citizen, and how they use it in practice. All the women in the bakery had previously told me, separately, about how Citizen notifications made them 'anxious', 'uneasy' or 'triggered'. Yet in practice, a notification of a violent incident just feet away was ignored, and seen as an inconvenient interruption, perhaps to mitigate these anxious feelings, or because Citizen represented an image of the neighbourhood that did not correspond to their view of it. While both are equally important when doing ethnography, it demonstrates the difference between discourse and practice: between how technology is spoken about and used, between describing affect and doing in practice. This highlights the importance of analysing Citizen app through the lens of affordances-in-practice. The use of Citizen is mediated by the blasé spirit of its users, who resist the real-time affordances, like incident notifications and the encouragement to 'go live'. 'Affordances are not intrinsic properties that can be defined outside their situated context of usage, but ongoing enactments by specific users that may vary across space and time' (Costa, 2018, p 3653), and as such are 'culturally and socially bound' (p 3651). If one neglects to look at Citizen app through the lens of affordances-in-practice, prioritizing localized practices and cultural specificities of use, such as Drew's cycle of deleting and re-downloading, a fuller, more nuanced picture of Citizen app can be omitted.

Moreover, as with Drew's cyclical use of Citizen, there is a push and pull to simulation. Its luring rhythm is disjointed and uncanny, yet can be simultaneously interesting, pulling Drew back in through the characteristic FOMO of a New Yorker. As described, such undulations are part of Drew's polyrhythmic urban everyday. However, for other interlocutors, Citizen's temporal modes made them feel 'spooky', 'unreal', endowing them with a sense of time out of joint. In short, Citizen use fluctuates among users, quite like the polyrhythmia of the city itself. Some embrace the push-and-pull cycles of delete and re-download, while others choose the pull of roller-skating and eating donuts, over the push of the simulated real time.

Conclusion

This chapter has explored ethnographically the ways in which Citizen app functions as a simulation, due to its gamified affordances of going live and real-time crime mapping, and its rhythmic impact on users. Such temporal regimes, including the interruption of real-time notifications, can conflict with users' past experiences and anticipations of their neighbourhoods, instilling feelings of uncertainty, dissonance, and fracture. Moreover, Citizen can also fail in its claim to provide real-time reporting, as notifications are received at different times, and historic incidents haunt the homepage for weeks or months after the fact. In response, some of my interlocutors switch off notifications, refuse to engage in the real time by going live, and exercise nonchalance, choosing instead to *live* in presence in their neighbourhoods, rejecting Citizen's isolated present. Others chose to engage with Citizen in cycles, in patterns that interact with the larger polyrhythms of the city. Rhythms fragment and undulate in their hands as they open notifications and scroll through their phones, pulling them in different directions: between indifference and intrigue, between going live and living; between the push of a real-time notification, and the pull of the last bite of a donut.

Acknowledgements

I would like to thank my editor for this chapter, Matan Shapiro, alongside the editors of this collection, Vita Peacock, Mikkel Kenni Bruun, and Claire Elisabeth Dungey, for their insights and patience. I would like to acknowledge my supervisors Rik Adriaans and Daniel Miller, and my PhD cohort for their support and guidance. I further thank the reviewer of this chapter for their direction and clarity. Finally, I thank my interlocutors for their time, generosity, and wisdom.

Notes

[1]   This chapter is based on long-term ethnographic research conducted both online and in the increasingly gentrified neighbourhoods of Bushwick and Bed-Stuy in Brooklyn, New York City (NYC), between March 2022 and September 2023. I utilized participant observation at community events, undertook autoethnography on the app, and interviewed more than eighty people, both in person and over Zoom. I also conducted two intensive group interviews, one year apart, with my primary interlocutors. My interlocutors comprised both present and past users of the Citizen app, and were often millennial or generation Z artists, performers, activists, and community leaders who had lived in the neighbourhoods for several years. Having lived in NYC from 2017 to 2020, my initial introduction to this population was through friends, before proceeding to utilize a 'snowballing sampling technique' (Low, 2008, p 55) to recruit interlocutors. I worked closely with a community gatekeeper, where I met other interlocutors while volunteering at their multi-purpose community space in Bushwick. I chose to work with this community as it was where I had both access and interest, as people were open to talking to me and recommending others I should speak with. All names have been pseudonymized and specific locations blurred to protect the identity of my interlocutors.

[2] Such as the false missile alert sent out in error to Hawaii residents in 2018.

[3] In terms of hyperreal media representations, New York City is the site of one of the most infamous: the terror attacks on the World Trade Center on 11 September 2001 (9/11). The images of impact, explosion, and collapse were continuously replayed, watched by my interlocutors, often while many of them were still in elementary school. 9/11 has been described as 'unreal', 'surreal', and 'like a movie' (Sontag, 2019b, p 17). 9/11 was unthinkable and yet terror attacks and apocalyptic accidents had been the object of the US's imagination, projected large and looming onto the screen, in the form of Hollywood movies. As Žižek argues, 'this fantasmatic screen apparition entered our reality. It is not that reality entered our image: the image entered and shattered our reality' (2012, p 19). A nation watched their screens transfixed, as the desert of the real appeared as dust cleared from ground zero (Žižek, 2012). The Citizen app is mediated by the cultural context in which it exists. Legitimatized by 9/11, the US moved into a state of hyper-securitization, normalizing the mass surveillance of civilians and creating a cultural landscape in which an app like Citizen could thrive.

[4] Other interlocutors had similar experiences of a delete/re-download loop. Often Citizen would be deleted due to 'anxiety' or 'for the sake of my mental health' and re-downloaded on a need-to-know basis, to confirm a local incidence seen on social media or in their neighbourhood.

[5] Some of my interlocutors used Citizen in confluence with their (eu)rhythmic experiences of the city, for example, utilizing the app to navigate protests. As with most technology, the use of Citizen is nuanced and fluctuates across the intersecting positionalities of users.

[6] This utterance originally traces back to Shakespeare's Hamlet; however, it is also the title of Phillip K. Dick's book *Time Out of Joint* (Dick, 2003), set in a Californian city in the 1950s, in which the protagonist gradually discovers the whole town is engaged in a staged fake to keep him fulfilled, thus alluding to the temporal nature of simulations.

[7] However, in practice often Citizen notifications are screenshot and shared in group chats, and sometimes members of those groups have chosen to turn off notifications or delete Citizen altogether. Thus, Citizen can continue to interrupt one's day even when one does not have the app.

[8] This is a pertinent comment considering Citizen's original moniker and the potential dangers of racial profiling and discrimination that arise with the 'go live' affordance. Citizen, in its suggestion to 'go live', asks users to make time-sensitive moral judgements on situations, bringing into question who does and does not look suspicious, a decision that could be animated by the threat of a racialized other. Further analysis is outside the scope of this chapter.

[9] 'Some' being the operative word here, due to numerous unfounded notifications which further fuel uncertainty.

[10] A term used for describing people who recently who moved to the city.

References

Akinnibi, F. and Wahid, R. (2022) 'Fear of Rampant Crime is Derailing New York City's Recovery', *Bloomberg*, 29 July. Available from: https://www.bloomberg.com/graphics/2022-is-nyc-safe-crime-stat-reality/ (Accessed: 25 February 2024).

Baudrillard, J. (1994) *Simulacra and Simulation*. Translated by S. Glaser. Ann Arbor, MI: University of Michigan Press.

Baudrillard, J. (2010) *America*. Translated by G. Dyer. London: Verso.

Bertoni, S. (2020) 'How Safety Startup Citizen Surpassed Twitter to Become Apple's Top News All Amid the George Floyd Protests', *Forbes*, 6 June. Available from: https://www.forbes.com/sites/stevenbertoni/2020/06/06/how-saf ety-startup-citizen-surpassed-twitter-to-become-apples-top-news-app-amid-the-george-floyd-protests/?sh=205ffe1559f1 (Accessed: 23 February 2024).

Bogard, W. (1996) *The Simulation of Surveillance: Hypercontrol in Telematic Societies*, Cambridge: Cambridge University Press.

Bolter, J. and Grusin, J. (2000) *Remediation: Understanding New Media*, Cambridge, MA: MIT Press.

boyd, D. (2012) 'Participating in the Always-On Lifestyle', in M. Mandiberg (ed) *The Social Media Reader*, New York: New York University Press, pp 71–6.

Brayne, S., Lageson, S., and Levy, K. (2023) 'Surveillance Deputies: When Ordinary People Surveil for the State', *Law & Society Review*, 57(4): 462–88.

Chordia, I., Erete, S., Hiniker, A., Parrish, E., Tayebi, T., Tran, L.-P., and Yip, J. (2023) 'Deceptive Design Patterns in Safety Technologies: A Case Study of the Citizen app', *CHI'23*, 23–28 April 2023, Hamburg, Germany [conference paper].

Citizen (2024) *Citizen*. Available from: https://citizen.com/ (Accessed: 23 February 2024).

Cole, S. (2010) 'Baudrillard's Ontology: Empirical Research and the Denial of the Real', *International Journal of Baudrillard Studies*, 7(2).

Costa, E. (2018) 'Affordances-in-Practice: An Ethnographic Critique of Social Media Logic and Context Collapse', *New Media & Society*, 20(10): 3641–56.

Der Derian, J. (1990) 'The (S)pace of International Relations: Simulation, Surveillance, and Speed', *International Studies Quarterly*, 34(3): 295–310.

Derrida, J. (1994) *Specters of Marx: The State of the Debt, the Work of Mourning and the New International*, Oxford: Routledge.

Dick, K.P. (2003) *Time Out of Joint*, London: SF Gateway.

Didion, J. (2008) *Slouching Towards Bethlehem: Essays (FSG Classics)*, London: Macmillan Publishers.

Eco, U. (1990 [1975]) *Travels in Hyperreality*, W. Weaver (trans.), New York: HarperVia.

Ellcessor, E. (2022) *In Case of Emergency: How Technologies Mediate Crisis and Normalize Inequality*, New York: New York University Press.

Fetterman, A.K., Baker, C.D., and Meier, B.P. (2023) 'Crime in Your Area: Use of Neighborhood Apps is Associated with Inaccurate Perceptions of Higher Local Crime Rates', *Psychology of Popular Media*, 13(2): 269–73.

Fisher, M. (2012) 'What is Hauntology?', *Film Quarterly*, 66(1): 16–24.

Fourcade, M. and Johns, F. (2020) 'Loops, Ladders and Links: The Recursivity of Social and Machine Learning', *Theory and Society*, 49(5–6): 803–32.

Gell, A. (1999) *The Art of Anthropology: Essays and Diagrams*. Edited by E. Hirsch, London: Routledge.

Genosko, G. and Thompson, S. (2006) 'Tense Theory: The Temporalities of Surveillance', *Theorizing Surveillance: The Panopticon and Beyond*, Edited by D. Lyon. London: Willan Publishing, pp 123–39.

Herrman, J. (2019) 'All the Crime, All the Time: How Citizen Works', *The New York Times*, 17 March. Available from: https://www.nytimes.com/2019/03/17/style/citizen-neighborhood-crime-app.html (Accessed: 23 February 2024).

Hölsgens, S. (2020) 'What Is an Interruption? An Interview with Lisa Stevenson', *Supplementals: Fieldsights*, 3 November. Available from: https://culanth.org/fieldsights/what-is-an-interruption-an-interview-with-lisa-stevenson (Accessed: 23 February 2024).

Jameson, F. (1991) *Postmodernism, or, The Cultural Logic of Late Capitalism*, Durham, NC: Duke University Press.

Kitchin, R. (2023) *Digital Timescapes: Technology, Temporality and Society*, NJ: Wiley.

Lefebvre, H. (2013) *Rhythmanalysis: Space, Time and Everyday Life*. Translated by S. Elden and G. Moore, London: Bloomsbury Academic.

Low, S. (2008). 'Fortification of Residential Neighbourhoods and the New Emotions of Home', *Housing, Theory and Society*, 25(1), 47–65.

Madianou, M. (2016) 'Ambient Co-Presence: Transnational Family Practices in Polymedia Environments', *Global Networks*, 16(2): 183–201.

Nath, A. (2016) 'Touched from Below: On Drones, Screens and Navigation', *Visual Anthropology*, 29(3): 315–30.

Pettman, D. (2015) *Infinite Distraction: Paying Attention to Social Media*, New York: Polity Press.

Powel, A., Stratton, G., and Cameron, R. (2018) *Digital Criminology: Crime and Justice in Digital Society*, New York: Routledge.

Riddell, A. (2023) 'Intersecting Positionalities and the Unexpected Uses of Digital Crime and Safety Tracking in Brooklyn', *Social Inclusion*, 11(3): 30–40.

Schwell, A. (2015) 'The Security-Fear Nexus: Some Theoretical and Methodological Explorations into a Missing Link', *Etnofoor*, 27(2): 95–112.

Seaver, N. (2019) 'Captivating Algorithms: Recommender Systems as Traps', *Journal of Material Culture*, 24(4): 421–36.

Simmel, G. (2012) 'The Metropolis and Mental Life', *The Sociology of Georg Simmel* (1950) [1903], Edited by K. Wolff, London: Routledge.

Sontag, S. (2019a) *On Photography*, UK: Penguin Random House UK.

Sontag, S. (2019b) *Regarding the Pain of Others*, UK: Penguin Random House UK.

Stewart, K. (2007) *Ordinary Affects*, Durham, NC: Duke University Press.

Stine, K., and Volmar, A. (eds) (2021) *Infrastructures of Time: An Introduction to Hardwired Temporalities*, Amsterdam: Amsterdam University Press, pp 9–38.

Vanolo, A. (2018) 'Cities and the Politics of Gamification', *Cities*, 74: 320–26.

Žižek, S. (2012) *Welcome to the Desert of the Real*, London: Verso.

6

Synchronizing Orbits and Deep Learning Algorithms: Satellite Surveillance and Civil Sea Rescue Missions in the Mediterranean

Andreas Stoiber

Introduction: Mind the gap

When I began fieldwork at the Regensburg-based non-governmental organization (NGO) Space-Eye, Walter Wissenschaftler,[1] a physics professor who played a crucial role in launching the Space-Eye project around 2018 and now acts as its scientific advisor, asserted:

> If we say we can look from above and document, then naturally half the population complains because they say, 'Well, then you can see me too when I'm in a bikini in my garden sunbathing'. Of course, we can't do that, and that's not our goal. But between what is actually fact, and what the population fears, there is quite a gap.

In the following, I explore this 'gap' when it comes to doing satellite surveillance 'for the good' as a civilian actor. I undertook ethnographic fieldwork between April 2021 and March 2022 on the voluntary work of Space-Eye members in Regensburg, Stuttgart, and Berlin, who deploy optical satellites and deep learning algorithms with the goal of supporting civil search-and-rescue (SAR) missions in the Mediterranean.

In this chapter, I show that within their coding practices, Space-Eye members must negotiate what Lefebvre (2009) called *polyrhythmia* – understood as multiple rhythmic demands that coexist simultaneously. Space-Eye members must synchronize the realities and rhythms of their (in)organic collaborators on land and sea, and in (cyber)space. The following paragraphs examine the polyrhythmia of these monitoring technologies, in the socio-technological practices necessary to operationalize them, and where organic and inorganic temporalities interact (Peacock, Introduction, this volume). By doing so, I problematize assumptions about the smoothness of (quasi-)real-time data processes in relation to satellite surveillance (Pollozek, 2020, p 678).

First, this chapter introduces the Space-Eye project, how and why it came about, and what socio-technological approaches Space-Eye members are working with. Second, it focuses on the kinds of temporal challenges that emerge in the technical encounters between Space-Eye members, optical satellites, and deep learning algorithms. These challenges show that Space-Eye's work is as much about compressing time as it is about compressing space. Thirdly, using the example of the 'European Data Relay Satellite System', I show that (quasi-)real-time satellite surveillance constitutes an active achievement that depends on overcoming temporal challenges, by patching together sets of unresolved temporal patterns and mechanical tempos, through specific infrastructural investments. In conclusion, I propose a preliminary politics of lag, that stresses the importance of being attentive to the infrastructural investments in satellite and artificial intelligence, and raises questions about ownership, funding, access, and who is being left out.

Space-What?

The Space-Eye project is part of other civil SAR techniques, which include ships, planes, (optical and radar) satellite data, and drone data. Satellites and drones offer the advantage that they can widen the search radius of ships by offering clues on where to look for boats in distress, compared with the view from ships, which is limited and weather dependent.

Sea-Watch started using the aircraft Moonbird (from 2017 to 2022 in collaboration with Swiss Humanitarian Pilot Initiative), Seabird 1 (since 2020), and Seabird 2 (since 2022) to help detect boats in distress and report them to the Maritime Rescue Coordination Centres and nearby vessels.[2] In 2017, civil SAR organizations such as Sea-Watch, Mission Lifeline, and Sea-Eye became subject to increasing criminalization and legal obstructions, resulting in the blockade of ships and planes. The Space-Eye project was initially conceived as a response to this hostile environment. Gerd Gründer, founder of Space-Eye, thought of using satellites to document what was happening in the Mediterranean while ships and planes were blocked.

The Space-Eye project started in 2018, with a technological and scientific focus on satellites and artificial intelligence. Rosa Roboter became the unofficial lead on the project. The idea was to train deep learning algorithms that were capable of processing satellite images of the Mediterranean to identify refugee boats. Space-Eye would then be able to cover the whole Mediterranean, and quickly filter out possible refugee boats in distress to give their approximate whereabouts to SAR ships nearby. Additionally, Space-Eye could sort through past satellite images, and look for images depicting push/pullbacks or human rights abuses.

However, members of Space-Eye struggled to gain access to data with which they could train their deep learning algorithms, and faced difficulties while attempting to operationalize the satellite images. During my fieldwork I noticed how a division between what we might call a humanitarian and a scientific side within the NGO emerged. They started to pick up on tasks such as first aid, material donations, and housing projects, which meant finding immediate solutions to problems that were manageable within a shorter timeframe through direct action. The 'humanitarian side' can make things happen within three weeks. Meanwhile, the work of the project's 'scientific side' requires years of building a socio-technological network and infrastructure (Figure 6.1).

The scientific work of Space-Eye is not restricted to the NGO itself. It is currently constituted by collaborations with the Augsburg- and Berlin-based NGO SearchWing and the Berlin-based PhD student Max Mustermann. They share the goal of supporting SAR missions through technological methods. There are four main socio-technological approaches.

Firstly, members based in Regensburg, and previously in Stuttgart, attempt to train a neural network on image classification instead of object detection

Figure 6.1: First attempt to trace the Space-Eye network

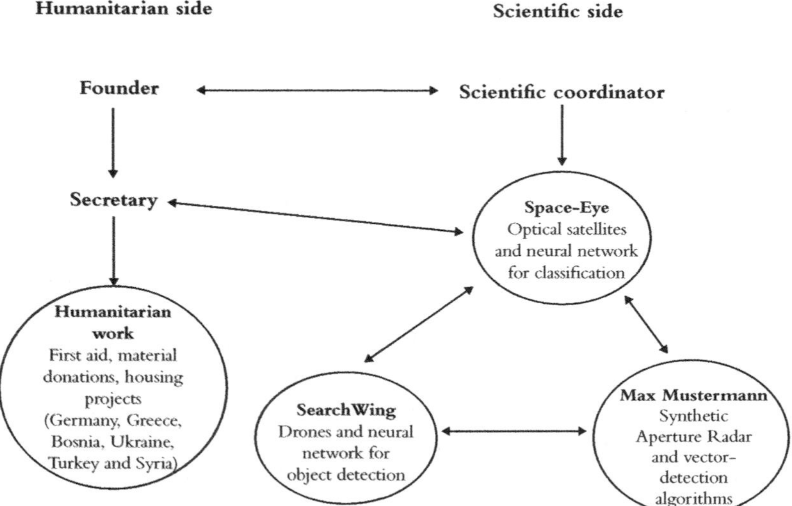

or facial recognition.[3] A neural network is a subset of machine learning and at the centre of deep learning algorithms. It is worth quoting Rosa Roboter at length to understand this further:

> Artificial intelligence is the really big umbrella term that stands above everything. Even a simple decision can fall into this category. Like 'if the power is too high, then my device switches off'. That can also be included as long as we would describe it as intelligent. One level below is machine learning. Machine learning can be defined as making decisions based on data. We no longer say that if the power is too high, you must switch off, but that the system learns for itself what 'too high' means. ...
>
> Under machine learning there are many different applications and one of them is neural networks or deep learning [algorithms]. ...] Neural networks are simply a connection of different so-called neurons, and they are *very* abstractly modelled on the human [brain] and consist of several layers of neurons. ... It is precisely this part of deep learning neural networks that is known for its black box, because there is very little information about what is actually happening between data input and output. A neuron simply processes its input data and produces an output. [It] is really just a mathematical component.

The term 'neural network' describes: a 'computational learning system that uses a network of functions to understand and translate a data input of one form into a desired output, usually in another form'.[4] In other words, a neural network constitutes 'a set of algorithms, modelled loosely after the human brain, that are designed to recognize patterns'.[5] Neural networks depend on training data to fine-tune their accuracy in the ways they classify and cluster data at high speed, and can be used for speech or image recognition. Image classification means the trained neural network in the case of Space-Eye would ideally be able to distinguish and classify refugee boats, as a distinctive pattern deviating from the blue water surface within satellite images. In the case of object detection, the trained neural network could sort out pictures with a pattern deviating from the blue water surface *and* show their geographical position for the ship to navigate to. Members of Space-Eye could use their neural network to skim faster through satellite images, spot potential refugee boats, and inform SAR ships and other actors nearby about the boat's geolocation. The nearby rescue ships can then navigate to the boat in distress.

Secondly, members of SearchWing build their own drones for usage by SAR ships. These drones start from the boats and fly a limited range while taking pictures automatically that are uploaded to an on-board computer. Then a neural network trained on object detection sorts out pictures with potential refugee boats and their geographical position, or other patterns other than the blue water surface. Thirdly, Max Mustermann uses synthetic aperture radar data from satellites and combines them with a machine learning model, similar yet distinct from the first approach due to the nature of the 'pictures' used and produced. Radar 'images' constitute a collection of microwave frequency ranges, representing returned radiation of material objects on the ground.

Fourthly, a group of Space-Eye members facilitate an 'Automatic Identification Signal' (AIS) as a sorting-out tool for their searches. AIS is used for navigating and securing naval traffic. Any 'official' boat has AIS to communicate its position, to secure smooth traffic or in instances of an emergency. Later, I focus on optical satellites and neural networks, and investigate the kinds of rhythms and mechanical tempos that Space-Eye members have to reconcile in their coding practices.

Reconciling polyrhythmia

Recent anthropological work has complicated our understanding of time and temporality. Time and temporality had been somewhat taken for granted and under-theorized (Munn, 1992; Guyer, 2007; Bear, 2016). However, anthropologists increasingly acknowledge 'composite and hierarchically assembled temporalities of most of the phenomena that [anthropology] explores' rather than seeing time as a universal singularity (Ssorin-Chaikov, 2017, pp 3–4).

Felix Ringel's concept of 'temporal agency' offers a starting point to study 'knowledge (about time) and the temporal dimensions of knowledge [practices]' (Ringel, 2018, p 29) as part of technical activities. Through Space-Eye's coding practices, space, time and movement have to be coordinated and assembled. The temporal dimension of these knowledge practices – or Space-Eye members' temporal agency –involves synchronizing the polyrhythmia resulting from the interaction of Space-Eye members with satellites, neural networks, and SAR ships through their coding practices.

I began my research in Germany during the COVID-19 lockdown in April 2021. Interviews with members of Space-Eye were therefore initially conducted via video chat. I asked my interlocutors about their past and current practices, as well as their future goals. Depending on who I was talking to, the answers (including the technological tools, collaborating actors, and infrastructures involved) would differ tremendously. It gradually became apparent that with each of the situated, socio-technological practices of Space-Eye, SearchWing and Max Mustermann, different relational and composite organic and inorganic temporalities were being negotiated. This led to distinct temporal progressions and rhythms of their individual monitoring tools.

The voluntary work of Space-Eye members can be seen as 'a temporary rhythm made up of a set of unresolved [bio-, physio-, and social] temporal patterns' (Mirmalek, 2020, p 93) that makes it susceptible to lags and delays. The resulting rhythms of these knowledge practices stem from bio-temporal patterns, meaning from the temporal properties and mechanical tempos of the technologies, such as satellites in orbit or digitally trained neural networks. They are furthermore connected to getting access to the infrastructures these technological elements rely on, the collaborations with actors and actants, and the actual temporal work patterns of Space-Eye members and its associates to bring them all together.

In the case of Space-Eye members, the 'indissolubility of space, time, and movement' becomes even starker. Members have to organize their digital knowledge practices to visualize, monitor, and enact the Mediterranean to support civil SAR ship crews around orbiting satellites in space, and therefore have to adapt to the physio-temporal patterns tied to the earth's axial rotation and Low Earth Orbits. A great deal of their digital work means taking into account, and attempting to merge, the local experiences of both orbiting satellites and roaming ships on the Mediterranean, as these constitute the primary sets of conditions around which Space-Eye's work must be ordered. But what does it mean to order one's voluntary work around the mechanical tempos of orbiting satellites in practice?

Between the temporal and the technological: orbits, pathways, and pipelines

Debates around technologies like artificial intelligence, big data, or satellite surveillance can be associated with a utopian vision, in the form of 'technological solutionism' (Morozov, 2014), or the opposite – a dystopian vision of techno-determinism (Fisch, 2018). Both narratives fall short when confronted with specific situated practices, such as Space-Eye members trying to combine satellite images and artificial intelligence to support SAR missions in the Mediterranean with their current access to academic research infrastructures.

Scholars have stressed the importance of situating and contextualizing where and how technological applications are *practised* (Mol, 2002) and the different actors (be they human or non-human), places, and times when technologies are used (Oppenheim, 2007). These 'encounters' with technology (Bissell, 2021) bear the potential for individual creativity, affective relationality, collective contestation, and organizational 'tinkering' that inhabit the potentiality to practise technology *differently*. Yet it is also within these situated practices of human–technology encounters that an interaction between place, time, and the expenditure of energy (Peacock, this volume, Introduction) takes place. An ethnographic engagement with the work of Space-Eye offers not only insights about the local practices of how one '*does*' artificial intelligence and satellite surveillance, but furthermore how within these practices a 'garland' of rhythms of human as well as the mechanical tempos of non-human bodies interact.

Space-Eye members' voluntary work therefore does not simply occur in time, but rather '[mediates] diverse temporal rhythms, representations, and technologies in an orchestration of human action towards their temporary reconciliation' (Bear, 2014, p 73). This process of achieving 'temporary reconciliation' of these diverging rhythms and temporal patterns tied to orbiting satellites, the training of neural networks, and the voluntary working capacities of individual Space-Eye members must be further synchronized with the rhythms of civil SAR missions on the Mediterranean with their own work 'rotations' resulting from the interactions of crew members, ships, and technological applications on board while searching for people in distress.

Investigating Space-Eye members' work centring around satellites and neural networks, Michael Fisch's concept of 'technography' offers us a starting point to understand human–machine relations not as a binary. Instead, he proposes to view them as 'iterations of a collective distributed across a technologically mediated milieu' and urges us to think '*with*, not just *about* technology' (Fisch, 2018, p 6, emphasis in original). Machines are, in other words, integral to human thinking and social becoming.

The Space-Eye project can be understood as a collective brought about by co-constitutional interactions through contextualized practices, materialities, and their rhythms between humans and machines. To do so raises our attention to how and where certain qualities of technologies enable, sustain, constitute, and restrict specific relations within the broader technological becoming of the Space-Eye project. To understand the possibilities and restrictions of Space-Eye and the temporal patterns, mechanical tempos, and rhythms that arise by collaborating with technological elements of earth observation and artificial intelligence, let us engage with the main qualities of optical satellites and artificial intelligence, specifically neural networks trained for classification.

Possibilities and restrictions

Optical satellites

What is the gap between the promise of constant satellite surveillance anywhere, anytime, and its possibilities and restrictions in practice? The sensor in optical satellites is passive to save energy and can only record the sunlight reflecting from the earth's surface.[6] If the satellite passes at night, the resulting image remains black, which means that optical satellites must be in a 'sun-synchronous orbit' (SSO).

These satellites roam within a 'Low Earth Orbit (under 2,000 km altitude)'[7] and are synchronous with the sun. The earth rotates around its own axis and orbits the sun, while satellites simultaneously orbit earth. A satellite in an SSO remains in the same 'fixed' position relative to the sun, while the earth rotates 'under' the orbiting satellite. It takes the earth around 90 to 120 minutes to rotate around its own axis 'under' a satellite in SSO to its 'starting point', as Daniel Düsentrieb, an aerospace engineering student based in Stuttgart, explained. These 90 to 120 minutes constitute the SSO's 'temporal resolution' as 'the time it takes for a satellite to complete an orbit and revisit the same observation area'.[8] The satellite thus passes different local spots on earth at the same local hour, either in the morning or in the afternoon.[9] While the earth itself is rotating, it also rotates around the sun. As Daniel elaborates:

> While the earth is rotating around the sun, I have to rotate the orbit of my satellites so that I always have the same angle to the sun. Then I always get the same exposure or the same lighting conditions for my photo …. Conveniently, the earth is not round, and the earth's gravitational field is not uniform, but is rather egg-shaped, or more precisely, elliptical. Even more precisely, it's more like a potato. I can conveniently adjust to fly through this gravitational field in such a way that with each orbit I get a little kick in the right direction to turn with the sun. In other words, I need to rotate my entire orbit by 360 degrees in a year. And in return, I can get through the earth's gravitational field at a [98 degree] angle, in a certain way, and I get this rotation for free. This is the so-called sun-synchronous orbit, which defines a very specific [north–west] direction of flight.[10,11]

Yet here a challenge arises. As Daniel specifies:

> I would expect to see the satellite again directly above me after 120 minutes. But unfortunately, the earth continues to rotate beneath the satellite during these 120 minutes. As the satellite is in orbit, it is detached from the earth's rotation and the earth rotates away from under the satellite …. This means that the next time you see your satellite again [at the exact same spot] will be after 12 hours …. While the earth rotates under the satellite, a certain distance is travelled, so to speak, during which I have not taken a photo. And the next time the satellite passes by, I will not be able to photograph the entire route. I can only ever photograph a narrow strip of 20 or 30 kilometres.[12,13] And that also determines how many satellites I need.

Here we can witness Lefebvre's (2009) principle that repetition is not synonymous with replication. New rhythms arise as the earth continues to rotate under the satellites. As Space-Eye members' work centres around the inorganic temporality of optical satellites, with each orbit this temporality changes. This inorganic temporality is a composite. It consists of the satellites' mechanical tempos which stem from their passive sensors, their temporal resolutions, and the physio-temporal pattern of their sun-synchronous orbits. Yet as the earth continues to rotate under the satellites in orbit, the satellite's trajectory differs with every iteration. This means that Daniel never gets exactly the same recorded strip of the earth's surface. Rather, he has to wait 12 hours until his satellite passes the same local spot. The result is that the narrow strips the satellite can record change with each repetition after 12 hours. It is to these changes to which the members of Space-Eye have to adjust their knowledge practices.

For Space-Eye and the case of the Mediterranean, the satellite of their current provider passes 'at a rough estimate 11:27 o'clock' each day, according to Rosa. This could be expanded to other satellites being located on different orbits while still being sun-synchronous. Space-Eye could get more pictures by purchasing from different providers. As Daniel explains:

> You can increase the temporal resolution by flying lower. But if you fly lower, a satellite doesn't last very long. Or you have many satellites and that's what [Space-Eye's commercial satellite image provider] does …. If you make constellations, then you get a lot of satellites that can come one after the other on the same orbit and then within … about half an hour, you always get a picture. But then, if you want to have a picture every day, it has to fly staggered, which is done with Sentinel [satellite missions developed by the European Space Agency for the EU's space programme 'Copernicus'], where they fly exactly opposite each other.[14] They have more or less the same orbit, but one is on one side of the earth and the other on the other side. And then they have a very good temporal resolution.[15]

As Daniel explained, Space-Eye is limited to a timeframe of pictures taken between 8 o'clock and 12 o'clock in the morning, when there are fewer clouds. Another factor slowing down the process of working with optical satellites is the 'downlink'. Downlink describes the delay because data can only be transmitted to the ground if the satellite in orbit is in visual range of a ground station.[16] A further delay is brought about by the difference between the recording of an image after it was sent 'down', and its provision by Space-Eye's commercial provider, which can take from four to 48 hours.

Let us return to Mirmalek's understanding of temporal rhythm and unresolved temporal patterns (2020). We witness the interplay of the 'bio'-temporal patterns of interacting organic and inorganic actors and the physio-temporal patterns tied to orbits and the axial rotation of the earth. The results are distinct mechanical tempos resulting from the 'lifespan' of optical satellites, their passive sensors, their temporal resolution, if they fly in a staggered way or not, how their orbit translates to strips on the map, their delay caused by the downlink and how clouds might interfere. The result is the 'indissolubility of space, time, and movement' (Peacock, this volume, Introduction) that must be temporarily reconciled within the social temporal patterns of Space-Eye members' work.

Ultimately, the work of Space-Eye members is as much about compressing time as it is about compressing space, exemplified by the issues of both temporal and spatial resolution inherent to optical satellites. Satellite surveillance epitomizes the very idea of successful 'time-space compression' (Harris, 2021, p 85). The work of Space-Eye is organized around technologies in space to support technologies and their crews in the Mediterranean, to offer them near 'real-time' information for their civil SAR missions. In the process it shows all the hidden boundaries and temporal challenges that arise for everyone involved. Compressing time becomes a vital issue. When it comes to connecting the reality of orbiting satellites to that of roaming ships, any lag or delay of information about a potential boat in distress might lead to a civil SAR ship not getting there in time to rescue people who would otherwise drown.

Neural networks

Space-Eye are limited to one picture per day. They are constrained by the inorganic temporalities of resolution and downlink, of their sun-synchronous satellites. This still offers a starting point to train the neural network. But here a new temporal challenge arises from how neural networks are trained. Space-Eye carries out supervised training of a neural network, rather than unsupervised training or enforcement training. The focus is on computer vision (pictures rather than audio) to enable the network to identify refugee boats in the images of Space-Eye's satellite image provider. Supervised learning means that Rosa submits pictures to the network that she has labelled. Rosa defines different categories that she relates to a numerical, quantitative value (0, 1), thereby making it processable for the neural network.

In the process, Rosa 'presents' the network with various images as input data, some labelled, others not. The network will work out its own criteria or pattern of how to distinguish the categories and then apply this to the unlabelled data. Rosa will then check if it has done so correctly or not. The network does not 'see' the image but just a summation of data points and sums. As Rosa mentioned, a classic example of a supervised neural network for computer vision is a network that is taught to distinguish pictures of cats and dogs. In this case, one would 'show' a neural network labelled images, meaning one assigned them a number for each category. Cats would be labelled '0', dogs '1'. Next to the labelled data, one would provide the network with thousands of other pictures of cats and dogs. Rather than predefining certain features, one would let 'it' figure out how to distinguish the two categories according to 'its' own criteria or pattern.

As part of training a neural network for the task of distinguishing boats from the surface of the Mediterranean, three core challenges arise: access to data, (spatial) resolution, and verification. For a neural network to be reliable, Rosa would need to show the neural network thousands of images. The first challenge for Rosa and the Space-Eye team was to put together their own dataset. Because of the specificity of their task, they could not rely on any of the standard datasets used in academic research. Furthermore, they had not found an example of a satellite image with a refugee boat in it.

The spatial resolution – meaning 'how big is a pixel on the ground' – currently available to Space-Eye via their commercial provider and the open-source data on the internet is around 3 metres × 3 metres per pixel. This means that the types of rubber boats commonly used by refugees (10–12 metres long and 3–4 metres wide) would be three pixels on the satellite images. Or, as Walter phrases it:

> We are currently working with resolutions that are atrocious, so something like three metres per pixel. In the military field, and technically possible, the resolution is less than 30 centimetres …. So, you have the following challenges in principle: There are satellites that are freely accessible or that are scientifically freely accessible. But these satellites usually have a poor resolution, or they don't have the spectral range that you want …. The moment I want something better, I either need money or I'm a military man.

During Space Eye's first labelling phase in August 2021, which I took part in, I found it challenging to distinguish anything from the blue background in the square sections of the processed satellite images, whereby the visualization with near-infrared spectroscopy can help.[17] But it is still nearly impossible to verify what it is that I had labelled, as there were not many ways to follow up on who or what was there. This generated creative approaches, in order to attempt to provide clarity on how a potential refugee boat might look on the images at Space-Eye's disposal. One of the members documented their time and GPS position while being out with their sailing boat on holiday, and Space-Eye members tried to find him via satellite.

Gaining access to satellite images with the resolution of Google Maps, for instance, is possible but is costly. This requires requesting and ordering satellite imagery for a specific region in advance, and buying pictures from multiple providers. Another way to gain access to satellite images with better spatial resolution is by applying to research institutes, like the European Space

Agency. This requires writing research proposals with academic researchers and their infrastructures, and waiting for these proposals to be accepted, which may take months.

The challenges that Space-Eye are dealing with in their work – for example, their attempt to successfully compress both time and space and to enhance their temporal and spatial resolution within socio-technological coding practices – were explained to me as a consequence of being 'merely' scientists and NGO actors on the project. The work of Space-Eye raises our awareness about certain 'temporal hierarchies' (Harris, 2021, p 96), 'temporal politics' (Ringel, 2018, p 11), or 'power-chronography' (Sharma 2013, p 14), that are related to the infrastructures of earth observation and artificial intelligence, and constitute limits to their usage for civilian ends. These boundaries can be both in relation of scientific use compared to military or corporate use, but also within the scientific field.

It is here that the multiple temporalities of global capitalism as well as military/security interest steps to the fore as being intertwined with these infrastructures. While Space-Eye members struggle to gain access, private corporations able to pay the price or military actors with the golden ticket walk by freely. In this case, we witness how military and global capitalist temporalities come *before* scientific temporality, both in abstract terms and additionally when it comes down to who gets their satellite images first, or '(near) real-time'. Or rather, we witness how the promise of speed as a universalized condition is contrasted with a reality of 'temporally experienced privilege and difference' (Sharma, 2013, p 19), whereby some forms of knowledge practice are advanced and accelerated if they are favourable to certain economic or military interests.

While there are challenges, there have been major leaps forward. Harry Hacker took the principle explained here and turned it on its head. Reaching out to SAR organizations, they agreed to share some of their logbooks in which they documented information about their sightings of refugee boats in distress. By scanning through the logbooks, he noted times, dates, and locations of sightings. Knowing where to look, and considering how the boat might have drifted in the time between the noted sightings and the time a satellite picture was taken, he gained access to satellite images of the surrounding area and built a tool for object detection. Object detection is a combination of *identifying* as in classifying into 'water' and 'not-water' and *locating* as in detecting the geolocation of objects.

While the former approach was 'We have a satellite image, find me the boats', Harry's approach is to say, 'I know whereabout the boat is, find me the satellite image'. By combining different algorithmic tools for this kind of object detection into a data pipeline, he was successful in finding various pictures of boats, which can further be used to train Space-Eye's classification-neural-network.

Circumventing temporal challenges through infrastructures

Throughout the fieldwork, I investigated the ways the same technological objects (satellites, drones, and artificial intelligence) are used by 'the other side', namely Frontex. One infrastructure that constitutes an interface between the work of Space-Eye and that of protecting EU borders is the EU satellite programme Copernicus. It consists of six satellite missions called 'Sentinel 1–6', that enable land, sea and atmosphere monitoring and observation through high-resolution optical imagery, radar imaging, and atmospheric spectrometry.[18] Most of the Copernicus data is advertised as free and open access for researchers and the wider public.[19] This led Space-Eye members to apply for access to Sentinel's higher-resolution optical data. Copernicus was formerly known as 'Global Monitoring of Environment and Security' (GMES), exemplifying the dual-use inherent to the programme. However, nowadays its environmental applications are foregrounded while its security applications are pushed into the background (Monroy, 2021).[20]

Frontex is one of the EU's fastest growing agencies, and supports EU member states with their surveillance and border control (see Kasparek, 2021). The agency researches and invests in the latest technological innovations for potential future application. Frontex started to use Copernicus satellites in 2014 as part of their border surveillance services 'in fighting cross-border crime and in countering terrorism'. The satellites provide 'near-real-time data on the EU's external land and sea borders, supporting the EU's external border surveillance information exchange framework (EUROSUR)'.[21] EUROSUR is based on optical and radar satellite data from the Copernicus programme and further (inter)national satellite providers. This (ideally) enables EUROSUR to automatically track and detect vessels. Through this system and platform, Frontex can allegedly calculate and detect anomalies, and predict vessel positions based on precise weather and oceanographic forecasts.[22]

To deal with the issue of downlink, meaning the delay due to data only being transmitted to the ground if the satellite in orbit is in visual range, Frontex uses the European Data Relay Satellite System (EDRS).[23,24] EDRS is part of the Copernicus framework and ideally ensures communication at all times. Three laser satellites facilitate a kind of 'space data highway' that 'establish[es] a connection between lower-flying observation satellites with a ground station over distances of 80,000 kilometres', resulting in a quasi-real-time transmission of satellite images anywhere on earth (Monroy, 2021, pp 19–20). The price for this space data highway is 'at least €520 million and is subsidized with large public sums as a public-private partnership between Airbus and the European Space Agency .... However, the owner of the 'space data highway' is Airbus, so the company markets the services alone' (Monroy, 2021, p 20).

What the EDRS exemplifies is that (quasi-)real-time satellite surveillance constitutes an active achievement *for some* rather than a given. EDRS constitutes one of various infrastructural investments in the fields of earth observation and artificial intelligence. Such infrastructures do not constitute a new overarching surveillance system. Rather they signify a 'patching together' of the multiple temporalities and paces to enable interoperability between existing data infrastructures (Pollozek, 2020, p 678). It constitutes a site where 'politics is translated from a rationality to a practice' (Appel et al, 2018, pp 15, 20). We can observe the divergence between the promise of 'real-time' satellite surveillance anytime anywhere, and its reality, which consists of all the composite and hierarchically assembled practicalities, rhythms, and temporal patterns that must be synchronized and patched together in the process.

Yet we can see that this patching together is only accessible for some. The 'same' satellite infrastructure(s) of the Copernicus programme play quite different roles in the collective brought about by the Space-Eye-project compared to that of the EUROSUR network. Both collectives are brought about by different contextualized practices and materialities involving interacting humans and machines and their (in)organic temporalities. The technological objects of optical satellites and neural networks entail the promise of speed and 'time-space compression'. Yet if one is neither a military person nor has unlimited financial capabilities, this promise dissolves and one is stuck with dealing with 'lags' and 'delay(s)'.

What we are left with are certain possibilities with simultaneous restrictions, be it due to the inorganic temporalities of optical satellites being tied to the physio-temporal pattern of sun-synchronous orbits, their passive sensors, the issues of temporal and spatial resolution, and further being 'slowed down' by the issue of downlink. Or it could be due to the inorganic temporality of training a neural network by providing a certain quantity of pictures with a decent resolution to 'speed up' the mechanical learning tempo of a neural network, to come up with its own criteria and pattern to distinguish refugee boats from the sea and for Space-Eye members to check up on its training's progression.

Thinking about Space-Eye's volunteer work, organized around satellites and neural networks with their organic and inorganic temporalities, makes us aware of the issue of access to certain infrastructures for better temporal and spatial resolution. This resonates with Marilyn Strathern's argument on the role of ownership in 'cutting the network' (Strathern, 1996). Positioned as as a critique of the open-endedness of networks within Actor-Network Theory she submits: 'Ownership is powerful because of its double effect, as simultaneously a matter of belonging and of property [...]. So where technology might enlarge networks, proprietorship can be guaranteed to cut them down to size' (Strathern, 1996, p 531).

Turning to these infrastructures of earth observation prompts the questions of 'Who knows?', 'Who decides?' and 'Who decides who decides?'. These questions relate to knowledge, authority, and power, and the 'axial principle of social order in an information civilization' (Zuboff, 2019, p 168). They reflect upon the ability to share or withhold knowledge, and who is in charge of such decisions, that is tied to earth observation infrastructures. These questions become quite concrete in the case of Space-Eye and earth observation infrastructures, where 'knowing' constitutes a specific, situated, socio-technological, practical achievement involving the reconciliation of multiple rhythms in the process.

We observe how these questions gain temporal importance, as being denied access to these infrastructures slows down Space-Eye members in their attempt at time-space compression 'for the good'. It slows down those in front of their screens, and those on board trying to find people in the water. They pose a closure of the future on the question of of how, and for whom, it is accessible in relation to the technologies of satellites and artificial intelligence, which involves 'not only the deceleration of technical advancements in certain domains but also an entrenchment of the same old visions of future societies, of power relations and ways of living' (Hong, 2022, p 373). In this case, the usage of satellites for military, corporate, and border security purposes is taken as a given, while we encounter various (temporal) challenges that arise when these technologies are enacted for a different kind of future and collective.

It is a closure that impacts the (techno)future(s) in the making, by members of Space-Eye within their alternative socio-technological practices. It further impacts the form of social becoming – and belonging – that is potentially brought about by this co-constitutional interaction in the future and the here-and-now. The collective that is brought about by the current hegemonic dialogical interactions of the EUROSUR-network does not seem to include people on the move as worth saving. Rather, people on the move are enacted as a security risk (Kasparek, 2021), exemplified by Frontex's research into future border technology applications. For people on the move this signifies a quite lethal closure, not of *the*, but of *a* future and who gets the opportunity to have one.

With the EDRS we get a glimpse from the 'other B-series' (Ssorin-Chaikov, 2017, p 15), the one that comes first. Or rather, the one that not only has the 'authority to share or withhold knowledge' (Zuboff, 2019, p 168), but also has the power to create the socio-technological and material basis through which knowledge is circulated, the speed of its circulation, and who gets access. It shows how the 'infrastructural ordering of time', as a 'macrophysics of power' (Crawford, 2021, p 81), is not solely given but can be actively reformulated through specific socio-technological or material investments and the creation of new infrastructural elements, in this case four satellites roaming geostationary orbit. It is the power to create new socio-technological infrastructural elements that 'configure time, enable certain kinds of social time while disabling others, and make some temporalities possible while foreclosing alternatives' (Appel et al, 2018, p 15).

We can witness here how spatialization constitutes a 'temporal act and activity' (Appel et al, 2018, p 16). It is through temporal agency that consistent 'near-real-time data on the EU's external land and sea borders' is brought about. Temporal agency relying on a socio-technological network transcending orbits and downlink through three laser satellites at the bargain price of €520 million of partly public money. The result is an infrastructural constellation that manages to watch in near real time how people on the move drown, while retrieving Frontex missions at sea were justified by 'framing the 'problem' as merely a lack of EU resources' (Mainwaring and DeBono, 2021, p 1034).

Conclusion: The politics of lag

Temporality – or arrhythmia – itself has become a tool and weapon in the context of EU migration control (Andersson, 2014). The EDRS offers a glimpse into the machinery, or rather the growing infrastructural 'hybrid collectif' (De León, 2015, pp 38–44), of EUROSUR and its temporalities of control. It constitutes an element in an 'economics of illegality' that facilitates technological innovations for all kinds of new policing applications. Because of that, defence contractors and border authorities are provided with ever more resources leading to 'precisely the opposite reality for those who are targeted: a world of slowness and stasis' (Andersson, 2014, p 806–7). Returning this to the reality of SAR missions, we encounter how lag and delay constitute the result of socio-material state actions such as criminalization that become a tool to target SAR organizations, slowing them down in their practices, whereby in the context of SAR, where compressing time signifies a vital issue, any lag becomes potentially fatal.

Faced with this discrepancy within both the means and ends of the 'other side' to the Space-Eye project, it is hard not to feel confronted with a cybernetically enhanced hydra, solely equipped with an Atari console. But getting access and being reliant on these infrastructures does not keep members, as exemplified by Harry Hacker's tool, from crafting unique pathways through their own forms of temporal agency. In the spirit of a cyborgian retelling of David versus Goliath, the image of their original encounter gracing the walls of the 'Goliathhaus' in the middle of Regensburg (Figure 6.2), what better place to spark hope?

A first step is to pragmatically develop the idea that where technology enlarges networks, ownership cuts them down. This means addressing these emerging satellite and artificial intelligence infrastructures, asking who has legal ownership over them and who is left out of decision-making. How could they nurture a different kind of collective? It would mean using situated socio-technological practices, and the infrastructures they rely on,

Figure 6.2: The 'Goliathhaus' in Regensburg

as a gateway to investigate 'lag' as the consequence of political decisions and infrastructural investments. These are manifested in composite and hierarchically assembled and patched-up rhythms, temporal patterns, mechanical tempos, and interacting (in)organic temporalities that signify (near) real-timeness for some, and the denial of a future for others.

It further raises our awareness to questions of technical/temporal imagination(s) and investigate how the *promise* of '(near) real-timeness' is tied to a specific kind of technofuture that constitutes a 'dominant formulation of temporality' (Ringel, 2018, p 27), one that 'enact[s] a hegemony of closure and sameness' and postulates 'the closure of possible worlds and temporalities to the one and only kind of progress' (Hong, 2022, pp 372–4). It thus forces us to investigate how time is folded within these infrastructures and how they fold time. It involves asking who (more in a network-, constellation-, or organization-sense rather than merely tied to specific individuals) is capable of, responsible for, and in charge of newly developing infrastructural elements that constitute an active achievement of time–space compression for some. How are these infrastructures funded? Whose time are they folding or accelerating? Whose are they slowing down? For what purposes?

This further involves tracing how our imagination of time is marked by dominant formulations of temporality, where the future is left to be colonized and occupied only by certain groups claiming the hegemony over its means and form(ulation) (Andersson, 2014). Hence it is crucial to engage actively with a 're-appropriation of the future [as] a political right, a right to aspire and to participate in the social practice of the imagination' (Ringel, 2018, p 30). Space-Eye offers a starting point for such a re-appropriation of the future, a technofuture which, although it has not happened yet, is already effective in the virtual (Fisher, 2014). In the case of Space-Eye, this technofuture is not even merely limited to the realm of the virtual, but *already* a future enacted within present socio-technological and infrastructural practices and as part of Space-Eye members' temporal agency. It is through their coding practices that Space-Eye members already enact surveillance more in the image of Big Mother (Peacock, this volume, Introduction). It is through their practices that surveillance acts as an anticipatory act which has the differential capacity to protect rather than to neglect in real time. While the Space-Eye project faces its limits in scope and resources, let us hope it can be one of many tears in the fabric of the closing curtain of securitized technofutures, a contribution to an alternative horizon of how technological progress and border practices could be, and *already are*, done differently.

Acknowledgements

I would like to dedicate this chapter to my uncle, Konrad Kutscher, who has supported my academic aspirations from the very start and believed in them at times more than I did. I would like to thank the members of Space-Eye and SearchWing, who have shown nothing but kindness to me and my project, and have provided me generously with their time, knowledge, ingenuity, and wit. I would like to express my deep gratitude to Tina Harris, Juan Ramón Mejía López, Dastan Abdali, Jenno Maaskant, and Tim Praha, whose support has been crucial in developing this chapter. Additionally, I would like to thank Mikkel Kenni Bruun, Vita Peacock and the SAMCOM team, as well as members of the STS x Anthropology reading group organized by Herbert Ploegman, Inge Dekker, and Salman Khan, for their constructive feedback on earlier versions of this chapter. Lastly, I would like to thank Beyond Borders Bucerius Start Up Scholarship provided by the Zeit Stiftung Bucerius.

Notes

[1] All names are pseudonyms.

[2] https://sea-watch.org/en/mission/airborne/ (Accessed: 25 October 2024).

[3] https://www.datacamp.com/tutorial/introduction-to-convolutional-neural-networks-cnns (Accessed: 25 October 2024).

[4] https://deepai.org/machine-learning-glossary-and-terms/neural-network (Accessed: 25 October 2024).

[5] https://wiki.pathmind.com/neural-network (Accessed: 25 October 2024).

[6] See online supplementary figure S1 at https://bristoluniversitypress.co.uk/rhythm-and-vigilance.

[7] https://privacyinternational.org/explainer/4595/satellite-and-aerial-surveillance-migration-tech-primer (Accessed: 25 October 2024).

[8] https://www.earthdata.nasa.gov/learn/backgrounders/remote-sensing#:~:text=Temporal%20resolution%20is%20the%20time,temporal%20resolution%20is%20much%20finer (Accessed: 25 October 2024).

[9] See online supplementary figure S2 at https://bristoluniversitypress.co.uk/rhythm-and-vigilance.

[10] For a visualization of the SSO, see https://www.youtube.com/watch?v=ylvgxNF3C0c (Accessed: 25 October 2024).

[11] See online supplementary figure S3 at https://bristoluniversitypress.co.uk/rhythm-and-vigilance.

[12] For a visualization, see https://www.youtube.com/watch?v=y_jM_BxQGvE (Accessed: 25 October 2024).

[13] See online supplementary figure S4 at https://bristoluniversitypress.co.uk/rhythm-and-vigilance.

[14] See online supplementary figure S5 at https://bristoluniversitypress.co.uk/rhythm-and-vigilance.

[15] For a visualization of Sentinel-2 'flying staggered' see https://www.esa.int/Applications/Observing_the_Earth/Copernicus/Sentinel-2/Satellite_constellation (Accessed: 25 October 2024).

[16] See online supplementary figure S6 at https://bristoluniversitypress.co.uk/rhythm-and-vigilance.

[17] See online supplementary figures S7 and S8 at https://bristoluniversitypress.co.uk/rhythm-and-vigilance.

[18] https://sentiwiki.copernicus.eu/web/copernicus-programme (Accessed: 25 October 2024).

[19] https://www.copernicus.eu/de/ueber-copernicus; https://www.esa.int/Applications/Observing_the_Earth/Copernicus/The_Sentinel_missions (Accessed: 9 June 2022).

[20] For the English version of the study from which quotes were taken, see https://digit.site36.net/2021/07/22/border-drones-part-1-unmanned-surveillance-of-the-eus-external-borders-by-frontex/ (Accessed: 9 June 2022).

[21] https://insitu.copernicus.eu/FactSheets/CSS_Border_Surveillance (Accessed: 25 October 2024).

[22] https://frontex.europa.eu/media-centre/news/news-release/frontex-to-implement-border-surveillance-services-as-part-of-copernicus-Z1r4A0 (Accessed: 25 October 2022).

[23] https://artes.esa.int/european-data-relay-satellite-system-edrs-overview (Accessed: 25 October 2024); for a visualization, see https://www.youtube.com/watch?v=_TnNmtm8l0I (Accessed: 25 October 2024).

[24] See online supplementary figure S9 at https://bristoluniversitypress.co.uk/rhythm-and-vigilance.

References

Andersson, R. (2014) 'Time and the Migrant Other: European Border Controls and the Temporal Economics of Illegality', *American Anthropologist*, 116(4): 795–809.

Appel, H., Anand, N., and Gupta, A. (2018) 'Temporality, Politics, and the Promise of Infrastructure', in H. Appel, N. Anand, and A. Gupta (eds) *The Promise of Infrastructure*. Durham, NC: Duke University Press, pp 1–38.

Bear, L. (2014) 'For Labour: Ajeet's Accident and the Ethics of Technological Fixes in Time', *Journal of the Royal Anthropological Institute*, 20(S1): 71–88.

Bear, L. (2016) 'Time as Technique', *Annual Review of Anthropology*, 45: 487–502.

Bissell, D. (2021) 'Encountering Automation: Redefining Bodies through Stories of Technological Change', *Environment and Planning D: Society and Space*, 39(2): 366–84.

Crawford, K. (2021) *Atlas of AI: The Real Worlds of Artificial Intelligence*. New Haven: Yale University Press.

De León, J. (2015) *The Land of Open Graves: Living and Dying on the Migrant Trail*. Berkeley: University of California Press.

Fisch, M. (2018) *An Anthropology of the Machine: Tokyo's Commuter Train Network*. Chicago, IL: University of Chicago Press.

Fisher, M. (2014) *Ghosts of My Life: Writings on Depression, Hauntology and Lost Futures*. Winchester: Zero Books.

Guyer, J. (2007) 'Prophecy and the Near Future: Thoughts on Macroeconomic, Evangelical, and Punctuated Time', *American Ethnologist*, 34(3): 409–21.

Harris, T. (2021) 'Air Pressure: Temporal Hierarchies in Nepali Aviation', *Cultural Anthropology*, 36(1): 83–109.

Hong, S. (2022) 'Predictions without Futures', *History and Theory*, 61(3): 371–90.

Kasparek, B. (2021) *Europa als Grenze: Eine Ethnographie der Grenzschutz-Agentur Frontex*. Bielefeld: transcript Verlag.

Lefebvre, H. (2009) *Rhythmanalysis: Space, Time and Everyday Life*. London: Continuum.

Mainwaring, Ċ. and DeBono, D. (2021) 'Criminalizing Solidarity: Search and Rescue in a Neo-Colonial Sea', *EPC: Politics and Space*, 39(5): 1030–48.

Mirmalek, Z. (2020) *Making Time on Mars*. Cambridge, MA: MIT Press.

Mol, A. (2002) *The Body Multiple: Ontology in Medical Practice*. Durham, NC: Duke University Press.

Monroy, M. (2021) 'Grenzdrohnen: Unbemannte Überwachung der Festung Europa', in Ö. Demirel, (eds) *Europäische Studien zu Außen- und Friedenspolitik*, pp 1–53.

Morozov, E. (2014) *To Save Everything, Click Here*. New York: PublicAffairs.

Munn, N. (1992) 'The Cultural Anthropology of Time: A Critical Essay', *Annual Review of Anthropology*, 21: 93–123.

Oppenheim, R. (2007) 'Actor-Network Theory and Anthropology after Science, Technology, and Society', *Anthropological Theory*, 7(4): 471–93.

Pollozek, S. (2020) 'Turbulences of Speeding Up Data Circulation. Frontex and its Crooked Temporalities of "Real-Time" Border Control', *Mobilities*, 15(5): 677–93.

Ringel, F. (2018) *Back to the Postindustrial Future: An Ethnography of Germany's Fastest Shrinking City*. New York: Berghahn Books.

Sharma, S. (2013) *In the Meantime: Temporality and Cultural Politics*. Durham, NC: Duke University Press.

Ssorin-Chaikov, N. (2017) *Two Lenins: A Brief Anthropology of Time*. Chicago, IL: HAU Books.

Strathern, M. (1996) 'Cutting the Network', *Journal of the Royal Anthropological Institute*, 2(3): 517–35.

Zuboff, S. (2019) *The Age of Surveillance Capitalism: The Fight for a Human Future at the New Frontier of Power*. London: Profile Books.

7

Surveillance in Small Acts: Health Code Rituals during the COVID-19 Pandemic in Xiamen, China

Karolina Kupinska

Introduction

I am sitting with Stone's mother during our interview in their apartment on the 43rd floor, enjoying the night view of Dongping Mountain, and the tea she has prepared for me. Stone is doing schoolwork in his room. As his mum is busy today, his father needs to assist their younger son with his homework – a task he is visibly unfamiliar with. We discuss educational surveillance and family education, after the implementation of the double reduction reform (*Shuang Jian*) in the Chinese education system. Suddenly I receive a notification on my phone. I have not yet reported my health status and whereabouts in the university system, and my department administrator reminds me of this task before the daily deadline of 7 pm. Even though sending the report requires only a few clicks and takes a short amount of time, I manifest my annoyance with the procedure.[1]

Stone's mother seems surprised by my reaction. She perceives my annoyance as an artefact of the fact that, 'Western people like freedom too much'. She reports the health data of her entire family to the school every day, and does not share my feelings of exposure and constraint. She calls it '*xiaoshi*' – a small thing, a petty thing, a trivial matter. 'Xiamen is very safe', she stresses several times, a moral logic whereby feeding data into the system will guarantee safety and good health.

This is a form of what I call 'small act' surveillance, during the COVID-19 pandemic in the city of Xiamen, China. I use the term 'small act' to

137

emphasize that surveillance during the pandemic was not only experienced (in the form of contact tracing and quarantine), but also performed by citizens through a series of quotidian acts. In China, pandemic surveillance consisted of numerous grids of surveillance, various authorities creating 'multiple surveillant assemblages, all linking back to provincially and centrally collected, stored, and analysed information' (Bernot and Cassiano, 2021, p 17). These pandemic surveillant assemblages created their own temporal regimes, visible either as an abrupt expression of state power, as in the case of lockdowns, or as the subtle, almost intangible temporalities of health codes. In line with Peacock (Introduction, this volume), I consider pandemic surveillance not only as constituted by the monitoring practices of the state and its institutions, but as a 'generator' of social life, of ritualized small acts and behaviours conforming to the temporal regimes pandemic surveillance had imposed.

Research background

This chapter is based on my ethnographic research on educational surveillance in Chinese families, conducted during the COVID-19 pandemic in Xiamen. This entailed both participant observation of their lives (in digital spaces and in person), as well as extensive interviews with parents and their school-age children.[2] Online we communicated through social media, particularly on WeChat – a platform deeply entrenched in the everyday lives of Chinese people (Chao, 2017).[3] I also engaged in informal interactions and conversations and shorter interviews with Chinese and foreign residents in Xiamen, who agreed to collaborate as research participants. All participants' names have been changed to English names for ease of reading. In addition, I used policy briefs on pandemic prevention, surveillance instructions, and official news on digital platforms to analyse themes related to the pandemic, surveillance, and other control measures. The research also involved documenting auto-ethnographic traces of my own experiences of living in Xiamen – a perspective framed by the limitations and conditions of being an international student at Xiamen University, living off-campus.[4]

My research participants belonged to the vague designation of the Chinese middle class of a second-tier city (Zhang, 2020).[5] Even if the total income of some of these participants may have decreased during the three years of the pandemic, some benefitted from the window of opportunity that COVID-19 offered, and were able to grow their new businesses significantly.

Chinese people were proud of the effectiveness of their efforts in fighting the virus, and could be disdainful of Western societies defending their freedoms against health surveillance (Liu, 2021). However, it should be noted that my interlocutors did not only take pride in how 'safe' China was compared to the rest of the world, but moreover in how 'safe' Xiamen was compared to other places in China. Unlike residents of cities like Shanghai, Xi'an, or Wuhan, where strict entire-city lockdowns were enforced, people in Xiamen only experienced a few outbreaks, which were contained relatively quickly. Critical voices against preventive measures were notably scarce. In November and December 2022, during protests in other cities, none of my interlocutors, to my knowledge, ever expressed criticism by posting a photo of a sheet of blank A4 paper (which became the symbol of protest) on their WeChat Moments.

This chapter was assembled more than a year after these interactions took place, when the COVID-19 pandemic was already considered by the World Health Organization (WHO) to be part of history.[6] It is thus a historical exploration of the temporalities surveillance measures produced, and the ruptures they caused in the lives of the Xiamen residents, in the knowledge that these measures did not continue after the formal end of the pandemic.

On temporal regimes of COVID-19 surveillance

Anthropologists have often conceptualized an emergency as a state of exception, whereby the power to impose legal and moral interpretations to reshape economic or political norms belongs to those who control the response. Emergencies have the potential to hence amplify both power, and vulnerability to it. In a state of emergency, norms that govern life may be suspended, and power structures entrenched (Beckett, 2013, MacPhail, 2014, Stellmach and Beshar, 2016, Lakoff, 2017, Jordheim and Wigen, 2018). As Didier Fassin and Mariella Pandolfi argue, 'A temporality of emergency derives from a desire to intervene' (Fassin and Pandolfi, 2010, p 16), emphasizing the 'now time' of action and the roles of those in command of the response. However, it is equally important to recognize that situated experiences may differ from how emergencies are framed by those in power, such as governments (MacPhail, 2014).

Here I employ the term 'ruptures' (Lynteris, 2014), in order to reflect on how the COVID-19 pandemic and its surveillance compelled residents of Xiamen to adopt new ways of experiencing time. Martin Holbraad and his co-authors apply the concept of 'ruptures' (Holbraad et al, 2019), to describe the multiplicity of differently experienced 'nows'. Ruptures look both backward and forward at once, and connote a forceful form of discontinuity. They also relate to memory and how the experiences of past traumas inform the present (Holbraad et al, 2019). Ruptures are venues for transformation, providing a temporal structure for the emergence of change.

I analyse the COVID-19 pandemic in China as a series of ruptures, causing post-disaster dynamics at three levels: national, institutional, and individual. On a national level, after an initial hiatus, the government used the outbreak to strengthen sentiment around the Chinese Communist

Party under the leadership of Xi Jinping. On 10 February 2020, Xi Jinping inaugurated the COVID-19 pandemic narrative by declaring a 'people's war against the novel coronavirus' (The State Council of the People's Republic of China, 2020). Surveillance was the weapon of choice. Institutionally, the Chinese government utilized this epidemic rupture to accelerate the digital transformation of government, economy, and society (Wu et al, 2020). To the repertoire of surveillance measures dating from the time of the SARS outbreak, Xi added digitalizatization of monitoring measures aimed at containment (Zhang, 2020). One aspect of strengthening pandemic control over society was the digitalization of the '*Meiri Jiankang Zhuizong Daka*' – a daily registration of citizen health records (Wu et al, 2020, p 307). On the interpersonal level, while others have examined the socio-temporal implications of outbreaks concerning epidemic surveillance and quarantine (Desclaux et al, 2017; Frankfurter, 2019), I present the surveillance enacted by citizens through digital reporting, as imposing a particular microsocial temporal regime.

What has been called epidemic intelligence is a particular kind of surveillance assemblage. It consists of the swift collection and analysis of disease-related data, in order to reduce the time between detection, diagnosis, and the introduction of control measures. Carlio Caduff argues that epidemic intelligence 'eventualizes' epidemics, producing 'a spectacle of eventfulness while blocking events from happening' (Caduff, 2014, p 41). It is not simply the neutral recording of information, but is an example of surveillance being simulated, in which coded information anticipates an event in order to shape its outcome (Bogard, 1996). In China, the foundation of this was contact tracing through health codes (*Jian Kang Ma*).

Developed as software extensions on two of China's most popular platforms, Alipay and WeChat, as early as February 2020, health codes became the tool of 'proving' one's 'health' status (Sun and Wang, 2022). Even though each province (and many cities) had specific health codes, the operation was similar. Schematically, three kinds of data fed the codes: personal information, users' geo-temporal locations,[7] and the likelihood of contact with virus carriers based on user networks and online transactions (Liang, 2020). The algorithm evaluated the data as safe, risky, or unsafe, and generated one of three colour indicators of the health code: green, yellow, or red. Health codes evolved during the three years of the pandemic, increasing the amount of data they generated and collected. They were sometimes faulty (Liu, 2022), paralyzing entire cities for hours. However, in Xiamen they operated without any major disruption until the end of the pandemic. Besides a health code, a travel code (*Xing Cheng Ma*) infrastructured through mobile network towers, showed counties visited by each user over the last seven days.

During outbreaks, pandemic monitoring was supported by 'special preventive measures': contact tracing extended to the precise movement trajectories of confirmed cases and close contacts within the city. It resulted in the 'closed loop management' of communities (meaning only registered people could enter or leave communities, company buildings, and facilities); quarantines (in medical facilities); localized lockdowns (such as 'no exit' spaces); the closing down or restriction of services and businesses (such as when restaurants could only serve takeaways); schools transferring to online lessons; and shops limiting the number of customers allowed inside.

During the days, weeks, and months free from the COVID-19 virus in Xiamen city, pandemic surveillance, based on health codes, created temporal regimes that dominated the rhythms of everyday life (Lefebvre, 2004). Mobile phone screens became the key loci of power – distributed in people's hands, empowering them to deter the danger of COVID-19 through acts of checking information, and scanning the codes on their phones. Enacting small act surveillance, they actively participated in 'observation before the fact' (Bogard, 1996). Participation in this simulated surveillance created the shared imagination of living in the 'future–past' (Bogard, 1996, p 34) and of being 'safe' in a 'safe' city.

Through micro-rituals of feeding the data into the system, which themselves set the rhythm of the day, the lives of Xiamen residents were governed by rhythmic multiplicity. What I consider the temporalities of the 'PCR test clock', 'reverse gear', and 'group responsibility' of pandemic surveillance will be described in what follows. In the simulation of pandemic surveillance, where all variations at each step are accounted for in advance, these regimes exhibit characteristics of hypercontrol. The Chinese government's decision to ultimately abolish health codes abruptly ended these ritualistic small acts and caused yet another rupture, with significant temporal and organizational consequences, in the personal lives of Xiamen residents.

The Chinese government has invested heavily in surveillance technology in recent years (Byler, 2022) and state and commercial surveillance are seamlessly integrated and apparent in everyday life. The involuntary nature of pandemic surveillance in China is important to highlight (Macnish and Henschke, 2023); however, as Lyon (2022) has argued, it emerged within an already complex combination of surveillance technologies, both digital and more traditional.

In his work on the AIDS pandemic, Charles Rosenberg (Rosenberg, 1992) introduced the concept of a dramaturgical form to describe the sequential unfolding of an epidemic. The outbreak emerges, develops, and eventually subsides, much like the plot of a theatrical play. Rosenberg's dramaturgy offers a frame through which to understand the chronology of epidemics, and highlights the dynamic and evolving nature of infectious diseases inside a population. It also emphasizes the social dimensions of epidemics, where societal behaviours, governmental responses, and medical interventions all contribute to the overall 'plot'. The following sections illustrate how different temporalities operated and created multi-layered ruptures during the four acts of the COVID-19 drama in the city of Xiamen.[8]

First act: the introduction to the pandemic

From December 2019 to 16 February 2020

The COVID-19 outbreak in Wuhan in late November 2019 did not happen in a vacuum (World Health Organization, 2021). The SARS 2003 epidemic had left indelible marks on China, creating a template that overwhelmingly shaped the response to COVID-19 (Dolan and Rutherford, 2020). Doctors were already attuned to the signs of epidemics (Li, X. et al, 2020), and authorities created a legal framework for implementing warning systems (Wang et al, 2020). The initial days of the COVID-19 outbreak in December 2019 put these systems to the test, and the failure of reporting mechanisms (Czernin, 2020) resembled the initial stage of denying the SARS outbreak (Eckholm, 2006). Soon afterwards, building on the experiences two decades earlier, the government and local authorities introduced procedures such as quarantine, social distancing, and measures severely restricting movements. Even the slogans of the mass mobilization campaign came from the time of SARS.[9]

Moreover, the news about the outbreak appeared before the Spring Festival holiday period. This temporal coincidence had important consequences, as many residents from Xiamen could spend the initial couple of months of the pandemic, characterized by uncertainty and lowered economic activity, in the safety of their family homes.

Statistically, with a confirmed patient carrying the virus, the COVID-19 pandemic started in Xiamen on 23 January 2020, with three recorded cases (Xiamen City Health Commission, 2020). Learning from the memory of SARS, many believed that they could avoid COVID-19 by self-quarantining. Some parents told me that in order to protect their children, they did not allow them to leave the house from January until the end of April (River, Cliff) or even May (Jasmin). Fear and anxiety stimulated extreme reactions, and the smell of bleach would linger throughout residential buildings for days. This period was characterized by desolate streets, closed restaurants, and almost empty supermarkets and shopping centres. Home delivery became a popular method of getting provisions, materialized by the piles of bags that accumulated at the gates of inner-city compounds and communities. Similar to rituals developed in Hong Kong during SARS (Lee and Wing, 2006), many families started the rituals of bleaching their homes, developing undressing procedures, and pressing elevator buttons with keys to avoid contaminating their fingers (despite the fact that elevators like those in my building were bleached every hour). Unsurprisingly, masks became the most sought-after item and were soon in short supply.

On 2 February 2020, the Xiamen city government introduced 'close loop management': prohibiting non-residents from entering buildings they were not registered to live in. Entering any venue required recording all personal information in special community registry books after having one's temperature taken. This temperature check was sometimes comical and eerie: guards would use 'thermometer guns' that were frequently faulty, resulting in imprecise measurements. To rectify this, guards would press the 'thermometer gun' against foreheads for a more accurate reading, pragmatically ignoring the potential presence of the virus and its 'distancing' and 'no contact' premises to fulfil the obligations of data collection. The yet-to-be-digitalized 'closed loop management' imposed on residents proved effective: within three weeks – by 16 February – the infection curve had flattened in Xiamen, with a total of just 35 cases.

Second act: proliferation

From 16 February 2020 to 30 July 2021

In Rosenberg's dramaturgy (1992), during the second act the epidemic spreads, and gains momentum. Xi Jinping's 'people's war against the novel coronavirus' proved to be effective, and from April to July 2020 there were no new cases reported in China. Afterwards, many regional clustered outbreaks occurred in different cities and surrounding areas, and the Chinese government chose to adopt an elimination strategy, the so-called 'Zero-COVID policy', described as 'active case finding and management' (Li, Z. et al, 2020). Zero-COVID became the collective framework for explaining and dealing with the disease.

After the initial containment in Xiamen, and for the next 18 months, the COVID-19 virus was absent in the city.[10] Companies and factories gradually restarted operations in March, and schools resumed in-person classes in May 2020. What was called 'getting back to a new normal' required huge caution. People applied a 'common sense' approach: children and grown-ups started to pay more attention to hygiene, washing their hands frequently (soap appeared in many public toilets), and ventilating rooms. Small gel alcohol bottles hung on students' backpacks. Due to the news of outbreaks that had started in logistic centres processing imported food, I was warned on many occasions against eating Norwegian salmon or Chilean cherries (Chen, 2021).

Masks were obligatory on public transport and in public space, and most people wore masks on the streets. Masks were also obligatory in schools, and, at first, even during physical education classes. Over time, despite biomedical reasoning that the virus would spread more easily in a crowded classroom of 50+ people than outdoors, students often discreetly removed their masks in the classroom – to breathe more comfortably, eat, or simply play – but continued to wear them in parks and on the streets. They felt they could trust their classmates more than strangers on the street, because each of them proved they were well each day by sending their health codes to their teachers (Sage).

Daily reporting and the sending of codes began in February 2020, when kids were confined to their homes attending classes online. Parents had to send two kinds of codes – health codes and travel codes – of all people living with them under the same roof on a given day. This blurred definition included parents, grandparents, and other relatives, including siblings (even though they were already linked to the parent's health code). In wealthier families, codes of 'stay-at-home helpers' had to be sent too. When travelling was permitted, visiting relatives' codes were also expected to be sent.

Sending codes set up a daily ritual for families, a new quotidian rhythm shared by all children attending educational institutions in Xiamen. Every day, Monday to Sunday, between the time children were out of school and 8:00 am the next day, mothers measured temperatures, collected codes, and uploaded data into the systems. Depending on each district, there were two time slots when parents had to submit the data: before 6:00 pm or before 8:00 am. In theory, pupils whose parents failed to send this data were not allowed to attend school. It was not made easy for them to forget. Teachers were responsible for gathering all the information, and were actively 'reminding' parents who did not fulfil their duties in time, by singling them out with the '@' sign in the class group chats.

The whole performance did not usually take long. If everyone in the extended family answered with their codes quickly, collecting the codes and uploading them in the system would only take a couple of minutes. Parents submitting the data to the school felt that this was a 'small matter' that took only 2–3 minutes of their day. 'Because every day I only need to spend 2–3 minutes to submit the data, for me, it doesn't have any impact', says Stone's mother. Another mother, from the working district, where data had to be submitted before 8:00 am, complained about the burden of taking temperatures from sleeping daughters and collecting the codes from sleeping in-laws before work. She was not happy with the arrangement; however, she did not oppose the idea of providing the information. This ritual, the active participation in the simulation of surveillance, simultaneously created a shared imagination of being safe from the virus, a simulation of pupils being safe in the school, and, consequently, of everyone being safe across the city.

It seemed that people were already used to being surveilled, being 'visible' to the state to such a degree, that this act of collecting codes and updating every day, seemed natural, even banal. As noted by Lyon, since the population in China are more used to constant ranking, the health code could be seen as just one more platform-assisted form of rating and ranking citizens (Lyon, 2022).

In their article about China's response to the pandemic, Cassiano et al (2021) explain how the surveillance ecosystem in which health codes are embedded gives smartphone users a degree of autonomy and personal flexibility, allowing them to make individual decisions about their activities. During this second act, when there was no virus in Xiamen and everyone's code was green, everyone accepted it as a tool of pandemic prevention, guaranteeing safety. However, when the COVID-19 virus was present in the city, these performed small acts of pandemic surveillance created multiple ruptures in the everyday lives of Xiamen residents.

Third act: stabilization and negotiating the public response

From July 2021 to December 2022

In the third act, the epidemic reaches an equilibrium. This does not mean that the disease disappears, but it becomes a constant partner to the affected population. Measures are implemented to control or manage the disease. When communities respond, it becomes another dramaturgical aspect of the epidemic, 'measures to interdict an epidemic constitute rituals, collective rites integrating cognitive and emotional elements' says Rosenberg (1992, p 285).

One month before the third act started, in June 2021, the health codes in Xiamen were upgraded. The first health code, used in the early stages of the pandemic prevention, showed only that a given person 'didn't have abnormal findings' as a green code. The second health code contained information about one's health status (again 'no abnormal findings' as a green code), vaccination status (a gold border surrounding the barcode), and the results of PCR tests in the last seven days. Then, in April 2022, the third version of the code was introduced. It showed 'low level of health risk' as a green code, vaccination status, as well as the numbers 24, 48 or 72 indicating how many hours had passed since the latest PCR test, and a 'scan' button to scan QR codes of every public venue a person had visited.

On 30 July 2021, when the first outbreak since the initial containment of the virus started in Xiamen, preventive measures were introduced that substantially transformed people's everyday lives. The imposed, non-negotiable Zero-COVID policy, sent many into quarantine facilities, which determined the rhythm of daily life for weeks. Here, however, I focus on the ruptures enacted by the discreet, almost invisible, small acts performed through the health codes, rather than the large-scale ruptures of lockdowns themselves.

With the epidemic situation changing rapidly, no one could be sure if a neighbour, a fellow passenger on a bus, another client in a store, a co-worker, or just a passer-by was not a potential 'case' – contact with whom might result in changing the colour of one's health code. One person infected in a compound could bring all residents into quarantine. This mechanism of what I call 'group responsibility' also worked through the new temporalities, undermining the autonomy that health codes were intended to provide.

Parents learned that having one yellow or red code in a family would cause the student to be banned from school. The mother of Rose, a third-grade middle school student, realized one day that her code had turned yellow. The daughter – healthy and having a green code herself – was forbidden to enter her school and forced to learn from her classmate's notes, as if she were sick. Only by repeating clear PCR tests every day for five days the mother's code returned to green, and the daughter to attend classes in person. After this experience, Rose's mother claimed she had no plans for upcoming holidays: 'I'm scared, what if my code turns yellow? I don't dare to go out because if my code becomes yellow, my daughter can't go to school [again].' Within a few minutes of conversation, Rose's mother mentioned being 'scared', 'anxious', 'feeling bad about it', and 'being too afraid to leave the house'. Group responsibility is an oft-neglected aspect of COVID-19 surveillance, which created another layer of temporal regimes: even though the student's own code was green, she could not go to school because of her mother's yellow code.

As previously mentioned, in addition to health codes, parents were required to submit travel codes that documented the counties they had visited over the previous seven days. Due to the rapidly shifting situation, counties classified as 'case-free' one day could be declared 'high-risk zones' the next. Given the biological temporality of the virus (Lynteris, 2014), the travel codes of those who had visited these areas could be retroactively affected. This ability to alter the past meant that no one's health status was ever truly 'safe', disrupting time as a form of linear progression. It was like briefly shifting a car into reverse, creating a new 'past' that altered how present and future were navigated. This reverse gear mechanism could suddenly change the health code status of even a passer-by, requiring additional screenings or even quarantine. The reverse gear temporality illustrated how the health code system changed the very concept of past and future, and influenced experiences and decision-making.

Stone's mother, who stressed the banality of sending daily health codes to school, admitted that it had had a great impact on her family life.

> Like before, his father went back to his hometown and when he was about to come back, in the afternoon the school sent a notice that if any student or a parent came back from that county, the child could not go to school. So, before his father came home, I told him not to. I said, don't come back, go and stay in a hotel. (Stone's mother)[11]

This way she did not have to upload his travel code to the system, and her sons could attend school. Stone's mother lost family time as a consequence of this small act. In another example, Iris's father, a factory owner in the neighbouring county of Quanzhou, decided to stay three weeks at the factory in order not to impact his daughter's school attendance, when COVID-19 cases were confirmed in Quanzhou in October 2022.

Travelling to visit parents was a risky endeavour, as the reverse gear of prevention measures could affect reported codes. Moreover, even during the summer holidays, teachers and children were 'advised' to stay in Xiamen, and strongly discouraged not to leave Fujian province. Pike's mother wanted to visit her elderly parents in Zhejiang, a virus-free province at the time, during the summer holidays of 2021. She was angry that her application for permission to travel was rejected. 'Nothing can be done', she told me, annoyed. As River's mother stated when discussing the issue of sending the health code: 'I've hardly seen my mother these three years. Even though she lives in Jinjiang, nearby[12] I couldn't visit her. She understands though.'

In times when the pandemic situation was changing fast, it was easier to 'play it safe'. As Stone's mother says, 'It was my birthday, and then my brother's wife's birthday. My parents wanted to come to visit, but I told them not to come as there was an outbreak [in the county they live in].' Once, during the course of fieldwork, I attended a wedding where the bride's parents could not be present as they were quarantined instead, because the risk status of their hometown had changed while they were en route to Xiamen.

As Wren's mother said, 'Now, moving around the city requires using your instincts. Luckily, yesterday we didn't pass by X neighbourhood, we crossed the street and walked on the other side. Otherwise, our code might have been yellow by now.' Another man, Alex, passed by a metro station where a person later confirmed as COVID-19 positive had bought breakfast at McDonald's that day. The next day he received a message calling for seven PCR tests within seven days, restricting him from leaving the house unless necessary, and not allowing him to use public transportation. As he described it, 'I don't even remember where I was yesterday, but they can tell me where I was at any moment in time'. Here there is a direct contrast between the information-gathering of the epidemic prevention system, directing his movements, and his own lack of knowledge and immobility.

The mechanisms of 'group responsibility' and reverse gear introduced disruptions into the fabric of time, extending beyond the original purpose of the system and resulting in unintended consequences. This phenomenon, known as function creep (Koops, 2021, see also Peacock, Chapter 8, this volume), occurred as the system, initially designed to ensure health and safety, expanded beyond its initial objectives. Surveillance, which was originally meant to provide safety guarantees for families and businesses, began to heavily intrude on and restrict family life. The health codes imposed novel temporal regimes, fostering self-regulated behaviours, as similarly exemplified by the PCR test clock.

The PCR test clock

By March 2022, PCR testing became commonplace, even without the presence of an outbreak. As one local beach security officer explains after checking my PCR test validity and registering me for a special permit to swim in the sea, 'The pandemic doesn't recognize borders'. In the last update of the health code, the code was showing not only a three-colour health and vaccination status, but also displayed how many hours passed since the last PCR test. From then on, the numbers 24/48/72 determined people's public lives. Different venues established their requirements for negative PCR test results and their validity: theatres, 48 hours; police stations, 24 hours; hospitals, 24 hours; hotels, 48 hours; parks, 72 hours; and swimming pools, 48 hours (or PCR tests done within 24 hours). This was seriously delimiting, requiring not only the passive sharing of information, but also active steps to get PCR testing done.

The validity of PCR tests became crucial in organizing daily life in Xiamen, as the scope of activities depended on how much time had passed since the last test. Much like a 24-hour clock governs routines – limiting what and how long one can do certain things – the PCR clock imposed similar constraints. People had to schedule their activities based on how long they had until the validity of a test 'expired' for a given venue. In this way, the PCR clock dictated not only what people could do, but also when, structuring daily life around the tests' validity.

Alex told me about a birthday party when some of the guests could not enter the venue due to 'invalid health codes', as even though their codes were green, the time since their last test was longer than demanded by the hotel. People either had to plan their activities according to the validity of their tests, or arrange time around the testing sites' operating hours to get tested as often as possible. As Nancy said, 'I got used to swabbing my nose. I test whenever I see a testing booth open, just to avoid trouble.' Once, when prevented from entering a police station because my test results were not in date, a guard advised me: 'Do tests more often. It's easy!'

Even though PCR testing centres were set up in many locations in the city at the time, most of them were open only during regular business hours, so that people who had to work office hours could not benefit from them. In the evenings, in front of the few testing sites operating late, there were queues of Xiamen's working residents getting tested for COVID-19. Or, to be more precise, they were updating information about their last PCR test in their apps, in order to have access to public spaces, services, and resources.

In many schools and kindergartens, there were testing sites on the premises to make testing easier for teachers and pupils. Describing her school routine during her lunch break, Marigold said: 'After finishing additional practice, there is 40 minutes to write homework. Then, if you need to do a PCR test, you must spend 10 minutes on testing. Yes, each person needs to do it once a week. Then you have like 30 minutes to nap.' Even though this whole procedure was not complicated, with testing sites inside schools, it took away precious minutes from pupils' rest time during the lunch break. On the other hand, the sense of safety that this simulated surveillance fostered led to paradoxical situations. Since the outbreak in autumn 2021, getting tested became the primary way to prove a 'healthy status', even though results took hours to update. During the next outbreak in the autumn of 2022, coinciding with the Mid-Autumn Festival and National Holiday, people lined up, masked, at testing sites to get swabbed, only to gather in crowds for outdoor activities like hiking, camping, and barbequing. Along the crowded seafront, most ignored social distancing and removed their masks, relying on the certainty provided by the act of performing the PCR test to relax and have a good time.

Fourth act: the end of the pandemic
After 7 December 2022

As Rosenberg articulates, 'epidemics ordinarily end with a whimper, not a bang' (1989, p 8). The COVID-19 pandemic in China was not an ordinary epidemic, as it finished abruptly on 7 December 2022, with the announcement of the decision of the State Council on another 'optimization' of the control mechanisms, this time signifying the 'lifting of protective measures' (The State Council of the People's Republic of China, 2022). On 13 December the health and travel codes went offline. This was received as the end of a historical epoch. As Pike's mother wrote in her WeChat post minutes before the travel code was about to become inoperative: 'The end of an era. Goodbye! Never to be seen again!'[13]

The end of the health code signified the lifting of pandemic monitoring, but not the end of the disease, as partial data published later showed soaring numbers of infections. The last data entry in the official statistical entry for Xiamen of confirmed cases is from 12 December 2022, after which local governments stopped publishing COVID-19 data. On 25 December, the Chinese government stopped publishing information on COVID-19 infections and fatalities.

In Xiamen, after monitoring measures were lifted, and the numbers of infected pupils were soaring, schools ended the semester on 15 December without the final exams taking place. Some parents I knew bunkered down in their homes, not going out from their apartments for weeks.[14] Others, especially those who were infected early and recovered quickly, behaved as if the pandemic was over, roaming freely through the city, often without wearing masks. Unable to get medical supplies and avoiding overcrowded hospitals, on WeChat, people shared home recipes for pear or orange syrup as a remedy for the COVID-19 cough. Food delivery companies ran out of stock of ingredients such as eggs, brown sugar, and the aforementioned fruit.

Open endings

The COVID-19 outbreak caused a multi-layered series of ruptures in the city of Xiamen. These ruptures appeared because of the presence of the virus, both in its biological form and in the state narrative of war upon the virus. The 'suspension of judgement' caused by the virus, both in the country and in the city, from January to February 2020, brought back the experience of the SARS epidemic. Throughout most of the three pandemic years, the COVID-19 virus was not present in Xiamen, as it was contained in quarantine facilities for inbound travellers. Residents could have experienced Xiamen as a safe haven. However, the official narrative of the pandemic maintained the virus's presence in the lives and the daily acts of its people: moulding experiences of work time, family time, and leisure.

Pandemic surveillance over various periods of time was not only experienced by residents as imposed measures, like quarantines or lockdowns. Health codes reassembled contact-tracing data into multiple assemblages with diverse effects at different periods and social localities. Like the Big Mother animated by this volume (Peacock, Introduction), health code-based surveillance managed the rhythms of life of urban dwellers. It was a generator of the small acts of surveillance due to the requirements of the system itself, imposing its own temporalities.

City residents actively performed small acts to serve the functioning of the monitoring system: scanning QR codes to enter different venues, feeding health code data to school reporting systems, and updating PCR test results. In this way it is important to emphasize that they were not only passive objects of monitoring. Sending health codes to schools made parents become warriors in the war against the COVID-19 virus. The active participation in pandemic surveillance, gave Xiamen residents the experience of living in a COVID-19 free 'future–past' (Bogard, 1996, p 34), in a world 'as if', in which acting 'as if' complying with the requirements of surveillance would guarantee safety (Seligman et al, 2008).

Ritualistic acts were the processes through which people in Xiamen created and engaged in a hypothetical safe world. The small act surveillance functioned as a ritual, serving as an 'orientation to action' (Seligman et al, 2008). People chose to submit to the surveillance acts, believing it was helping to sustain normality. The obligation to send data to schools became a ritual, 'as if' sending the health codes could guarantee children's safety. People raced against the PCR test clock, as if updating PCR test results in the health code system was the primary way of preserving their health. These became the core instrument for the construction of social relations and shared temporalities. Yet although they brought the feeling of being together in time, they also generated feelings of worry, fear, and helplessness during outbreaks, when the system's function creep (Koops, 2021) retracted the autonomy it promised, and instead imposed these three forms of temporality.

All these ritualistic acts became the content of the pandemic experience. Small act surveillance requirements determined how people understood the pandemic as a reality that came into being, due to these powerful measures implemented by the state. This power was achieved not only through mechanisms of quarantine or restrictions on movement. It was also realized by acts of obedience, adherence to temporal regimes that cut into the fabric of time. Surveillance mechanisms, like the PCR test clock or reverse gear, showed how time was constructed in ways that relied on the verification and validation that state power could offer (Marx, 2016).

Compliance with the requirements of the state that used to provide safety turned out to be useless, when the special measures and surveillance mechanisms ceased to exist on 13 December 2022. The state's narrative about winning the war against the pandemic did not correspond with the experiences of those sick with the virus recording videos, and taking pictures of overcrowded hospitals. 'The end of the pandemic' in the state narrative brought yet another break, another suspension of certainty.

Acknowledgements

I would like to sincerely thank all the research participants who generously shared their experiences which form the foundation of this chapter. My deep gratitude also goes to the organizing team of the 'Times of Surveillance' workshop, whose event sparked the inspiration for this work. I am especially thankful to Vita Peacock and Claire Elisabeth Dungey, whose guidance, meticulous editing, and patience have been invaluable throughout the process.

Notes

[1]   Daily reporting was an obligatory task of all students at Xiamen University – including international students who were outside China.

[2]   I conducted 12 of these interviews with parents, and seven with children.

[3]   WeChat provides messaging, video conferencing, gaming, mobile payment, and the sharing of photographs, videos, files, location, and app extensions for many other commercial services, including health codes and travel codes during the pandemic.

[4]   Unlike many international students who left for winter holidays (and could not return after the Chinese government cancelled visas in March 2020), I did not leave China during the pandemic.

5   In China, cities are categorized into different tiers based on factors such as economic development, population size, infrastructure, and overall urbanization.

6   According to the WHO, the COVID-19 pandemic ended on 5 May 2023 (World Health Organization, 2023) '.

7   Children (and possibly older people), who did not have phones themselves, had health codes generated in extensions in applications on parents' phones.

8   As epidemic data released by the National Health Commission of China shows, temporal division into stages for Xiamen city does not match the stages on national level.

9   'Millions of hearts with one mind battle against SARS' ('Wanzhong yixin, kangji feidian') and 'Millions of hearts with one mind battle against pandemic' ('Wanzhong yixin, kangji yiqing'), based on Zhang (2006).

10   It existed in the quarantine system for international travellers.

11   Stone's mother admitted that not all parents were willing to pay such a price for 'honest reporting' and some used to '*PS yixia*' (meaning using Photoshop-like tools to make alternations in reported codes).

12   It is located 60–80 kilometres from Xiamen.

13   'The end of an era. Goodbye! Never to be seen again!' (yiduanlishi de jieshu! Zaijian! Zai yebujian! 一段历史的结束。再见！再也不见！)

14   Many of those who stayed at home to avoid infection in the early days decided to risk infection during the later phases of winter holidays, being afraid that if kids did not get through COVID-19 during winter break, unavoidably they would get ill during the second semester causing them to lose some school time, like Cliff's mother.

References

Beckett, G. (2013) 'The politics of emergency', *Reviews in Anthropology*, 42 (2): 85–101.

Bernot, A. and Cassiano, M.S. (2021) 'China's COVID-19 Pandemic Response: A First Anniversary Assessment', *Journal of Contingencies and Crisis Management,* 30(1): 10–21.

Bogard, W. (1996) *The Simulation of Surveillance. Hypercontrol in Telematic Societies.* Cambridge: Cambridge University Press.

Byler, D. (2022) *Terror Capitalism: Uyghur Dispossession and Masculinity in a Chinese City.* Durham, NC: Duke University Press.

Caduff, C. (2014) 'Sick Weather Ahead: On Data-Mining, Crowd-Sourcing and White Noise', *The Cambridge Journal of Anthropology,* 32(1): 32–46.

Cassiano, S.M., Haggerty, K., and Bernot, A. (2021) 'China's Response to the COVID-19 Pandemic: Surveillance and Autonomy', *Surveillance & Society,* 19(1): 94–7.

Chao, E. (2017) 'How WeChat Became China's App For Everything', Fast Company, 2 January, Available from: https://www.fastcompany.com/3065255/china-wechat-tencent-red-envelopes-and-social-money (Accessed: 15 October 2024).

Chen, S. (2021) 'Coronavirus on chilled salmon may be infectious for over a week', South China Morning Post, 8 September, Available from: https://www.scmp.com/news/china/science/article/3100637/coronavirus-chilled-salmon-may-be-infectious-over-week (Accessed: 16 August 2023).

Czernin, J. (2020) 'Dr. Li Wenliang and the Time of COVID-19', *Journal of Nuclear Medicine*, 61(5): 625–25.

Desclaux, A., Dioumel, B., Ndione, A., and Sow, K. (2017). 'Accepted Monitoring or Endured Quarantine? Ebola Contacts' Perceptions in Senegal', *Social Science & Medicine*, 178: 38–45.

Dolan, B. and Rutherford, G. (2020) 'How History of Medicine Helps us Understand COVID-19 Challenges', *Public Health Reports*, 135 (6): 717–20.

Eckholm, E. (2006) 'SARS in Beijing: The Unraveling of a Cover-Up', in A. Kleinman and J. L. Watson (eds), *SARS in China. Prelude to Pandemic?*. Stanford (California): Stanford University Press, pp 122–32.

Fassin, D. and Pandolfi, M. (2010) *Contemporary States of Emergency: The Politics of Military and Humanitarian Interventions*. New York: Zone Books.

Frankfurter, R. (2019) 'Conjuring Biosecurity in the Post-Ebola Kissi Triangle: The Magic of Paperwork in a Frontier Clinic', *Medical Anthropology Quarterly*, 33(4): 517–38.

Holbraad, M., Kapferer, B., and Sauma, J. (2019) 'Introduction: Critical Ruptures', in M. Holbraad, B. Kapferer, and J.F. Sauma (eds) *Ruptures: Anthropologies of Discontinuity in Times of Turmoil*. London: UCL Press, pp 1–26.

Jordheim, H. and Wigen, E. (2018) 'Conceptual Synchronisation. From Progress to Crisis Millennium', *Journal of International Studies*, 47: 421–39.

Koops, B.J. (2021) 'The Concept of Function Creep', *Law, Innovation and Technology*, 13(1): 29–56.

Lakoff, A. (2017) *Unprepared: Global Health in a Time of Emergency*. Oakland, CA: University of California Press.

Lee, D.T.S and Wing, Y.K. (2006) 'Psychological Responses to SARS in Hong Kong – Report from the Front Line', in A. Kleinman and J.L. Watson (eds) *SARS in China. Prelude to Pandemic?* Stanford: Stanford University Press, pp 133–47.

Lefebvre, H. (2004) *Rhythmanalysis: Space, Time and Everyday Life*. Translated by S. Elden and G. Moore. London and New York: Continuum.

Li, X., Cui, W., and Zhang, F. (2020) 'Who Was the First Doctor to Report the COVID-19 Outbreak in Wuhan, China?' *Journal of Nuclear Medicine*, 61(6): 782–83.

Li, Z., Chen, Q., Feng, L., Rodewald, L., Xia, Y., Yu H., et al (2020) 'Active Case Finding with Case Management: The Key to Tackling the SARS-CoV-19 Pandemic', *The Lancet*, 396(10243): 63–70.

Liang, F. (2020) 'COVID-19 and Health Code: How Digital Platforms Tackle the Pandemic in China', *Social Media + Society*, 6(3): 1–4.

Liu, C. (2021) 'Chinese Public's Support for SARS-CoV-19 Surveillance in Relation to the West', *Surveillance & Society*, 19(1): 89–93.

Liu, C. (2022) 'Seeing Like a State, Enacting Like an Algorithm: (Re) assembling Contact Tracing and Risk Assessment during the COVID-19 Pandemic', *Science, Technology, & Human Values*, 47(4): 698–725.

Lynteris, C. (2014) 'Introduction: The Time of Epidemics'. *The Cambridge Journal of Anthropology*, 32(1): 24–31.

Lyon, D. (2022) *Pandemic Surveillance*. Cambridge: Polity Press.

Macnish, K. and Henschke, A. (2023) 'Introduction', in K. Macnish and A. Henschke, (eds) *The Ethics of Surveillance in Times of Emergency*, Oxford: Oxford University Press, pp 18–38.

MacPhail, T. (2014) *The Viral Network: A Pathography of the H1N1 Influenza Pandemic,* Ithaca, NY: Cornell University Press.

Marx, G.T. (2016) *Windows into the Soul: Surveillance and Society in an Age of High Technology*. Chicago, IL: University of Chicago Press.

Rosenberg, C.E. (1989) 'What is an Epidemic? AIDS in Historical Perspective', *Daedalus*, 118(2): 1–17.

Rosenberg, C.E. (1992) *Explaining Epidemics and Other Studies in the History of Medicine*. Cambridge: Cambridge University Press.

Seligman, A.B., Weller, R.P., Puett. M.J., and Bennett, S. (2008) *Ritual and its Consequences. An Essay on the Limits of Sincerity*. Oxford: Oxford University Press.

The State Council of the People's Republic of China (2020) 'Xi Jinping investigates and guides the prevention and control of the new coronavirus pneumonia epidemic in Beijing', 10 February, Available from: https://www.gov.cn/xinwen/2020-02/10/content_5476997.htm (Accessed: 28 August 2023).

The State Council of the People's Republic of China (2022) 'Press Conference of the Joint Prevention and Control Mechanism of the State Council', 9 December, Available from: https://www.gov.cn/xinwen/gwylf lkjz219/ (Accessed: 16 September 2023).

Stellmach, D. and Beshar, I. (2016) 'Introduction: Special Issue on the Ethics of Anthropology in Emergencies', *Journal of the Anthropological Society of Oxford–Online*, 7(1): 1–15.

Sun, Y. and Wang, W.Y. (2022) 'Governing with Health Code: Standardizing China's Data Network Systems During COVID-19', *Policy and Internet*, 14: 673–89.

Wang, L., Yan, B., and Boasson, V. (2020) 'A National Fight Against COVID-19: Lessons and Experiences from China', *Australian and New Zealand Journal of Public Health*, 44(6): 502–07.

World Health Organization (2021) 'Listings of WHO's Response to SARS-CoV-19', 29 January, Available from: https://www.who.int/news/item/29-06-2020-covidtimeline (Accessed: 25 November 2023).

World Health Organization (2023) 'WHO chief declares end to SARS-CoV-19 as a global health emergency', 5 May, Available from: https://news.un.org/en/story/2023/05/1136367 (Accessed: 25 November 2023).

Wu, J., Zhang, F., Sun, Y., Zhu, Y., and Liu, C. (2020) 'Fight Against SARS-CoV-19 Promotes China's Digital Transformation: Opportunities and Challenges', *Chinese Academy of Sciences*, 35(3): 306–11.

Xiamen City Health Commission (2020) 'Pneumonia epidemic situation caused by the new coronavirus infection in Xiamen City, Fujian Province on January 23, 2020', Available from: https://hfpc.xm.gov.cn/xwzx/tzgg/202001/t20200123_2418817.htm (Accessed: 28 August 2023).

Zhang, H. (2006) 'Making Light of the Dark Side: SARS Jokes and Humor in China', in A. Kleinman, and J.L. Watson (eds) *SARS in China. Prelude to Pandemic?* Stanford: Stanford University Press, pp 148–70.

Zhang, Q. (2020) 'Xi Jinping presided over the 12th meeting of the Central Committee for Comprehensive Deepening Reforms and emphasized the improvement of major epidemic prevention and control systems and mechanisms and the improvement of the national public health emergency management system', Xinhua Agency, Xinhuanet, 14 February, Available from: http://www.xinhuanet.com/politics/leaders/2020-02/14/c_112 5575922.htm (Accessed: 26 February 2023)

Systems Past, Present, and Future

8

Privacy as Unfolding: German *Netzpolitik* and the Legacy of Colonial Registration

Vita Peacock

Introduction

> Many people come and tell me, 'I don't have anything to hide'. It is *not* about hiding. It is about feeling the freedom and the safety to develop your personality, to develop your interests. I will never know whether I like this piece of music or not before I listen to it. And for this possibility, I believe this is the basis of democracy, of any free thinking, feeling, breathing society. We need these kinds of spaces in terms of time, in terms of information, data, surveillance.

In these utterances from a privacy advocate in Germany, privacy is decoupled from association with a dubious desire for secrecy, and presented as a space of temporal unfolding. It is one characterized by uncertainty, and by the potential for subjectivation and sensual delight that are able to occur when outcomes are not pre-determined. This yields an analogical leap from the subjective value of not being surveilled, to the value that obtains for societies at large, and the potential for democratic participation that accrues in the presence of 'breathing' room.

In this chapter I elaborate this view as it emerges through the discourses and imagery of privacy and data protection advocates across Germany, in an assembly known as *Netzpolitik*.[1] The view is inherently temporal, one that continually animates secondary memories of German twentieth-century history, to obviate dark futures it knows to be possible. The history of Nazi censuses in 1933 and 1939, and the pivotal role of machines in assembling, sorting, and weaponizing census data, provides much of the historical basis for suspicion of mass information collection, and the inherent political dangers of making human life and exchange machine-readable. Memory, here, is also understood in a broader sense to include the development of law: the means by which laws encode, and subsequently reproduce, the values of a place and time. Germany's Basic Law (*Grundgesetz*) which came into effect in 1949, and its conscious application to a growing world of information technology in 1983, provide both a language as well as a set of legal tools, to sustain the concept of free development in the face of mass information processing, known as informational self-determination (*Informationelle Selbstbestimmung*).

In characterizing what these actors advocate for and consequently oppose, I introduce a notion of surveillance as fixing. I understand fixing here in temporal terms – that is, *intemporal* terms – as the gamut of technological efforts to stabilize phenomena in order to contain them. To fix is to hold a person or thing artificially still. Fixing carries with it the moral ambiguity of surveillance, as it can on the one hand signify repair, holding something still with the aim of mending it.[2] In this chapter, however, I explore fixing as a historically specific political technology that emerged alongside the colonial state, to fix certain populations within certain territories. Indeed, the same intemporality is contained within the word 'state' itself, principally defined as a condition in which a person or thing exists 'at a particular time' (Simpson, 1989, pp 550–51).

This notion speaks to two important literatures. The first is the terrain of conceptual work on classification or 'sorting' (Douglas, 1966; Gandy, 1993; Bowker and Star, 1999; Lyon, 2003), which has shown how phenomena, including but not limited to human beings, are ontologically stabilized through the act of being categorized. The second lies in historical studies of passes, permits, and identity cards (Torpey, 2000; Caplan and Torpey, 2001; Bennett and Lyon, 2008; Lyon, 2009; Breckenridge, 2014). These have examined how forms of identification, initially paper, and now increasingly digital, developed as critical components of the bureaucratic management of the modern world that sought to constrain the movement of human bodies across it. These two literatures have many overlaps, but here I splice them fully together. Rather than considering classification as something inherently 'human' (Bowker and Star, 1999, p 1); and sorting and identification as the product of consumerization, globalization, and the risk society (Gandy, 1993; Amoore, 2008; Lyon and Bennett, 2008), I posit their co-emergence in the late colonial period, through systems of mass registration and the prescriptions on movement that attended them. *Fixing* certain persons within delimited areas for political reasons, necessarily entailed *fixing* their identities – frequently in the face of bountiful evidence to the contrary. Although the scale and speed of the effects of Nazi censuses were not comparable, at the level of information technologies – both in how human beings were categorized, and as well as the actual machines that were used to process this information – they had substantial precursors and successors across the colonial world and its aftermath.

Contemporary privacy and data protection advocates in Germany display a heightened sensitivity to having their identities fixed, particularly by computing. Yet, as William Bogard argues, from the 1980s onwards surveillance itself broadly underwent a qualitative shift. It altered in many domains, from being a static subject–object relationship, seeking to document and contain, into the dynamic 'flow control' enabled by computational modelling (Bogard, 1996, p 44). Contemporary forms of surveillance based on simulation can be a more plastic endeavour than these historical modalities. The enduring memory of the latter, however, within *Netzpolitik,* continues to exert an impact upon the present, in a dynamic Henri Lefebvre calls 'the rhythm of history' (2009, p 51). There are periods when the past effaces itself, he says, and periods when it returns. And in the return of memory there is always modification. Here, historical concerns around state registration mutate into concerns around the variety of agencies operating in the digital world, which in various ways obstruct the possibility of indeterminacy.

Privacy as unfolding

An agreed definition of privacy is inessential for participating in the life of German privacy advocacy. Nonetheless, although definitions are offered as personal takes, they hover around certain themes, metaphors, and signifiers. Privacy is often represented as a space (*Raum*) that allows a transition from one state to another, particularly in the form of intellectual development. This is partly afforded by the word 'privacy' in German – *Privatsphäre* – which retains a spatial orientation in its inclusion of the concept of a sphere. For example:

> You need spaces (*Räume*) to be by yourself, without feeling oppressed
> by public life. It's also a question of how you inform yourself online.
> What sites do I click on? How do I form my own opinions? (*sich bilden*)

In this process of development, failing and being imperfect are legitimate outcomes. For another privacy is:

> The possibility of being oneself, without absolutely hitting the nail on
> the head with every word in a sentence.

Visual and verbal metaphors of the organic world, specifically of plants and vegetation, may be used. Privacy is described as an 'inner garden', or 'the soil on which anything can grow'. In these cases, infractions thereof may take mammalian form, as human intruders or destructive wild animals. As in the opening extract, presenting privacy as a site of organic life – as something 'feeling, breathing' – permits a shift between interior intellectual growth, and spaces for the growth of democratic society.

Partly because of the enigma of privacy itself, the discursive emphasis may be placed directly upon digital or informational self-determination.

> I want to know, I want everyone to know, where is the data about me? Who has it? What are they doing with it? And how can I prevent people from doing something with it that I don't want them to?

Citing self-determination is a more or less explicit reference to a landmark ruling in 1983, by the former West Germany's Federal Constitutional Court, guaranteeing citizens the right to informational self-determination. Nominally a response to the emerging capacities of electronic technology to store, process, and transmit personal information, the ruling sought to curtail the construction of an 'image of the personality' (*Persönlichkeitsbild*, cited in Hannah, 2010, p 102), beyond the knowledge and control of the affected individual. Informational self-determination is the retention of agency over this image, what in the language of surveillance studies is called a 'data double' (Haggerty and Ericson, 2000).

The ruling was forged from the first two articles of German Basic Law, which guarantee general protection for the rights of the personality. The first is Article 1, that the value of every human being is inviolable; while the second is contained in Article 2, that every human being has the right to the free development (*Entfaltung*) of their personality. When announcing the ruling, the justices explained their reasoning in detail.

> Whoever cannot with sufficient certainty oversee which information regarding them is known in specific areas of their social environment, and whoever is not able to some extent to estimate the knowledge of possible communication partners, can be essentially limited in their freedom to plan or decide on the basis of their own self-determination ... This would restrict not only the chances for the unfolding (*Entfaltung*) of the individual personality but also the general welfare, because self-determination is an elementary functional condition (of possibility) for a free democratic order. (Translation in Hannah, 2010, p 102)

In this reasoning, the protection of the personality, and by implication society, takes an explicitly temporal form. It is the citizen's right to 'plan or decide', in other words to act in the present upon the future, that is being safeguarded.

Let us pause briefly on the specific term used to indicate this future orientation – *Entfaltung*. *Entfaltung* – literally un-fold-ing – can be translated as evolution or development. Yet this form of development across time is a not linear one, and therein synonymous with the use of the word in the Anglophone world, which would lie closer to the German *Entwicklung*. *Entfaltung* also means blooming or blossoming, and can be used with direct reference to plant life to indicate a biological dynamic that is allowed, through its environment, to realize itself, to become larger. *Entfaltung* also means to expand. In turning towards surveillance as fixing, it is worth keeping some of these associations in mind. Here, not being surveilled becomes a space in which change can occur, and in which the modality of change is not mechanical but organic, a principle of growth and becoming larger, of bearing flowers and fruit.

Surveillance as fixing

The history of surveillance is imbricated with endeavours to restrict or otherwise determine the physical mobility of certain human bodies (Torpey, 2000; Caplan and Torpey, 2001). The incarceration of those categorized as criminal (Foucault, 2019; Jefferson 2020), is only the thick end of a much larger wedge extending to many historical forms of monitoring and containing persons for social purposes. Before the advent of modernity, prescriptions on movement in Europe were arranged within feudal relations: travel passes, badges, letters, insignia, and so on, that contained details of the bearer's position within a feudal order, and their relationship to a master or sovereign. These documentary and material artefacts could include their 'distinguishing characteristics', such as hair colour (Groebner, 2001, p 24), height, or a curiously placed mole, but it was only in the wake of the transatlantic slave trade, and the growth of the plantation economy, from the seventeenth century onwards, that prescriptions on movement developed a definitively racial character. This being said, the passes violently regulating the mobility of those labouring on the plantations were still inscribed within feudal proprietary relations – containing details of the bearer, their owner, and where and for how long they were permitted to travel (Lyon, 2009; Browne, 2015).

It is only towards the turn of the twentieth century that nation-states claimed fully for themselves what Torpey (following Marx and Weber) calls a 'monopoly of the legitimate means of movement' (2000, p 4). The development of the modern passport system, and the state registration systems that attended them, circumvented the old estate hierarchies and established the right to move as emanating directly from a state polity (see Steinwedel, 2001). Torpey argues that this was the effect of the unprecedented migratory flows that characterized the late nineteenth century between and across national borders, calling it (via Alan Dowty): 'The closest approximation to an open world in modern times' (2001, p 256). To state this, though, neglects the experiences of colonized and otherwise constrained peoples in the same historical moment. It thus simultaneously constitutes an analytic disconnect, because of the ways in which the colonial world, even after independence, in India and Argentina, formed a critical venue for scientific experimentation with the first biometric technology (Ruggiero, 2001; Breckenridge, 2014), namely fingerprinting, which was later hitched to the passport system.[3]

In this long history of identification, methods of fixing persons to particular localities, have simultaneously been modes of fixing the meaningful aspects of who this person is, and therefore how they become visible as subjects of surveillance before a given socio-political order.[4] The distinctive aspect of the late colonial moment at the turn of the twentieth century came in the second strut of this double-fix, as identities took on a pseudo-biological character, artificially stabilized using nascent anthropometric techniques and dubious notions of racial descent. By the late nineteenth century, a kind of mania for fixing had taken hold. This was particularly the case in Britain, where the emerging field of eugenics provided an ideological basis to cement the asymmetries of a fragile imperial order, particularly in the wake of several colonial rebellions, by doubling down on apparently 'permanent' characteristics (Levitan, 2011, p 163). Although this has since been thoroughly deconstructed, this moment in world history generated a particular social, political, and technical intersection that still to some degree shapes the structure of state surveillance today. As nation-states asserted themselves as the primary mediators of political visibility and the right to move, this was entangled with ideas of identity as biological, and critically, a set of information technologies that cemented the relationship between both.

Central to these were forms of mandatory registration such as the census. As Simone Browne says, a census is a particular strategy of the state to 'fix' its occupants within certain predefined categories (2015, p 56). In this respect, the census is a distinctly synchronic endeavour that provides a polity not only with 'a collective image of the present, but of the past and future' (Darrow, 2015, p 146). The West German activist Götz Aly has gone further to argue that a census is no less than 'a frontal attack on the imagination and of the intelligent posing of questions *for* the future' (cited in Hannah, 2010, p 46, emphasis added). While it is certainly the case that the holding of censuses was prompted by political concerns throughout the eighteenth and nineteenth centuries, and was vital to the ascendance of the state-qua-state, as with any information technology censuses remain politically ambivalent. Their political potentials hinge on what questions are asked, and the social uses to which this information is put. Throughout the nineteenth century the categories continued to change, and although questions about race and ethnicity had appeared much earlier, particularly in the US and the Caribbean, it was in the context of ideas about 'healthy' populations that these questions and their answers began to assume a central importance in the enumerating process (Levitan, 2011, p 150).

One of the reasons why censuses were held only once every number of years was that they were enormously labour-intensive. Not only could they involve hundreds of thousands of enumerators going door-to-door to collect the answers, but also an immense sorting process afterwards. When German-American engineer Herman Hollerith, while working at the US Census Bureau in the 1880s, developed an automated system for collecting and sorting this information, the technology was quickly acquired by census and statistical departments all over the world, and was used in the US census of 1890 as well as the Russian Empire census of 1897. His idea was apparently inspired by observing a train conductor record physical characteristics of passengers that could then be read by other conductors, by punching holes into their ticket rather like a 'punched photograph' (cited in Black, 2001, p 24). Hollerith developed a card with standardized holes, each representing a different characteristic, which could then be fed into a reader and sorted accordingly. Millions of these punchcards could now be sorted and resorted at speed, each card functioning, as Edwin Black says, like a 'nineteenth-century barcode for human beings' (2001, p 25). Hollerith machines made human life machine-readable and machine-sortable. They took the fixing, synchronic modality of the census and accelerated it.

Fears of being fixed, unable to move, unable to change, are expressed across *Netzpolitik*. When a group of activists collect short interviews with several leading privacy and data protection advocates across the German-speaking world, on why they support a ban on facial recognition in the public sphere, several articulate their opposition explicitly using the language of physical movement:

> I consider automated video recognition with biometric characteristics to be a great danger to our democracy, because after that we can no longer move freely. (Markus Beckedahl. Founder re:publica and netzpolitik.org)

> I am against facial recognition in the public sphere because in a free liberal democracy, it is important that people can move around unobserved. To be able to exercise your fundamental right to freedom of assembly and also to simply have a democratic debate, it is important that you are not monitored with every step you take (*auf Schritt und Tritt*). (Thomas Lohninger. Managing Director, epicenter-works)

> Democracy means that people can ... move around in public space, that they can participate in demonstrations, for instance, or that they

can go to advisory centres. (Ulf Buermeyer, Chairman, Gesellschaft für Freiheitsrechte)

Meanwhile, the widely revered Federal Commissioner for Data Protection and Freedom of Information, Ulrich Kelber, emphasizes the biological fixing of identity that facial recognition enables. For Kelber, its danger inheres in the fact that, 'you cannot change your face like you can change your password'. The landmark constitutional ruling that secured the right to informational self-determination in Germany, took place in the context of sustained mass protests in the former West against plans to hold a national census (Hannah, 2010). It is now time to turn towards Germany's own history of censuses, and the way in which concerns about machine-readability have infused the German data protection movement since the 1970s.

Machine-readable people

One of the first laws passed by the Nazi government after coming to power in Germany in 1933 imposed a census of the population and its minorities. The general census posed questions about marriage and fertility, to advance its natalist policies for those it defined as ethnically German. It avoided questions about birthplace, which were reserved for the special censuses for Jews and foreigners that took place in addition to the general census, and sought out far more detail for those in these groups. For the 1933 census, punchcards with 60 columns were designed by the *Deutsche Hollerith-Maschinen Gesellschaft*, or Dehomag, a German subsidiary of IBM, the American corporation that now owned and leased Hollerith machines across the world. Its tabulators were used to sort the cards once collected; yet even with the Hollerith system, the 1933 census still involved around half a million enumerators, which included forced labour.

Numerous scholars have observed that, contrary to historical attempts to fix human identities along certain categorical lines, human beings are better thought of as fluid and subject to change (Longman, 2001; Amoore, 2008; Lyon 2009). This observation is furnished with an extra dimension, if we recall sources that suggest that those in charge of fixing processes partly understood this too. The year following the 1933 census, Erwin Cuntz, a lawyer from southern Germany, began to formulate his proposal for a 'registry of the populace', ordered by year of birth. As he wrote in a letter to Hitler:

> One need only proceed with the knowledge that man is a versatile and self-directing being. The principle of organization should therefore not be the counting of something that can *constantly change* and that does change for millions of people, namely the place of residence. Rather, it should be something that *always stays the same*, namely, the date and

place of birth, and, in a more developed framework, race and family origin. (Cited in Aly and Roth, 2004, p 35, emphasis added)

By the time the second Nazi census was carried out in 1939, providing the information for the deadly *Volkskartei* (the national identity card), Hollerith machines had become much faster, now able to count up to 12,000 punchcards every hour. Although this remains a site of historical debate, Götz Aly and Karl Heinz Roth (2004) and Edwin Black (2001) argue that without these machines – that are a precursor to the modern computer – the ensuing genocide could not have happened at the speed and the scale that it did.

Deep reservations about making human beings machine-readable, have erupted in Germany at several flashpoints in the decades since. The political context for the 1980s census boycott movements in the former West was provided not only by the failed attempt to reintroduce the census, but also a technique that had been used by the police to publicized effect in the 1970s: the *Rasterfahndung*. The *Rasterfahndung* was a primitive form of dragnet search that could be used to identify certain individuals out of a collective grid of social characteristics. This invoked outrage in the former West, not only because it treated all those whose data constituted the grid as potentially suspect, but because of the automated nature of targeting itself. As the boycott movement gathered momentum, its defining symbol became the barcode (Hannah, 2010, pp 58–61). Barcodes appeared at protests, on posters, in photographs, on bodies, and on the Berlin Wall. As a nascent technology to track and inventory physical products by giving each a unique readable code, the barcode presented the movement's opposition to the census overtly in terms of objectification and machine-readability.

Barcodes appear again with the emergence of *Netzpolitik* in the early twenty-first century, but are largely supplanted by the more contemporary image of the bot. In 2018, the EU submitted its proposal for a new law which would compel internet platforms to install 'upload filters' – software that could automatically detect and block certain kinds of content – nominally with the aim of protecting against copyright infringement online. A record five million signatories joined a petition against the Copyright Directive (which passed into law in 2019), with many more thousands in Germany communicating their opposition through social media and emails to their representatives (EDRi, 2019). When members of the EU hostile to the campaign dismissed the online opposition as 'bots', this prompted the motto for a protest movement that assembled the following spring: *Wir sind keine Bots* (We are not bots).[5] Protesters across dozens of German cities held up signs and placards either emphasizing that they were not bots, or satirically suggesting that they were. Beneath the jokes however, the protests against upload filters in 2019 expressed and reanimated profound concerns about machine-based monitoring and its impact on public life. As an open letter from a number of German privacy organizations articulated it:

> Free development (*Entfaltung*) and creativity within the framework ... of the Copyright Directive, as well as the diversity of content on the Internet as a whole will be threatened.[6]

While the movement unhooked the immediate link between machine-readability and mortal threat, the former was still presented as an attack on the ability of culture to develop in ways that are unforeseen. In the mobilization against upload filters, there is hence a meaningful pivot, as a historic focus on the state swivelled towards new constraints introduced by protecting the property rights of internet companies.

The *Stasi* and the GDR

Carrying out this research has involved confronting the *Stasi* as an ethnographic fact. Not as one which emerged, by and large, from within the fieldsite, but from people and places beyond it. When describing my research on the comparative strength of privacy sensibility in Germany, the response of my interlocutor has often been to reach directly for the *Stasi* as the major causal explanation. *Stasi* is an abbreviation of *Staatssicherheit*, and refers to the Ministry of State Security (hereafter MfS) that was the institutional base for the large-scale covert intelligence operation of the former German Democratic Republic (GDR). These responses are not without good reason. The story of the *Stasi* – of how East German citizens were invited or coerced to spy on one another on an extraordinary scale on behalf of the regime – is much more widely known that the story of punchcards produced by IBM. The popular German-language film *The Lives of Others* (Donnersmarck, 2007), along with other books and stage productions, have positioned the *Stasi* story as part of public culture in the Anglophone world (Oltermann, 2019). Indeed, it seems representative that, when I visit the former MfS headquarters which is now the Stasi Museum, part of the building is closed off for filming. An important aspect of its appeal as a subject of art may be its intensely human character. Here, macropolitics finds intimate expression in relations of voyeurism and betrayal, as well as episodes of resistance (Funder, 2011). Other less salubrious reasons I will elicit beneath.

The association between surveillance in Germany and the GDR can also be reinforced by its own institutions. Figure 8.1 is a display inside the Humboldt Forum, a large world-facing exhibition site recently erected on the grounds of the former East German Palace of Culture. The display, which occupies much of the corridor, is an actual surveillance monitor from the former building. As the blurb says, this and other monitors were

Figure 8.1: A surveillance monitor from the former Palace of Culture, on display in the Humboldt Forum

Source: Photo by author

used, inside and outside the building, to 'Keep it under close surveillance … employees were checked, visitors observed, telephones tapped, and central areas monitored by cameras'. It goes on to discuss the systematic spying on dissidents. The display is striking, not only because of its reproduction of the association between surveillance and the GDR for an international audience, but because surveillance itself is being symbolically equated with an object that resembles a computer.

As a form of memory work it is somewhat misleading. Not only, as the many other artefacts on display at the Stasi Museum attest, was the MfS willing to experiment with many forms of surveillance technology beyond video, but there was a much greater emphasis on surveillance as a human-oriented operation (see Verdery, 2019). The MfS employed over a dozen different categories of informer, each with its own function and form of knowledge, the number of which steadily increased over 30 years to reach a peak in the 1980s of approximately 180,000 people (Gieseke, 2015). It would be more accurate to symbolically equate Nazism with a computer than the GDR. The far shorter Nazi regime relied far more overwhelmingly on machine-readability than human intelligence, and made a fetish of ways of knowing populations that were entirely impersonal (Dumont, 1986).

In 2022, I visit the offices of one of Germany's oldest digital rights organizations, Digital Courage, in Bielefeld in the former West Germany. Shortly after arriving, I am offered a tour by one of the members, as a way of orienting me in the site. The tour resembles what geographers call a 'spatial narrative' (Ryan et al, 2016), rehearsing the indissolubility of space and time by telling both as an embodied story. They show me the single downstairs room in which the association began in the 1980s, and all the ways it has changed and expanded in the intervening years. At the same time, they weave in the memory of the site before, during, and after the Second World War. Bielefeld was once a centre for linen production, and many of the linen factories were turned into munitions factories during the conflict. As a consequence, it was bombed heavily. They point across the road towards a space where one of these factories had once stood, and explain that the building we are now standing in was erected in the area flattened by the bombardment.

Later on, we sit down for a long conversation, and I ask about them about the significance of the *Stasi* for their own political convictions. '*Auch*' – that too – they reply. This *auch* is a metonym for the relative position of the *Stasi* in *Netzpolitik* as a whole. Instead of being the core historical motive for those within, the *Stasi* is positioned as another expression of larger patterns in the region with regards to authoritarian surveillance, against which citizens must remain vigilant. As another offers with grim irony, 'We are the masters of surveillance'. It should be noted too that, as a social world, *Netzpolitik* is predominantly shaped by associations founded and registered in the former West Germany, and by people born either after 1989, or in the former West.[7] While it encompasses influential voices of those such as Constanze Kurz, who were born and raised in the GDR, their experiences are narrated publicly as personal. This distinguishes them, as a discourse, from the deeper history of fascism, which takes the form of collective memory that unites the former East and West.

From indeterminacy to self-determination

One characteristic of technological infrastructures that has been recognized by scholars is known as 'function creep' (see also Kupinska, Chapter 7, this volume). Function creep is the phenomenon whereby a technical system designed for one particular purpose gradually comes to be used for another. Function creep is a theory of social change around technology, and to that extent a theory of temporality, in which this temporality is creeping – so slow and so quiet as to be almost imperceptible. Gary Marx, in his study of US undercover policing, develops the more specific concept of 'surveillance creep' (1988, p 2). He argues that, 'As powerful new surveillance tactics are developed, the range of their legitimate and illegitimate use is likely to spread. Where there is a way, there is often a will' (Marx, 1988, p 2). The history of surveillance is replete with examples in which monitoring technologies designed for one, more benign, purpose begin to be used for another, less benign. Although less common, the reverse can equally be true. For instance, it is in the registration system established in the 1930s through which residents of Germany today access numerous welfare benefits (Kempner, 1946).[8]

To Marx's concept of surveillance creep, we can add another party who plays a role in its occurrence. Although substantially, surveillance creep is not exclusively a matter for those in command of a particular technological apparatus, its capacity to occur also relies to some extent – particularly in conditions of greater transparency – upon those whom it implicates in its information collection. In this regard, surveillance creep particularly flourishes in those contexts where this party presumes political stability and continuity. In other words, it assumes that regardless of who is controlling the technology, the ends of information-gathering will remain the same.

This presumption is largely absent from *Netzpolitik*, where participants display a heightened sensitivity to the possibility of political change. The future (*Zukunft*) is a term that appears often, not as a promise of technological optimism, but as potential threat. For instance:

> Snowden says, 'Freedom of opinion is also important for people who don't have an opinion. Maybe they will have one, one day.' But that also means, of course, it's not just that I have something to hide now, the question is, what will happen in the future? If we already have all these instruments, what will happen if the AfD (*Alternativ für Deutschland*) comes to power?[9] Who is then suddenly in the focus? Who is it then that will be surveilled? And then they already have all the data. So it wouldn't affect the majority at first. It won't affect me for the time being, but it would affect refugees, for example, who are always the first to be targeted. And of course I can say that it will only affect

other people. It won't affect me. So I have nothing to hide, but who knows if I will have something to hide in the future?

In the quotation at the start of this chapter, the interlocutor recalls the people who tell them that they have nothing to hide. This is a reference to an oft-repeated refrain in both English and German (*nichts zu verbergen*): that if citizens of democratic polities have nothing to hide with respect to criminality, then they have nothing to fear with respect to new forms of surveillance. Yet, as a moral arithmetic, it fails to account for the possibility of creep to which such technologies can be prone. In direct contrast, the previous extract rehearses the sensitivity to creep in *Netzpolitik*, and in this sense the prevailing diachrony of their positions. While my interlocutors disavowed the claim that they have nothing to hide, one that imagines surveillance within static political conditions, the assertion that they 'will have something to hide' positions it instead with regard to a future which is inherently unknown. In this context, tropes of unfolding and self-determination do not simply organize a praxis around technology (though they do that, too), but can also be construed as a more ambitious attempt to hold the reins of historical change. The potentiality for future difference arises out of the fact of historical difference, in a rhythm of history that still has beats to play.

The double-fix that characterized the late colonial period, and was reterritorialized within the borders of Europe, did not end there. Censuses, and the passes that derived from them, continued to be central tools of colonial governance, particularly across the African continent, in the second half of the twentieth century. The *kipande* system in British Kenya (Al-Bulushi, 2021), and the Belgian registration system in the Congo (Van Brakel and Van Kerckhoven, 2014), were employed as political technologies to tie labour to land, by fixing identity through residence, age, race, and other markers, and fixing these identified bodies through the prescriptions on movement that attended them. In Rwanda, it was the colonial endeavour to 'fix' identity into one of three ethnic groups (Longman, 2001, p 346) that provided the categorical basis for the subsequent genocide. Meanwhile in South Africa, the identical technological apparatus provided by IBM – punchcards in the 1950s and computers by the 1970s – was used to manage the pass system of Apartheid. Just five years after war in Europe ended, the South African government passed a law to build 'four separate population registers that fixed racial identities in perpetuity' (Breckenridge, 2014, p 168).

In response to these conditions of involuntary visibility, the political value of not being seen emerges as a strand of anti-colonial thinking. Édouard Glissant outlines a right to opacity, as a way of reasserting subjective and relational humanity in the face of colonial objectification (1997). More recently, Clare Birchall has imported Glissant's concept into the terrain of digital rights discourse, as a viable alternative to privacy itself (2021). Another iteration can be found in Browne's *Dark Matters* (2015). Combining Steve Mann's concept of sousveillance (Mann et al, 2002) – the surveillance that takes place from below to confront the surveillance from above – with the metaphor of darkness, Browne makes the case for a 'dark sousveillance' (2015, p 12). Dark sousveillance is not only a means of rejecting a hostile demand for visibility, but also contains the potential to redefine the very terms through which visibility occurs. A dark sousveillance can 'plot imaginaries … hopeful for another way of being', she offers (Browne, 2015, p 21). It is in this sense a temporal idea. From historical sources that document different responses to enslavement in eighteenth-century America, Browne similarly reclaims the generative value of indeterminacy. Like unfolding, dark sousveillance creates space not to hide within the privacy of the self, but to conceptually transform public life.

Conclusion

In view of the deeply distributed history of registration, it is worth reflecting again on why the East German regime retains such a powerful sway on the cultural imagination in the history of surveillance, particularly in Germany. This imagination surfaced once again in a particularly public way in May 2018, the week when EU General Data Protection Legislation came into effect. Mark Zuckerberg declared at a tech conference in Paris that it was 'because of the *Stasi*' that Germans were so sensitive about privacy.[10] In anthropological terms, we might think of the *Stasi* in the manner of the scapegoat. By attaching the sins of a collective to a person, animal, or thing, and then ritually banishing or sacrificing them, small-scale societies were morally purified (Frazer, 1998). By harnessing surveillance in Germany to the *Stasi*, binding it tightly to the arm of a regime that no longer exists, it achieves a purification of the present that consigns the dangers of new forms of surveillance to the past as well.

Instead, as the legal and cultural concept of self-determination, and its echo in anti-colonial theory, attests, it is a question with profound implications for the present and its non-linear development into the future. Emblematic of some of these contradictions, the old GDR monitor at the Humboldt Forum has several active surveillance cameras peering out over it, whose presence and purpose remains undiscussed. In these contemporary conditions, who is being fixed, and who is allowed to bear flowers and fruit? Documenting the colonial techniques of censuses and census tabulation that bookended Nazi Germany invites a more active response to these questions. It suggests the need to rethink the settlements and contracts that were implicitly or explicitly drawn up with the making of the modern world, and the ways in which these still can determine how many of us today become visible.

Acknowledgements

Versions of this chapter were presented as the keynote lecture at the symposium 'Human Agency, Digital Society, and Data-Intensive Surveillance' at the Paris Institute of Advanced Study in 2023, and the Senior Research Seminar in the Cambridge Department of Social Anthropology in 2024. I would like to thank the hosts of both these events, Anders Albrechtslund and Natalia Buitron, respectively, as well the audiences, for their responses and remarks. I would also like to extend my deepest gratitude to all the privacy advocates in Germany who engaged with me and this project, and the European Research Council for supporting it at every stage (grant no. 947867).

Notes

[1]   I conducted approximately fourteen months of ethnographic research between 2019 and 2023 among the associations, activists, and concerned citizens in the sphere of German civil society that calls itself *Netzpolitik*. This included participation in meetings and events alongside formal interviewing, the collection of publicly available digital and analogue material, and archival research in local district courts (*Amtsgerichte*).

[2]   Joel Robbins alerted me to this dynamic. Like fixing as surveillance, fixing to allow repair has mechanical connotations. Think, in this case, of a plaster-cast around an injured leg, or a bicycle on a stand having its wheel changed. This is distinct from forms of repair that arise through movement.

[3]   Edward Higgs issues a valuable *mea culpa* on a comparable disconnect. In a later return to his influential 2004 publication on the English Information State, he says, 'I failed to grasp how the British in the Victorian period were already laying the foundations of much more extensive forms of surveillance in their Empire ... one might argue that modern methods of surveillance in the West reflect the importation into metropolitan societies of the methods formerly used to control colonised peoples' (2014, p 18).

[4]   See also Szreter's discussion of Oliver Cromwell's use of the parish registration system to cement Protestant hegemony in sixteenth-century England (2012).

[5]   Musical supporters of the movement also produced its own eponymous theme tune (Willboy, 2020).

[6]   https://digitalegesellschaft.de/wp-content/uploads/2018/02/OffenerBrief_UploadFilter_Voss.pdf (Accessed: 27 January 2025).

[7]   This data is drawn from publicly available information, in *Amtsgerichte* and online.

[8]   By registering myself and my family in Berlin-Brandenburg during the period of fieldwork, I was awarded the right to free nursery care for my daughter at the age of three to four.

[9]   This interview took place in 2019, four years before this prophecy was realized in Thuringia (Connolly, 2023).

[10]   The conference is called Viva Technology and takes place annually in Paris.

References

Al-Bulushi, S. (2021) 'Citizen-Suspect: Navigating Surveillance and Policing in Urban Kenya', *American Anthropologist*, 123(4): 819–32.

Aly, G. and Roth, K.H. (2004) *The Nazi Census: Identification and Control in the Third Reich* (First English Language Edition). Translated by E. Black. Philadelphia: Temple University Press.

Amoore, L. (2008) 'Governing by Identity', in C.J. Bennett and D. Lyon (eds) *Playing the Identity Card: Surveillance, Security and Identification in Global Perspective*. London; New York: Routledge, pp 21–36.

Bennett, C.J. and Lyon, D. (eds) (2008) *Playing the Identity Card: Surveillance, Security and Identification in Global Perspective*. London; New York: Routledge.

Birchall, C. (2021) *Radical Secrecy: The Ends of Transparency in Datafied America*. Minneapolis, MN: University of Minnesota Press.

Black, E. (2001) *IBM and the Holocaust: The Strategic Alliance Between Nazi Germany and America's Most Powerful Corporation*. London: Little, Brown and Company.

Bogard, W. (1996) *The Simulation of Surveillance: Hypercontrol in Telematic Societies*. Cambridge: Cambridge University Press.

Bowker, G.C. and Star, S.L. (1999) *Sorting Things Out: Classification and its Consequences*. Cambridge, MA: MIT Press.

Breckenridge, K. (2014) *Biometric State: The Global Politics of Identification and Surveillance in South Africa, 1850 to the Present*. Cambridge: Cambridge University Press.

Browne, S. (2015) *Dark Matters: On the Surveillance of Blackness*. Durham, NC: Duke University Press.

Caplan, J. and Torpey, J.C. (2001) *Documenting Individual Identity: The Development of State Practices in the Modern World*. Princeton: Princeton University Press.

Connolly, K. (2023) 'Far-right AfD Wins Local Election in 'Watershed Moment' for German Politics', *The Guardian*, 26 June. Available from: https://www.theguardian.com/world/2023/jun/26/far-right-afd-wins-local-election-watershed-moment-german-politics (Accessed: 4 July 2023).

Darrow, D. (2015) 'Census as a Technology of Empire', *Ab Imperio*, 2002, pp 145–176.

Donnersmarck, F.H. (2007) *Das Leben der Anderen*. Wiedemann & Berg Filmproduktion, Bayerischer Rundfunk (BR), ARTE.

Douglas, M. (1966) *Purity and Danger: An Analysis of Concepts of Pollution and Taboo*. London: Routledge & K. Paul.

Dumont, L. (1986) *Essays on Individualism: Modern Ideology In Anthropological Perspective*. Chicago, IL: University of Chicago Press.

EDRi (2019) *Upload Filters: History and Next Steps, European Digital Rights (EDRi)*. Available from: https://edri.org/our-work/upload-filters-status-of-the-copyright-discussions-and-next-steps/ (Accessed: 4 July 2023).

Foucault, M. (2019) *Discipline and Punish: The Birth of the Prison*. Translated by A. Sheridan. London: Penguin Books.

Frazer, J.G. (1998) *The Golden Bough A Study in Magic and Religion*. Oxford: Oxford University Press.

Funder, A. (2011) *Stasiland: Stories from Behind the Berlin Wall*. London: Granta.

Gandy, O. (1993) *Panoptic Sort: A Political Economy of Personal Information.* London: Routledge.

Gieseke, J. (2015) *The History of the Stasi: East Germany's Secret Police, 1945–1990* (Translation edition). Translated by D. Burnett. New York and Oxford: Berghahn Books.

Glissant, É. (1997) *Poetics of Relation.* Translated by B. Wing. Ann Arbor: University of Michigan Press.

Groebner, V. (2001) 'Describing the Person, Reading the Signs in Late Medieval and Renaissance Europe: Identity Papers, Vested Figures, and the Limits of Identification, 1400–1600', in J. Caplan and J.C. Torpey (eds) *Documenting Individual Identity: The Development of State Practices in the Modern World.* Princeton: Princeton University Press, pp 15–27.

Haggerty, K.D. and Ericson, R.V. (2000) 'The Surveillant Assemblage', *The British Journal of Sociology*, 51(4): 605–22.

Hannah, M.G. (2010) *Dark Territory in the Information Age: Learning from the West German Census Controversies of the 1980s.* Farnham: Ashgate.

Higgs, E. (2014) 'Further Thoughts on The Information State in England... since 1500', in K. Boersma, R. van Brakel, C. Fonio, and P. Wagenaar (eds) *Histories of State Surveillance in Europe and Beyond.* London: Routledge, pp 17–31.

Jefferson, B.J. (2020) *Digitize and Punish: Racial Criminalization in the Digital Age.* Minneapolis, MN: University of Minnesota Press.

Kempner, R. (1946) 'The German National Registration System as Means of Police Control of Population', *Journal of Criminal Law and Criminology*, 36(5): 362.

Lefebvre, H. (2009) *Rhythmanalysis: Space, Time and Everyday Life.* Translated by S. Elden and G. Moore. London: Continuum.

Levitan, K. (2011) *A Cultural History of the British Census: Envisioning the Multitude in the Nineteenth Century* (1st edn). New York and Basingstoke: Palgrave Macmillan.

Longman, T. (2001) 'Identity Cards, Ethnic Self-Perception, and Genocide in Rwanda', in J. Caplan and J.C. Torpey (eds) *Documenting Individual Identity: The Development of State Practices in the Modern World.* Princeton: Princeton University Press, pp 345–358.

Lyon, D. (2003) *Surveillance as Social Sorting: Privacy, Risk, and Digital Discrimination.* London and New York: Routledge.

Lyon, D. (2009) *Identifying Citizens: ID Cards as Surveillance.* Cambridge: Polity.

Lyon, D. and Bennett, C.J. (2008) 'Playing the ID Card: Understanding the Significance of Identity Card Systems', in C.J. Bennett and D. Lyon (eds) *Playing the Identity Card: Surveillance, Security and Identification in Global Perspective.* London; New York: Routledge, pp 3–20.

Mann, S., Nolan, J., and Wellman, B. (2002) 'Sousveillance: Inventing and Using Wearable Computing Devices for Data Collection in Surveillance Environments', *Surveillance & Society*, 1(3): 331–355.

Marx, G.T. (1988) *Undercover: Police Surveillance in America*. Berkeley; London: University of California Press.

Oltermann, P. (2019) 'Wired up: East Berlin thriller makes National Theatre a surveillance centre', *The Guardian*, 16 May. Available from https://www.theguardian.com/stage/2019/may/16/berlin-1968-national-thea tre-anna-ella-hickson-communist-east-germany-headphones (Accessed: 4 July 2023).

Ruggiero, K. (2001) 'Fingerprinting and the Argentine Plan for Universal Identification in the Late Nineteenth and Early Twentieth Centuries', in J. Caplan and J.C. Torpey (eds) *Documenting Individual Identity: The Development of State Practices in the Modern World*. Princeton: Princeton University Press, pp 184–96.

Ryan, M.-L., Foote, K., and Azaryahu, M. (2016) *Narrating Space / Spatializing Narrative: Where Narrative Theory and Geography Meet*. Columbus: Ohio State University Press.

Simpson, J.A. (1989) 'State', *Oxford English Dictionary*. Oxford: Clarendon Press.

Steinwedel, C. (2001) 'Making Social Groups, One Person at a Time: The Identification of Individuals by Estate, Religious Confession, and Ethnicity in Late Imperial Russia', in J. Caplan and J.C. Torpey (eds) *Documenting Individual Identity: The Development of State Practices in the Modern World*. Princeton: Princeton University Press, pp 67–82.

Szreter, S. (2012) 'Registration of Identities in Early Modern English Parishes and Amongst the English Overseas', in S. Szreter and K. Breckenridge (eds) *Registration and Recognition: Documenting the Person in World History*. Oxford: Oxford University Press.

Torpey, J. (2000) *The Invention of the Passport: Surveillance, Citizenship, and the State*. Cambridge: Cambridge University Press.

Torpey, J.C. (2001) 'The Great War and the Birth of the Modern Passport System', in J. Caplan and J.C. Torpey (eds) *Documenting Individual Identity: The Development of State Practices in the Modern World*. Princeton: Princeton University Press, pp 256–70.

Van Brakel, R. and Van Kerckhoven, X. (2014) 'The Emergence of the Identity Card in Europe and its Colonies', in K. Boersma, R. Brakel, C. Fonio, and P. Wagenaar (eds) *Histories of State Surveillance in Europe and Beyond*. London: Routledge, pp 170–85.

Verdery, K. (2019) 'Comparative Surveillance Regimes: A Preliminary Essay', in S. Low and M. Maguire (eds) *Spaces of Security: Ethnographies of Securityscapes, Surveillance, and Control*. New York, NY: NYU Press, pp 57–77.

Willboy (2020) *Wir sind keine Bots*. Available from: https://www.youtube.com/watch?v=E4-6pj3NkC4 (Accessed: 27 June 2023).

9

Playtime:
Monitoring and Surveillance
in NFT Sociality

Matan Shapiro

Introduction

A networking event was held in a London pub. I arrived early and started talking with Laura, the organizer, about exciting new business opportunities in cryptocurrency investment. Then, a middle-aged woman arrived. She introduced herself as 'Angie', and after a brief chat tried to convince us to invest a few hundreds of pounds in what she defined as a 'blockchain investment' that will yield tens of thousands in return. Laura answered bluntly that the offer sounded like an invitation into a pyramid scheme. Angie insisted that it was legitimate, nonetheless. More people arrived in the meantime, and we were all caught up in other conversations. Angie stayed in the pub for another 30 minutes, pitching her lines and writing up some contact numbers. When she finally left the pub, Laura approached me. 'That woman was a typical scammer', she determined. 'These people never stay until the end. They try to collect emails and phone numbers so they can follow up the next day. That's how they work, *and they are wasting our time*'. When I inquired further what 'wasting time' meant in this context, Laura said:

There are artists here trying to promote their digital art and explore new ways to making money. All these scammers put up a good show so it's difficult to know who to trust and from whom you should stay away. If you find out [that] you were trying to make a partnership with someone who is not honest you just ended up wasting your time.

Laura was right to suspect Angie. In 2021 more than $3 billion was stolen from cryptocurrency exchange platforms or from individuals using them, with overall security breaches rising more than 40 per cent *every year* since the first major cryptocurrency theft took place in 2011 (Derrick, 2021). In 2022 millions of dollars were also stolen in different non-fungible token (NFT) swindles, including three major fraudulent schemes related to the once-prestigious lifestyle brand 'Bored Apes Yacht Club' in April and May 2002. The ever-present possibility of fraud in this social landscape assigns a ghostly mystique to the figure of the 'scammer', who could appear suddenly in your inbox using the email address of your best friend, or might even turn out to be a middle-aged woman you accidently met in a pub.

In this chapter I will focus on Laura's and other self-defined 'honest' traders' perceptions of timelessness, loss of time, or 'waste' of time, which they associate with the ongoing requirement to identify potential 'scammers'. Rather than analyse these ideas as pertaining to a rational risk aversion strategy, I examine them as forms of play, which create a suspension of everyday economic calculations, while introducing a measure of uncertainty into nearly every encounter with other traders, online or offline. NFT playtime in fact *replaces* the 'Big Motherly' monitoring of mundane economic rhythms (Peacock, Introduction, this volume), consequently generating the temporal precision of new economic and political rhythms (see Thompson, 1967; also Peacock, Introduction, and Polan, Chapter 10, both this volume). Based on fieldwork I conducted in 2022 with NFT traders and collectors in London, I advance the assumption that play theory may shed new light on the contemporary expansion of surveillance online, which is becoming ubiquitous not only in blockchain-related social circles but also other digital milieus.

NFTs

In October 2008, a person or group of people using the pseudonym Satoshi Nakamoto, in a cryptography mailing list, published an academic paper titled 'Bitcoin: A Peer-to-Peer Electronic Cash System' (Nakamoto, 2008). Satoshi, as cryptocurrency investors (especially Bitcoin adopters) have come to call them, described a decentralized system for the production of electronic money that innovatively solved what programmers and game theory experts call 'the problem of double spending' online. The solution reliably enabled peers to send and receive digital tokens, while ensuring that: (1) there is no fear of duplication (sending the same token twice); and (2) there is no need to go through a 'trusted third party' (Nakamoto, 2008), such as banks, to audit and guarantee the authenticity of the transaction.

Satoshi called this system 'the blockchain', an automated digital ledger in which every 'peer' holds a copy of the entire history of transactions. The blockchain thus registers all transactions between peers in real time, while verifying which of these transactions is fraudulent and which is honest. At the same time, using an algorithmic process called 'mining' (Zimmer, 2017), the blockchain also produces a set number of digital tokens that are released back into the network to produce value.[1] Every 10 minutes, the system seals this data in a virtual 'block', which contains a detailed record of all the transactions that were registered in the last 10 minutes on the ledger, *as well as* the details of the single computer that 'solved' the encrypted riddle from which the new coins were created. Every such 'block' is then assigned with a time-stamp sealing, which cannot be altered because it is protected by a cryptographic formula that makes it effectively tamper-proof (Antonopolous 2016). The signed block is immediately linked to the block that preceded it, which is already linked to the previous block, thus generating a 'chain' of verified blocks that stretches diachronically all the way back to the first block ever produced on the relevant blockchain. While Satoshi's blockchain produces only one type of digital tokens – the infamous Bitcoin – later blockchains could handle other cryptocurrencies, and in recent years also began monitoring the transactions of entirely different sets of decentralized tokens, such as NFTs.

NFTs, as their name suggests, are digital tokens whose storage on the blockchain turns them into tradeable goods or assets, much like Bitcoin and other cryptocurrencies. These tokens can be image files, music files, video files, or any other type of file which the creator/owner would like to register as theirs. Many NFTs are stored on the Ethereum blockchain – currently the main network used for the trade and exchange of cryptographic digital assets – but there are other existing blockchains that host NFTs. All these networks transparently show the different owners each NFT has had from the moment it was created and posted online (in a process similar to 'mining', which is called 'minting'), along with their changing prices through time. This enables all peers on the network to track the trajectory and value transformations of each NFT ever posted. Meanwhile, the cryptographic code assigned to each individual NFT guarantees its authenticity as a 'one-of-a-kind' item. Each NFT can then become an object for commodification, its value derived from the sums of money people are willing to pay for owning it. Since each NFT is singular and unique, it cannot be exchanged for other NFTs. While cryptocurrencies are all the same (or 'fungible', meaning that any single bitcoin is fully identical with any other bitcoin), NFTs can only be bought for the price tag that their owner has set in advance, whether that price is designated in cryptographic money or in state-owned fiat money.

For example, imagine you created a beautiful picture of a cactus on your digital drawing pad, and you now wish to make a profit by selling it online to cactus enthusiasts. The process is fairly simple – first, you create a digital wallet for yourself, which is essentially a hub, or a postal address, used exclusively for sending and receiving money online. Access to the wallet is exclusively yours, and is protected by a personal password that only you can change. Then, you will be able to connect your wallet to a blockchain of your choice (for example, Ethereum); each blockchain has different advantages and challenges, including varying transaction and storage fees, which means that some form of comparison is required if you wish to reduce the overall costs. Once that is done, you can link your wallet address to any of the many NFT marketplaces online (for example, OpenSea, Rarible, or NBA Top Shot), and upload to this marketplace the file you wish to sell. The file is then presented online side by side with graphs and other information regarding its trading and ownership history. Since NFTs represent ownership or proof of authenticity of a unique item, they can also be used to designate membership in a community, ownership of virtual or physical property (for example, land or a house), celebrity and lifestyle symbols, brand development and marketing, purchasable icons in the gaming industry, or any other object that requires nominal legal singularity and whose value can be derived from its scarcity (or rarity).

NFTs are not, however, attractive merely due to their potential financial value. Many of the traders and collectors I met in different public meetups in London or online were merely experimenting with this new form of digital asset 'for fun'. There are currently many online self-described NFT 'communities' and forums where collectors interact, including physical meetups or drinking nights. On the Discord network, for example, NFT enthusiasts engage in conversations on diverse issues, ranging from new 'hot mints' recently available on the market, to warning about 'scams', selling tickets to or publicizing information about related events, and NFT-related news in the gaming industry. Likewise, NFT communities hold digital art contests, exhibitions, and online treasure-hunt games aimed at finding and winning NFTs on different platforms (much like a *Pokémon Go!* game). In 2023, these have been expanded to include prestigious Web3 and metaverse events or parties,[2] which bring together creators, technologists, and entrepreneurs to chat, foster partnerships, and make friends, meeting in a random pub online using avatars. While there is an underlying economic value to these engagements, most of the time they fall under the category of play, as I now outline.

Play in NFT sociality

Since the 1950s, scholarly analyses of play have shifted the theoretical focus from a view of play as a 'free' activity (Huizinga, 1970 [1939]), to a view of play as a communicational vehicle in the ongoing negotiation and transformation of social values (Caillois, 2001 [1961]). When people reach a tacit understanding, 'This is Play' (Bateson, 2000 [1972], pp 177–193), they establish a communicational framework that is structurally separated from non-play events (Caillois, 2001 [1961], Handelman, 2021). The term 'framework' refers here to the implicit understanding that actions during playtime are *not* subjected to the same moral judgements and normative interpretations that non-play actions would require (Bateson, 2000 [1972]). For example, if during play I 'shoot' my playmate and she 'dies', I might have to accept some form of reaction or sanction within the rules of the game – whatever they are – but nobody will think of calling the police, and any sanction will dissolve after the game is over. If my playmate *really* dies, however, the moral and legal weight of everyday life will take over the play scenario and I will most likely go to prison, even if the tragedy was an accident. Playfulness thus allows persons to experiment with types of symbolic interaction that expand the possibilities of everyday non-play conduct, but this can rarely fully replace non-play resonances and real-world consequences.

The temporality of play thus suspends reality while not entirely ignoring the boundaries, conventions, norms, and rules that usually govern the flow of mundane life (Stromberg, 2009). This temporal bracketing, which enables participants to frame their activity as playful, accompanies several structural components (Huizinga, 1970 [1939]). These are: (1) people engage in play freely, rather than being coerced into it; (2) a clearly defined set of rules or norms constitutes an acknowledged playful order, which must be accepted by all the participants for the play or game to be considered effective or 'fun'; (3) when play activities become productive, especially with regards to the creation of wealth, they become instead a form of labour. Roger Caillois (2001 [1961]) argues that this set of structured characteristics contains four main types of human playful activities. He uses Greek terms to classify them as (1) *agon* (competition); (2) *alea* (chance, luck); (3) mimicry (make-believe, role-playing, imitation); and (4) *ilinx* (often translated to English as 'whirlpool' and referring to the sense of losing control over one's body or cognition).[3]

The world of NFT investors is playful in at least three aspects. To begin with, NFTs are a type of collectibles, much like traditional hobbies that include the collection of stamps, artworks, stickers, old swords, and so on. Collection and trade in NFTs include elements of *agon* (competition) and *alea* (chance), much like financial edgework activity that involves speculation and risk (for example, stock exchange investment; see Smith, 1999; Borch 2007). Although notions of profit do form part of this activity, NFT trade is rarely undertaken as a main source of income or a 'job', pertaining more to the realm of 'leisure' or 'hobby', as an interlocutor called Philip once told me at a meetup. The distinct temporality of this 'hobby' or 'leisure' activity is thus differentiated from labour, thereby suspending the regular rhythm of everyday sociality (Stromberg, 2009). Framing NFT trade as *playtime* therefore generates a designated *rhythm* that is taking place exclusively in the world of the masked, which is elusive and deceiving for all those who take part in it. The repetition of this rhythmic game of mirror across many relevant encounters, online or offline, pulsates side-by-side with the rhythm of everyday economic encounters, thus turning NFT playtime into a distinct temporal and spatial universe that is nevertheless exciting for those who dwell in it because it is never predictable (see Handelman, 2021). Playtime rhythm of collectibles, in short, continues to define NFT sociality intrinsically during negotiations on value. As Vita Peacock argues, following Lefebvre (2009) and Deleuze (1994), in the Introduction to this volume:

> Besides bodies, critical for rhythm is repetition, whether at exact intervals such as the thud of a metronome, or irregular repetitions such as seasons or tides. Like Gilles Deleuze (1994), repetition for Lefebvre is never simply replication. Though repeated, every repetitive occurrence takes place in conditions of difference, and therefore possesses the potential to reshape subsequent rhythms.

Secondly, and as a consequence, NFT sociality is playful because its ever-pulsating rhythm produces a thrill similar to that experienced in gaming. The digitality of NFTs, which, after all, are encrypted images made of pixels, turns the act of collecting them from a slow task of accumulation into a fast-moving rush to win a jackpot, as is the case with *ilinx* (whirlpool) forms of play. That is so because the rhythm of exchange relations here opens a new space of sensory and cognitive immersion that requires concentration, devotion, and risk taking, all of which are key elements in gaming (Vanolo, 2018). In fact, the aesthetics that dominate NFT sites build heavily on video game graphics, which include dark background, colourful icons, animated avatar profiles, and 'airdrops' of 'free' merchandise (such as items from an NFT series, discount codes, and entry tickets to related events). These gaming techniques structure a space in which 'trade' maintains a sense of playful unseriousness (Holloway, 2019), which is distinct from the more calculated world of cryptocurrencies trade, now already defined by some investors as 'decentralized financial investment' (DeFi).

Thirdly, at the level of daily encounters, NFT sociality is playful because it includes a high degree of role-playing, mimicry, and performance, online or offline, which inject a measure of uncertainty to most encounters in this space (Faustino et al, 2022). As the opening vignette indicates, perpetual awareness to detail, and a measure of suspicion, is built into NFT meetups, where traders meet primarily to discuss, drink, share information, and strike partnerships that could yield money in the future. To understand how this relates to play, it is important to emphasize the double nature of uncertainty. In games, a measure of uncertainty means that the result can never be known in advance (Ashtari and de Lange, 2019). If the final score of a football match was predetermined, the game would have no value. Secondly, uncertainty is anchored in the duplicity of symbols, actions, and messages. A broomstick that represents a horse during play is *simultaneously* a broomstick and a horse (Handelman, 1998). In play, as Don Handelman (1998, p 68) says, 'one thing is another, but it could be both and therefore neither'. Handelman argues that this second sense of uncertainty is endemic to any form of play, inducing doubt to the extent that players sometime wonder whether the playtime is no longer playful.[4] It is this deeper sense of uncertainty that I wish to explore in relation to play in the NFT world.

Uncertainty

While blockchains are considered 'immutable' digital environments – that is, it is difficult to hack them – swindlers can use deception, performance, and make-believe play to steal money from 'honest' traders. For example, some fraudsters have created fake NFTs that mimic genuine digital art or collectibles, selling these counterfeit NFTs to unsuspecting buyers. Phishing schemes are another preoccupation, wherein a person or organization would set up fake NFT marketplaces or websites to trick users into providing their private keys or wallet information. Once obtained, scammers can steal cryptocurrencies or NFTs from these wallets. Problems can also emerge from the fact that there is little or no legal regulation on financial activities taking place on blockchains. For example, organized groups of 'scammers' can artificially inflate the price of an NFT through coordinated buying, hyping (or 'booming'), and social media promotion. After the price has surged, they sell off their entire holdings, and convert the money into normative state–regulated currencies such as the dollar or euro, which often results in a value crash. Preoccupation with fakery, 'scamming', and fraud in NFT sociality also emerges from the fact that these tokens are traded 'on one's own responsibility', as a trader called Jonathan told me in an interview. Trading platforms are not accountable for each user's activities, and they are therefore not expected to reimburse sellers or buyers unless the platform's own account is being hacked.

A Reddit post written in mid-2022 by the pseudonymous user Reecekidd illustrates this logic. Published on the Ethereum Reddit forum and written in first-person prose, the author recounted how he fell into a series of NFT scams while trying to buy and later also mint NFTs (that is, create and connect an NFT into a blockchain). The narrative presents Reecekidd as a dumbstruck newbie blinded by the possibility of quick profiteering in the emergent Web3 ecosystem, whose lack of technical knowledge increasingly leads him to ignore warning signs, take more risks, and make more mistakes. Reecekidd writes:

> I clicked on the verify link [to join an NFT Discord community] and a login popped up. This was strange. My wallet is a Google Chrome

plugin that should always keep me logged in. Did it time out for a security measure? I typed in my password without thinking. The plugin accepted it. But it said for additional security information, it needed my secret phrase ... I went and got my secret phrase and entered it. When I entered it, nothing happened. It just said error. I entered my password and secret phrase for the second time. This is when I realized I had f***ed up. What I had entered my password and secret phrase into wasn't the official plugin. It looked the same, but it belonged to some randomer living in a shack in a different country ... A better person than me would have realized they needed to be more careful. But I'm not a better person. I still wanted my NFT. I figured I had some time before the randomer would steal all my money. Like all addicts, I looked for my next hit.[5]

Reecekidd exposed in this post only some of the common schemes used by scammers to deceive and dupe unsuspecting newcomers. Readers who commented on the post generally belittled and laughed at Reecekidd, for having identified these schemes always just a moment too late, and for having continued to fall into new traps as he went along. A reader named OxPendus, for example, writes:

You're actually just too dumb for this. And I don't mean that in a rude way. You have the self awareness to realize the mistakes you made but you feel for everything in the book and it was all driven by your desire to get rich quick. Stop and ask yourself 'is it likely that the guy who fell for multiple scams in one day without deep technical knowledge will end up striking gold and making it rich from a few pixels?' No. The answer is no. You're not that guy. I have sympathy for the pain you're in now but it's entire [sic] self inflicted due to greed. You need to accept the fundamental lesson that you are an outsider in this space – you're the sucker everyone else is making the millions from.

Other readers understand the parody in between the lines, however. Rather than reflect incidents that happened to a single person, the story seems to have wittingly used a composite personality to ridicule or accentuate a series of real-life events common in the hype of NFT trade that at the time was booming. A commenter named Psukhe, who may have realized the joke, summarizes its moral lessons as a form of advice to other newcomers:

Great post, fear of missing out [FOMO] and the allure of easy money is strong. It causes you to panic, and there are so many scams out there. Sorry it happened to you but consider it a $300+ lesson. Your journey was probably similar to many others, people can read this post and not make the same mistakes. Make sure to disable DMs [Direct Messages] in new discord servers you join, there are inflated fake discord user numbers, discords mods and admins can get hacked and send out links in official channels. *Don't move so fast that you forget to take the time to double check* … Good luck out there!

NFT traders act in an environment drenched with suspicion, which is subjected to a continuous sense of uncertainty, which thus has a transformative appeal and power that lasts beyond the designated temporality of the play itself, as it constitutes a general attitude (Handelman, 2021). Partly this ongoing atmosphere of suspicion is preserved because, unlike financial transactions that go through credit card companies, blockchain-enabled transactions do not enjoy legal protections. Cryptocurrency and NFT transactions are also irreversible, so it is nearly impossible to retrieve lost or misdirected funds. In fact, as fraudsters increasingly improve their tactics, NFT collectors, creators, and sellers have increasingly also begun exercising extra caution, conducting due diligence, and identifying potential risks. As Psukhe claims in the previous extract, traders must move slowly and 'take the time to double-check' who they are interacting with, thus ultimately turning the act of monitoring into a distinctly temporal issue.

Temporal monitoring

Surveillance in the playful world of NFT traders is a serious business, which is enacted rationally to either protect or steal money. Without monitoring – both in the sense of self-control, self-discipline, and self-tracking, and in the sense of observing and measuring others in the 'space' – there can be no financial securitization. Once you are in this game, you need to know what you are showing to whom, who is an ally and who is a foe, and what types of masks or deceptive strategies swindlers might use to put their hands on your money (or money-like tokens, such as NFTs). There is a spatiality to this act of monitoring – you need to verify that things are correctly positioned in their digital space. An account out of place, a transaction going to the wrong address, and so on, can result in economic loss (see Thompson, 1967). You must therefore scan the horizon constantly for those who fake in contrite spirit, who seek direct scamming (Swartz, 2022). Monitoring under these conditions has two main manifestations.

At the technical level, experienced NFT collectors would first verify that they were investing in genuine assets. To do that, they can use designated sites where you can audit the token to determine how likely it is to be fraudulent.[6] They would typically check whether the cryptographic code that identified a token they wished to buy was registered on the Ethereum network, the main blockchain used for storing NFTs; read the comments section in different sites that scan blockchain tokens to verify their authenticity; Google-search to see if a personal page or a site of the seller can be located; check blacklists that are published by both scanning sites and exchange platforms on a regular basis; and verify that the token they are buying is registered on the main exchange platforms. One of the rules of thumb is in fact *never* to post NFTs on – or buy them from – unknown or newly created marketplaces.

Meanwhile at the level of social interaction, monitoring focuses on verifying the identity of interlocutors on common digital platforms that traders use for networking and communication. These mainly include LinkedIn, Reddit, Twitter (now called X), Telegram, Discord, and several meetup applications, which are used to organize social events offline. On Discord channels, which host most NFT self-proclaimed 'communities', moderators continuously publish warnings and actively encourage members to double-check any interaction they have with others online. Since all peers are equal in their ability to track and produce information on the blockchain, and the many relevant forums used to sustain NFT sociality online, both honest and dishonest NFT traders must monitor themselves and other users all the time. This creates a social landscape characterized by total visibility: everyone keeps watching everyone else's movements to make sure they cannot be harmful to them, on the one hand, or expose them as 'scammers' on the other. For example, a moderator in an NFT Discord community, in March 2022 published the following warning:

We've heard one too many stories of people in the NFT community losing their assets or getting scammed. We typed up this guide to help you avoid the most common scams and keep your accounts and wallets safe.

Rule #1: *Don't click on links from strangers.* If you need to get somewhere, try googling it or going through a project's official twitter accounts.
Rule #2: *Disable Discord DMs* from server members, and *enable two factor authentication.*
Rule #3: If in doubt, open a ☐| HELPDESK [chat box] before you do *anything*.

Rule #1 is most important – don't click on links or connect to sites someone has asked you to visit … *Keep an eye out for similar messages and report them!*

As in the film *Brazil* (1985), a social landscape drenched with suspicion transpires here through a continuous demand to monitor everything.[7] Business opportunities, financial security, and the sheer ability to trade or collect all emerge from the ability (and skill) to use surveillance as integral to any other social calculation. Abiding by rules of thumb meant to protect so-called 'honest' traders, thus becomes a vector of individual control designed to produce securitization and independence. For example, in a Reddit post from 2023, a user called FSmertz described a potential scammer who provoked their suspicion. They ask community members for their opinions, as they were still interested in receiving their commission in case it was a genuine buyer. The full message reads:

> Got a private message a couple of days ago on Instagram asking if I can do a painting for her. I said yes and now she is very keen to put the money into my account right away via PayPal before I have a chance to discussed [sic] more details. Her profile name is very common and is the same name as a famous American actress. She only has four post [sic], the oldest being a mouth [sic] old. I ask her if we can do a different payment method than paypal [sic] but said she can only do paypal [sic]. I've heard about paypal [sic] scams from other artist and worried this may happen to me. Am I being paranoid or should I just take the commission?'

Based on the description, all responders agree that the potential customer must have been a scammer, advising FSmertz to 'run-away', 'block', and 'delete'. One of them provides the following answer:

> Its [sic] could be a scam. I had a personal experience from Instagram a few months back. They pretended to have put the money in my account, than [sic] an email was sent that I was to refund $200 due to [use of] different currencies. My partner helped me and rang PayPal and read the email to customer service and they were excellent in determining it was [a] scam just by the 'invoice number'. *Be vigilant, your time is too valuable to waste on these nonces* [sic].

The call for vigilance, seen as a time worth investing in order to avoid wasting investors' time later on, is reiterated during physical meetups I attend in London. In another meetup organized by Laura and Jim, her co-organizer, for example, the initial welcome speech includes a direct appeal to 'those of you in the room who are after the easy money' not to promote illegitimate or fraudulent NFT products. 'You will be wasting our time, and also yours', said Laura. In an interview with Wanderlei, a Brazilian-born London-based artist who has, in recent years, been selling his art via Instagram, he likewise mentions the 'loss of time':

> I work on [both] my prints and digital pictures for weeks at a time, you know. I design them based on traditional symbols and images [from

Brazil] and this is a lengthy process. I print them physically, take photos, and post them on my Instagram page. Because of all that investment, not just of money and material but also energy and all those weeks or even months [for production], I just don't want to take the chance that someone will scam [sic] me. I am [not] going to waste my time and eventually likely also to lose money. I don't need this.

Naturally, then, active swindlers also monitor the persons they are attempting to scam. Gus, a research interlocutor from London, shares a screenshot of a conversation on Telegram with an unknown person, using the alias Sherron T. Moore. 'Sherron' approached Gus unexpectedly, and at some stage during their conversation dropped in the word 'Ayale'. Gus quickly Googled the word and discovered that it is a Yoruba term used by West African fraudsters to test if their interlocutor might also be a 'scammer'. Gus thus replied with an 'Ayale' of his own, and the conversation swiftly moved to pidgin as the 'scammer' on the other side of the screen assumed he or she was talking with a colleague. The entire conversation between them is short, and does not include a direct reference to time. It is reasonable to assume, however, that partly the dropping of 'Ayale' sometimes at the beginning of the conversation is itself a monitoring technique aimed at 'saving' time.

In all these accounts, acts of wasting/saving time advance a double meaning. On the one hand, they are related to the labour-intensive and productivity-oriented aspects of art at large, and the creation of NFTs, in particular, which can be quantified as either loss or gain of money. On the other hand, however, 'wasting/saving time' in the context of NFT sociality is also related to the temporality of play itself, which should adhere to certain rules to be considered play at all. 'Waste of time' in that sense is the time lost for *dishonest play*, a breaking of the rules which upon its discovery retrospectively obviates the meaning of the entire playtime, turning it in fact into a form of unproductive labour on the side of the scammer. 'Saving time', then, from the point of view of those same swindlers, is thus aimed to reduce the time spent/wasted while trying to play/work (that is, to 'scam' through) a worthless game.

One of the consequences of the normalization of this temporal logic is an erosion of panoptic sensibilities, which Michel Foucault (2004, p 1) associated with the advent of 'bio-power', 'the set of mechanisms through which the basic biological features of the human species became the object of a political strategy, of a general strategy of power'. The body is increasingly becoming secondary within a regime of truth that assumes the ongoing preservation of masks all the time (Mathiesen, 1997). The game of surveillance that ensues within such a regime, which in the case of NFT sociality is enacted as part of the wider playtime of trading and collecting, abolishes the importance of corporeality, as it shifts attention from the ontological, the material, and the authentic, to the graphical, the ethereal, and the performed. The temporal implications of this transformation, as I now turn to explicate, are confining as much as they may be regarded liberating, at least as this relates to the tension between experimentalism and securitization in the unregulated space of crypto-asset trading.

Analysis

David Lyon (1994; 2007) uses the term 'post-panoptic surveillance' to describe a diffusion of power relations in the deployment of monitoring. As opposed to the panoptic model of surveillance (Foucault, 1991), which is spatially confined and which assumes an unbridgeable yet clearly observed distance between those who monitor and the subjects of monitoring, post-panoptic surveillance is spatially dispersed. It assumes concealed forms of monitoring as much as it uses other forms openly (for example, CCTV), to deter and restrict potential deviance in the public sphere. Post-panoptic surveillance turns the top-down exploratory gaze of the panopticon into a heterogeneous, space-level, all-encompassing inspection, which can be employed in any direction and towards any 'target' (Albrechtslund and Lauritsen, 2013). The sociality around NFT trade is 'post-panoptic' because it makes ongoing monitoring a *necessity*. In a reality marked by playful performances, masking, pretensions, uncertainty, and suspicion, constant monitoring simply becomes the natural thing to do and the most important survival strategy, both at the technical level and as a skill required to navigate social relations (See Staples, 2013 [2000]).

Post-panoptic surveillance technologies thereby perpetuate the spell of Prediction (with an uppercase P) as a preferred method for designing anticipated futures (Hong, 2022; compare Kitchin, 2014). The establishment of post-panopticism on a large scale helps distribute the idea that Prediction is positive and necessary. In the case of NFTs, as I demonstrated earlier, Prediction relates to anticipating and thwarting 'scams' as integral to regular encounters. However, this same process also works to validate facts retrospectively by seeking to concretely identify objects such as names (for example, scammers) or events (for example, a phishing attack in a forum). In NFT sociality, retrospective identification of a scam can be disheartening, as some of the responses to Reecekidd's post quoted previously make clear. This duality reveals a normative dimension that organizes NFT trade – the requirement to identify a potential trap translates into the promulgation of suspicion and the reification of certain values, especially regarding the binary distinction between 'honest' and 'fraudulent' actors. Time dedicated 'now' to risk aversion – manifesting in the disposition to 'double-check' everything – becomes a murky liminal territory between legitimate and illegitimate datafication of play-forms (van Dijck, 2014), which are retrospectively defined as a 'wasted time' in case a fraud has indeed been detected.

Hong's analysis exposes a double temporality that is intrinsic to post-panoptic realities: on the one hand, surveillance works progressively to justify the truth of Prediction, but on the other hand, it works recessively to justify hegemonic moral values (of which Prediction is an essential part; Hong, 2022). Prediction in that sense, paradoxically, extends a concrete, grounded vision of the present, which often relies on abstract notions of order and control (Frois, 2013; Kitchin, 2014) and on concrete agents that wield the power to sanction (Zuboff, 2019). The operative and pre-emptive temporal logics that drive surveillance practices in NFT sociality can thus be seen to universalize themselves, becoming ubiquitous as they are applied, and thus also extending the real or imaginary threat conditions for which they were invented in the first place. Surveillance as a tool aimed at protecting the self, consequently drives the perfection and innovation of better monitoring technologies, which deepen and totalize the present order even further into the future (Hong, 2022).

The temporality of post-panoptic monitoring in the world of NFT collectors thereby generates a game of hide-and-seek, in which power itself is constantly disguised and revealed unexpectedly (Lyon, 2018). Arising from within the ranks as it sinks back into anonymity, the power to swindle and the power to defend oneself against swindling is embedded in the ability to track and observe others almost all the time (Maras and Wandt, 2019). Those who appropriate and operationalize better monitoring and tracking techniques gain a significant advantage, a fleeting dominance over nearly arbitrary others. Sometimes this comes at the expense of others, as with outright 'scamming', and sometimes it is a mere fencing technique. When NFT traders normalize acts of monitoring and surveillance as boundary-making techniques that securitize their funds in the present for a sense of a more certain future, they effectively mimic the exploratory gaze employed by hackers and scammers, a gaze they are otherwise trying to block or evade. This scrutinizing gaze, allegedly characterizing only those malicious actors seeking a scamming opportunity, here emerges almost by definition as an ethical common demeanour in a sociality defined by play, masking, and accelerated movement. The very act of masking, which is endemic to both play and barter, becomes essential for NFT playtime activities at large.

An empirical game of hide-and-seek in this context opens possibilities to think about self-expression in situations of algorithmic visibility (O'Neil, 2016). A traditional *panoptic* approach assumes that self-expression under a scrutinizing gaze produces docility and a desire to satisfy the observer. Resistance in this situation can only be practised in dead spots, where observers cannot exercise their power. Self-expression in *post-panoptic* realities has contrarily been celebrated as inherently resistant and even liberating because it appropriates surveillance to the goals and interests of the observed (Albrechtslund, 2008). Here, technologies of visualization and representation (such as chats) become emancipatory tools for genuine personalized desires, on the one hand, or means to manipulate and commercialize an audience voyeurism on the other (Staples, 2013 [2000]). But what do we do with self-expression in and around blockchain-based sociality, wherein every single peer is simultaneously the observer and the observed? What do we do with power and resistance in a 'networked' environment composed of a multiplicity of tightly interconnected peers, who always watch one another while being watched by everyone else?

Conclusion

Rather than social persons in the sociological sense of the term, which always includes bodies as the ultimate space of political contestation, a temporal logic of surveillance in the world of NFT collectors contributes to the emergence of purified perspectives, from which people can explore or even scrutinize others. I here follow the late John Perry Barlow, a pioneer of techno-utopianism in cyberspace and a renowned American poet. In 1990, Barlow published an account of his first experience with a virtual reality machine in which he claims that he was 'reduced to a point of view' (Turner, 2006, p 165). Amazed by the lack of corporeality of the experience, Barlow described how everything suddenly became possible within a three-dimensional cyberspace. Barlow claimed that the adoption of this gaze, a reductionism into a position of a total observer, also entailed epistemological transformations. Operating freely as a 'point of view' in the context of NFT monitoring, ultimately demands not only technical knowledge (that is, how to verify the authenticity of tokens), but also: (1) the embodiment of a new set of moral codes that distinguish right from wrong (that is, what kinds of half-truths are acceptable and which ones would be considered deception); and (2) the implementation of these moral codes through concrete acts of ethical decision-making (that is, when it is okay to 'DM' [direct message] someone, proper ways to speak with others online and offline about NFT trade, and so on).

Playtime, as it is empirically grounded in acts of surveillance, goes beyond NFT trade or even the involvement in other, more risky, blockchain assets. Among many contemporary examples, the gamification of cityscapes seems to be especially relevant for the intensification of a post-panoptic temporal dynamic of surveillance, that builds distinct playtimes and play-spaces wherein all interactions are closely monitored (Ruffino, 2014; Maras and Wandt, 2019). 'In its essence', argues Alberto Vanolo:

> gamification concerns the mobilisation and implementation of ludic
> elements – or, better to say, videoludic elements – in order to manage

'serious' and 'real' issues … By introducing game mechanics such as rankings, scores, badges, levels, rewards and virtual currencies in apps and websites originally distant from gaming cultures, software designers and policy makers aim at stimulating public engagement and virtuous social behaviours. (Vanolo, 2018, p 320)

Gamification apps in urban spaces are often designed to increase awareness to sustainability issues by incentivizing the users to engage in fun activities and play scenarios, thereby ultimately impacting and modifying behaviours (Kitchin, 2014). In that sense they also sometimes work to coerce, tacitly, or even enforce, certain types of behaviours in public. The same temporal logic undergirds NFT monitoring, wherein 'awareness' is integrated into mundane actions to predict present as well as future threats. I hope this chapter will encourage colleagues to conduct more research on this process.

Notes

[1]   Mining is an ongoing competition between computers to decipher a complicated cryptographic code, which conceals a set number of digital coins. The first computer to decrypt the code 'extracts' these coins from its digital storage and gets to keep them. They are then traded online on designated platforms using other types of currency, either digital or state-controlled fiat money.

[2]   Web3 refers to emergent decentralized internet infrastructure, which, unlike Web2 applications, enables content creators to own and commercialize their data using blockchains and NFT-like digital signatures. Metaverse is a general category for the use of virtual reality (VR) headsets to engage in virtual environments in a more immersive way than is usually enacted today. Whereas VR glasses are now mainly used for gaming, metaverse activities can include many other mundane activities, such as professional meetings in workplaces and online concerts.

[3]   Caillois distinguishes between structured games, which, following Huizinga (1970 [1939]), he calls *ludus*, and unstructured and spontaneous play, which he calls *paidia*. The four types of play occur in each of these modes.

[4]   On the one hand, duplicity in play affords flight of the imagination, but on the other hand, it can cause confusion and breakdown that would spill over into mundane reality. This is so, as Gregory Bateson (1972) argued, because any playful action *could* be interpreted as if it was entirely serious. For example, I once watched a performance of a clown that included controlled, yet deliberately abusive interaction with the audience. About halfway through the stint, one of the volunteers, who was drunk, suddenly stood up, grabbed a half-empty beer bottle, and broke it on the clown's head. He then screamed that he would not tolerate such abuse and ran away before security could reach him. This radical reaction resulted from the uncanny feeling that the clown's words *could* have been serious, rather than playful.

[5]   https://www.reddit.com/r/ethereum/comments/tz7p9w/i_fell_for_every_nft_scam_in _10_minutes/?rdt=57683 (Accessed: 26 February 2025).

[6]   Such as www.dappradar.com (DAPP = Decentralized Apps) (Accessed: 26 February 2025).

[7]   Gilliam's dystopic parody playfully ridiculed some of the darker fantasies of the genre by using different signs that were embedded in the set. For example, a poster that was hung on the office wall of one of the protagonists read: 'Don't suspect a friend, report him'. Another poster, however, read: 'Suspicion breeds confidence'.

References

Albrechtslund, A. (2008) 'Online Social Networking as Participatory Surveillance', *First Monday*, 13(3): 1–10.

Albrechtslund, A. and Lauritsen, P. (2013) 'Spaces of Everyday Surveillance: Unfolding an Analytical Concept of Participation', *Geoforum*, 49: 310–16.

Antonopoulos, M.A. (2016) *Mastering Bitcoin*. Sebastopol: O'Reilly Media.

Ashtari, D. and de Lange, M. (2019) 'Playful Civic Skills: A Transdisciplinary Approach to Analyse Participatory Civic Games', *Cities*, 89: 70–9.

Bateson, G. (2000) [1972]). *Steps to an Ecology of Mind*. Chicago, IL: University of Chicago Press.

Borch, C. (2007) 'Crowds and Economic Life: Bringing an Old Figure Back In', *Economy and Society*, 36(4): 549–73.

Caillois, R. (2001 [1961]) *Man, Play, and Games*. Urbana, IL: University of Illinois Press.

Deleuze, G. (1994) *Difference and Repetition*. London: Athlone Press.

Derrick, J. (2021) 'Crypto security breaches are up 850% in the last decade', Invezz.com. Available from: https://invezz.com/news/2021/12/16/cryptocurrency-security-breaches/ (Accessed: 27 January 2025).

Faustino, S., Faria, I., and Marques, R. (2022) 'The Myths and Legends of King Satoshi and the Knights of Blockchain', *Journal of Cultural Economy*, 15(1): 67–80.

Foucault, M. (1991) *History of Sexuality Vol. 1: An Introduction*. New York: Vintage Press.

Foucault, M. (2004) *Security, Territory, Population: Lectures at the Collège de France, 1977–78*. Edited by M. Senellart. Translated by G. Burchell. London: Palgrave MacMillan.

Frois, C. (2013) *Peripheral Vision: Politics, Technology, and Surveillance*. New York and Oxford: Berghahn Books.

Handelman, D. (1998) *Models and Mirrors*. Oxford: Oxford University Press.

Handelman, D. (2021) *Mobius Anthropology: Essays on the Forming of Form*. Edited by M. Shapiro and F. Jackie. New York and Oxford: Berghahn.

Holloway, D. (2019) 'Surveillance Capitalism and Children's Data: The Internet of Toys and Things for Children', *Media International Australia*, 170(1): 27–36.

Hong, S. (2022) 'Predictions Without Futures', *History and Theory*, 61(3): 371–90.

Huizinga, J. (1970 [1939]) *Homo Ludens: A Study of the Play Element in Culture*. London: Maurice Temple Smith Ltd.

Kitchin, R. (2014) 'The Real-Time City: Big Data and Smart Urbanism', *GeoJournal*, 79(1): 1–14.

Lefebvre, H. (2009) *Rhythmanalysis: Space, Time and Everyday Life*. Translated by S. Elden and G. Moore. London and New York: Continuum.

Lyon, D. (1994) *The Electronic Eye: The Rise of Surveillance Society*. Cambridge: Polity Press.

Lyon, D. (2007) *Surveillance Studies: An Overview*. Cambridge: Polity Press.

Lyon, D. (2018) *Surveillance, Power, and Everyday Life*. Oxford: Oxford University Press.

Maras, M.H. and Wandt, A.S. (2019) 'Enabling Mass Surveillance: Data Aggregation in the Age of Big Data and the Internet of Things', *Journal of Cyber Policy*, 4(2): 160–77.

Mathiesen, T. (1997) 'The Viewer Society: Michel Foucault's Panopticon Revisited', *Theoretical Criminology*, 1(2): 215–34.

Nakamoto, S. (2008) Bitcoin: A Peer-to- Peer Electronic Cash System. Open Access Online. Available from: https://bitcoin.org/bitcoin.pdf (Accessed: October 2023).

O'Neil, C. (2016) *Weapons of Math Destruction: How Big Data Increases Inequality and Threatens Democracy*. New York: Crown.

Ruffino, P. (2014) 'From Engagement to Life, or: How to Do Things With Gamification?', in M. Fuchs, S. Fizek, P. Ruffino, and N. Schrape (eds) *Rethinking Gamification*. Lüneburg: Meson, pp 47–68.

Smith, C.W. (1999) *Success and Survival on Wall Market*. Oxford: Rowman & Littlefield.

Staples, W.G. (2013 [2000]) *Everyday Surveillance: Vigilance and Visibility in Postmodern Life*. Oxford: Rowman & Littlefield.

Stromberg, P.G. (2009) *Caught in Play: How Entertainment Works on You*. Stanford, CA: Stanford University Press.

Swartz, L. (2022) 'Theorizing the 2017 Blockchain Ico Bubble as a Network Scam', *New Media & Society*, 24(7): 1695–713.

Thompson, E.P. (1967) 'Time, Work-Discipline, and Industrial Capitalism', *Past & Present*, 38(1): 56–97.

Turner, F. (2006) *From Counterculture to Cyberculture: Stewart Brand, the Whole Earth Network, and the Rise of Digital Utopianism*. Chicago, IL: University of Chicago Press.

van Dijck, J. (2014) 'Datafication, Dataism and Dataveillance: Big Data between Scientific Paradigm and Ideology', *Surveillance & Society*, 12(2): 197–208.

Vanolo, A. (2018) 'Cities and the Politics of Gamification', *Cities*, 74: 320–26.

Zimmer, Z. (2017) 'Bitcoin and Potosí Silver: Historical Perspectives on Cryptocurrency', *Technology and Culture*, 58(2): 307–34.

Zuboff, S. (2019) *The Age of Surveillance Capitalism: The Fight for a Human Future at the New Frontier of Power*. New York: Public Affairs.

10

Growth's Imagination: Startups and the Cruel Intimacy of the Internet's Business Model

Lake Polan

Introduction

In September 2014, Sam Altman welcomed a room of Stanford undergraduates to the first session of an advanced computer science course titled *How to Start a Startup* (henceforth, 'Startup School'). At the time, Altman was President of Y Combinator, a startup 'accelerator' with an outsized presence in Silicon Valley's high tech and venture capital communities. Like any good lecturer, Altman immediately established his authority and identified course goals. Only nine years beforehand, he told them, he had also studied computer science at Stanford. After dropping out to found a startup, he sold it and turned to investing. By 2014, Altman and his Y Combinator partners had invested in more than 700 startups. While most of the guidance they offered founders was startup-specific, approximately 30 per cent, Altman estimated, was generally applicable. With Startup School, he and his guest lecturers – each a Y Combinator partner or alumni with experience creating a 'billion dollars-plus' company – would now publicly share that knowledge for the first time. Reproducing the talks given to Y Combinator's own participants, Startup School would impart the formerly privileged practical knowledge needed to appreciate startups as 'the way of the future', and pursue that distinctive entrepreneurial aspiration, 'hyper growth and eventually building a very large company'. Biographically aligning his students' present with his own past, Altman's introduction diagrammed an imaginative pathway towards their own future-saturated futures. It thus provided a taste of the strategic labour in and of entrepreneurial time (see Munn, 1992; Bear, 2014,

196

2016), which Startup School reveals to be central to venture capitalist–entrepreneur relations.

Despite my husband's occasional hopes, when I watched the video recordings of *How to Start a Startup* in 2017, posted to YouTube in testament to the startup gospel, it was not out of latent entrepreneurial zeal. Rather, as part of an ethnographic study of privacy as it has been taken up as an object of technological intervention in Silicon Valley, I was tracking an increasingly powerful cultural figure of recent origin, understood within tech communities to be implicated in the problem of privacy's future. American law and popular culture have long figured privacy's fate as intertwined with technological progress. Since the 1890s, Americans have regularly responded to new communications technologies, including photography, the telegraph, and the telephone, as potentially 'fatal' privacy threats (Nelson, 2002; Nissenbaum, 2010). Recent decades may have seen a tempering in the public outrage precipitated by privacy violations (Zuboff, 2019, p 20). Even so, since the 1960s, Americans have anxiously catalogued the new forms of public and private surveillance facilitated by computers, digital databases, and the internet (Brin, 1998; Nissenbaum, 2010).

Nonetheless, between 2014 and 2018, as I prepared for and conducted fieldwork among corporate privacy engineers in San Francisco and beyond, my interlocutors consistently cited not technology, but rather something like technology's animating value logic when naming the ultimate cause of privacy's decline. Across blogs, tweets, conference presentations, and interviews, internet engineers and computer scientists professionally engaged in preserving privacy, characterized its ongoing erosion as a structural feature of what they sometimes called 'the internet's business model' (see, for example, Schneier, 2013). Under this logic, if the commercial internet has developed into a system of total surveillance (Masco, 2017), it is neither because of some inherent feature of internet technology, nor because 'Zuckerberg, Brin and Page are scheming, sinister masterminds' (Zuckerman, 2014). Rather it is because the surveillance-based advertising that internet corporations adopt to 'capture' value from the users attracted to their (apparently free) content and services compels them to collect ever-more invasive personal data.

Pioneered by Google following the 2000 dot.com crash (Zuboff, 2019), by 2016, the internet's business model accounted for a preponderance of the annual revenue generated by both Silicon Valley's iconic startups and the web's sprawling long-tail of individual websites. When I arrived in San Francisco in October that year, the privacy engineers I met, and the broader tech communities in which they circulated, had identified the model as the source of the harms they increasingly recognized to flow from the internet. Even as they laboured to build privacy protections into tech products and services, they were largely resigned to the idea that the web as we know it – as a 'free', universally accessible, global information commons (Berners-Lee et al, 1999) – could no more survive without the model than it could without its underlying physical infrastructure. To secure privacy's future, they said, a new business model had to be found, one capable of replacing surveillance-based ad targeting as the default means of funding the web. At once inevitable doom and potential salvation, the business model concept defined an imaginative limit to Silicon Valley's techno-moral aspirations.

Technology, of course, has never stood alone in the rogues' gallery of American privacy. Privacy's foes include the institutions and logics of American policing (Browne, 2015) and national security (Masco, 2017). The public's supposed moral failings – its embrace of self-disclosure (boyd, 2014) and 'refusal' to take personal responsibility for privacy – continually vex privacy's defenders. In their seminal 1890 call for legal privacy rights in the US, Warren and Brandeis acknowledged that privacy-threatening technologies co-emerge with 'novel business practices'. Even so, the business model's rapid emergence as a culturally legible explanation for privacy's decline marks a historical shift in both American understandings of privacy and theories of corporate malfeasance.[1]

At first pass, business model-based explanations for privacy's decline side-step the popular American treatment of technology as an autonomous, socially determinative force (Smith, 1994). In so doing, however, they trade one such force for another. Such explanations deflect responsibility for the internet's harms away from its technologies, but also from the entrepreneurs, product managers, engineers, and corporations professionally invested in it as a commercial medium. Business model-based explanations gesture towards an indictment of capitalism, but in highly circumscribed form, limiting critique to a situated competitive strategy pioneered by, and closely associated with, the venture capital-backed corporate form.

Business school professor Shoshana Zuboff argues that a parasitic logic of accumulation has overtaken the commercial internet, inaugurating an increasingly hegemonic economic order, an 'age of surveillance capitalism' (Zuboff, 2019). Zuboff's theory broadly aligns with my interlocutors' analysis of the internet's business model. While business models figure peripherally in her account, Zuboff similarly characterizes internet companies as economically beholden to the ever-intensifying surveillance of human behaviour. Across 700 pages, she considers how technology companies unilaterally claimed human experience as raw materials of capitalist accumulation. Rejecting technological determinism, Zuboff characterizes surveillance capitalism as the product of specific individuals (2019, pp 85–9). She further catalogues a set of political, economic, and technological circumstances, and institutional forms and strategies which, she argues, respectively, cleared the ground for surveillance capitalism and shepherded its emergence.

Less clear, in the partially articulated accounts of Zuboff and privacy engineers, are the institutionally situated affective processes and ethical claims in play. Startups by definition have no history of revenue and, often, no actual products. Investors value them on the basis of narratively elaborated, future-oriented abstractions like 'the felt possible of future … profit' (Sunder Rajan, 2007, p 19). If capitalism is generally defined by actors' systemic orientation towards open if uncertain futures' (Beckert, 2016), this is doubly true of speculative ventures like internet startups. According to Laura Bear (2020), as a form of future-oriented labour, speculation seeks to accumulate capital by intervening in the ethical orders that underwrite economic action. In explaining surveillance capitalism's spread, Zuboff (2019, p 165) cites the 'palpable magnetism' of Google and Facebook's early success. She provides little insight, though, into the institutional structures and interactions through which entrepreneurs become reconciled to surveillance-based business practices as justified, if not required, by some compelling image of the social good.

In this chapter, I attempt to recuperate the moral imaginaries and affective labour obscured in these accounts through an ethnographic study of the business model. In so doing, I take up this volume's call to attend to changing contemporary configurations of surveillance and time. I do this, however, by considering not how people use surveillance technology to manage the rhythms of life, but rather how surveillance emerges from the efforts of entrepreneurs, under venture capitalists' tutelage, to summon flows of speculative capital by managing the contradictory rhythms of technological development, market competition, and government regulation. First, tracing the brief history of the business model concept, I show that management experts have come to valorize business models in general as a vital domain of strategic corporate creativity and determinant of technological success. Despite this, business models are only ambiguously present in the reflexive mythology of startup success narrated in Startup School. Attending to this mythology, I draw out the distinctive figure of exponential corporate growth that investors like Altman promote, in the place of the internet's business model, as both normative ideal and pragmatic technique for achieving startup success. Detailing the 'sociotechnical imaginary' (Jasanoff, 2015) enacted through such veneration, I argue that the pathologies attributed to the internet's business model are better understood as emerging from the way Silicon Valley's socially authoritative stories of growth take the model up, structuring its temporal logic and suturing it to a drive for totalizing accumulation. In the concluding section, I shift focus to the 'unscalable' interpersonal work that Startup School describes as key to startups' distinctive capacity for realizing the future in the present. In so doing, I identify a recurrent cycle of what Berlant (2011) might call cruelly intimate solicitation, seduction, and betrayal as a key temporal experience of the modern internet, and show how it emerges from entrepreneurs' attempts to mediate the conflicting rhythms of technology, the market, users, and venture capital itself.

'Say it and move on'

For my interlocutors, the internet's business model has become a necessary rubric through which to understand the relationship between privacy, the internet, and technology corporations. It bears observation, therefore, that the business model concept originated only in the mid-1970s. According to scholars of corporate management, engineers and economists first deployed the term to describe the novel use of electronic spreadsheets to model the likely financial effects of business operation changes (Magretta, 2002). In the mid-1990s, when the term entered the public lexicon, it did so alongside the internet's commercialization. Circa 1995–2000, technology entrepreneurs, investors, and journalists used the term heterogeneously as a stand-in for a company's revenue model and to refer to the new transaction and pricing forms introduced by online commerce[2] (Porter, 2001). In his 2000 account of wealth creation in Silicon Valley, journalist Michael Lewis (2000, p 256) thus dismissed the business model as an obfuscatory buzzword of the dot.com bubble: 'it glorified all manner of half-baked plans. All it really meant was how you planned to make money.'

Following the 2000 dot.com crash, when the initial period of internet-related market euphoria concluded, the business model took on the more precise meaning it carries today. Management professors and consultants converged on a definition of business models as simplified, conceptual representations of a corporation's sustaining value logic (Fielt, 2013). Business models, so defined, model how corporations reproduce themselves, first creating and delivering value to users and then capturing part of it as revenue and profit.

Whatever ambiguities still surround the concept, the corporate management literature uniformly insists that business models matter. The literature specifically portrays business models as a vital domain of strategic creativity, one potentially more important than technology itself to startup success (see McGrath, 2010). So valorized, business models have become an object of intense public interest, elaboration, and formalization. Business schools and consultancies teach business model innovation. The internet is rife with advice on business model design and selection.

Given the cultural ferment surrounding them, business models are notably absent from Silicon Valley's quasi-archival materials[3] and reflexive mythology. That is, when one observes entrepreneurs and investors discussing startups, or reviews examples of startup business models, there is little to suggest that they wield the influence over corporate behaviour that some attribute to them.

Consider as illustration the stories told in Startup School about achieving startup success. Across 20 lectures, Startup School dedicated sessions to topics including product development, hiring, company culture, strategy, and management. Business models, however, merited neither their own class nor recognition in Sam Altman's list of the key contributors to startup success ('a great idea, a great product, a great team, and great execution'). Indeed, business models received sustained consideration only twice. In the twelfth lecture, for example, Aaron Levie, co-founder of Box, a file management company, discussed business models as a means of managing technological revolution. Aligning with the corporate management literature, Levie observed that when new enabling technologies disrupt an industry, businesses adapt by innovating not just on their products but also on their business model. Levie separately clarified, however, that startups serving consumers (rather than other businesses) really only have two options. They must either charge directly for their products or 'provide advertising' on them, that is, adopt the internet's business model.

Later, in Lecture 19, Michael Seibel, a Y Combinator partner and former entrepreneur, discussed the role of business models in fundraising. According to Seibel, to secure venture capital, entrepreneurs must always be prepared with a funding pitch no more than two minutes long. Using the simplest language possible, he specified, entrepreneurs should first explain in one sentence 'what your company does'. In a second sentence, entrepreneurs should then describe their target market's size such that investors immediately understand, 'Oh wait, if we're big, if we really blow this company up, it could be worth billions of dollars.' In sentence three, entrepreneurs address 'traction', communicating that they are 'moving fast and that this isn't some long slog'. Only subsequently, after sharing the unique market insight crystallizing 'all the reasons you guys are going to kill the competitors', should entrepreneurs answer — again in one sentence — 'How does your company make money?'.

> You know your business model. I see so many founders run away from this question because they think things like, 'If I say advertising people are going to be like, "Oh, that's stupid."' Just say it! Don't run away. If it's advertising, say advertising … This was a check mark that I just wanted to write: 'And then I am going to monetize it.' Instead I am writing a big question mark. So do the thing that everyone else in your industry does to monetize 95 per cent of the time. Say it and move on.

Seibel's commentary here confirms a role for business models in securing venture capital financing. Like Levie, however, Seibel suggests this role is largely formal. In Seibel's depiction, pitch meetings are opportunities to secure a startup's future by conjuring promissory visions of its potential (see Sunder Rajan, 2007). To achieve this effect, a pitch must induce what we could consider an epistemic and affective change in investors, an 'Aha! moment' indexing new market insight and palpable fantasies of future wealth. In Seibel's telling, however, no particular burden falls on the business model in narratively conjuring such imaginative pathways towards market control. As he elaborated in a 2016 blog post, unless a startup's product somehow reconfigures its market, founders should be 'honest with themselves' (Seibel, 2016). 'By and large', startups that haven't 'figured it out' during early fundraising are going to 'make money by growing big and turning on advertising'. Founders should just admit they will monetize with advertising 'when clearly that [is] the only answer'. From this perspective, when pitching, the question of the business model speaks less to a startup's money-making potential than to its founder's perceived competencies. Specifically, by claiming the internet's business model, founders acknowledge that the 'monetization problem' (Zuboff, 2019, pp 73–85) has already been 'figured out'. They thereby demonstrate their ability to adhere to the distinctive economy of attention and effort, which as we shall see, venture capitalists promote as a condition of entrepreneurial success.

Exponential growth

I include Seibel's lecture here to foreground the ambiguity, even the hint of disdain, that Silicon Valley gatekeepers attach to the business model concept, but also to draw out the alternative figure they valorize in its stead. Note how just as he diagnoses the internet's business model with a certain negative charisma, Seibel indexes a significant investment in an animating ideal of 'growing big'. Recall that in his introductory remarks Sam Altman similarly identified 'hyper growth' as the aspiration uniting Y Combinator-funded entrepreneurs. One might reasonably assume growth to be the goal of any capitalist enterprise, but growth as mobilized here takes a particular form that is central to Silicon Valley's self-understanding. According to Y Combinator's founder, Paul Graham, as a kind of corporation, startups are in fact distinguished not by producing technology, being newly incorporated, or relying on venture capital, but by being designed from inception for rapid growth. Under Graham's (2012) influential mantra, 'The only essential thing is growth. Everything else we associate with startups follows from growth.'

The organization of high-tech communities around this ideal is evidenced everywhere in Silicon Valley. As Michael Seibel explained, for example, demonstrating growth's emergence ('traction') is necessary to attract initial venture capital interest. It's on growth's basis that investors ultimately bestow stratospheric valuations on businesses with no revenue history (Graham, 2012; Beckert, 2016). Meanwhile, under headlines about the next startup 'unicorn', business and technology journalists feverishly track who has growth and who'll have it next (see, for example, Feldman, 2023).

The growth ideal thus valorized in Y Combinator's orbit is characterized by totalizing ambition. At a 2017 conference for female entrepreneurs, Y Combinator partner Jessica Livingston (2017) observed that one day you start a site for college students, 'and pretty soon you realize you could expand to sign up the whole world if you wanted to'. If Livingston thus posited planetary reach as a possible startup outcome, Sam Altman embraced it as an explicit goal. While most successful startups initially focus on a small market, he lectured, a startup's core idea should be one that can expand in ambition and eventually create 'a path to world domination'. An entrepreneur should be able to say regarding her initial idea, 'Today only this small subset of users are going to use my product, but I'm going to get all of them. And in the future almost everyone is going to use my product.'

The totalizing ambition of growth extends to the dimension of time. As suggested, Y Combinator's partners predicate success not just on growth, but growth that is specifically hyper, rapid, even 'exponential'. Growth in such formulations is sublime, occurring at speeds, which *pace* Altman (2014), exceed human experience and comprehension. As Silicon Valley's critics rightly note, exponential growth thus also necessarily exceeds the regulatory grasp of human institutions (see Zuboff, 2019). But as depicted in Startup School, pursuit of the exponential is keyed not to the temporality of governance, but rather to the temporalities of technology and the market. On the one hand, startups must grow exponentially so entrepreneurs can stay abreast of the 'leading edge' of their technological field.[4] On the other hand, good startup ideas often turn on insights into future market growth. Only through exponential growth can startups keep pace with their target markets as they expand, thereby crowding out potential competitors. In both instances, implicit in the ideal of exponential growth is an understanding of time as a destructive, external obstacle that must be overcome to accumulate and realize value (see Bear, 2014).[5] Reformulated in the conceptual language of this volume, we might say that exponential growth is animated by a belief that only by drawing the distinct rhythms of startup development, technological progress, market competition, and government regulation into certain difficult-to-achieve configurations can entrepreneurs avoid the arrhythmic collapse that awaits the majority of internet startups.

By now, the tendency of high-tech markets to discount present revenue in favour of speculative future profit is widely recognized (Fortun, 2001; Sunder Rajan, 2007; Beckert, 2016, pp 135–53). Observe, however, that Startup School's growth stories systemically orient entrepreneurs towards the future in multiple ways. Such discounting of the present is evident, for example, in the explanation offered for why Silicon Valley's best product ideas often initially appear 'trivial' or 'pointless' (Altman, 2014). According to Altman, given startups' globalized competitive environment, when entrepreneurs identify a potential product that 'sound[s] really good', that is, addresses an obvious need, they should assume 'Google or Facebook will do it'. The supposed strangeness of Silicon Valley's best ideas thus only appears as such when evaluated according to *present* consumer sensibilities. But, as indicated, the most promising startup ideas are understood to be those that address not today's markets, but markets as they will evolve in the future.

Future bias is further evident in the recommendation that entrepreneurs aspire to 'liv[e] in the future'. In his lecture on 'How to Have Ideas', for example, Paul Graham cautioned that intentionally trying to identify startup ideas at best produces ideas 'that are not only bad, but bad and plausible sounding'. Instead, he advised, entrepreneurs need to turn themselves into the kind of person that has startup ideas 'unconsciously'. Specifically, entrepreneurs should treat startups as an 'ulterior motive to curiosity' by developing domain expertise in some technological field and working on personally compelling problems. Thus figured, entrepreneurship involves the kind of ethical self-formation through the labour of creativity that Boellstorff (2008) calls creationist capitalism. 'If you think of technology', Graham said, 'as something that's spreading like a sort of fractal strain, every point on the edge represents an interesting problem.' To approach technology's leading edge is thus to outmanoeuvre the normal flow of time, effectively 'ratchet[ing]' oneself into the future where 'ideas that seem uncommonly prescient to others will seem obvious to you'.

In his work on the Indian and US biotech industries, Kaushik Sunder Rajan (2007) observes that an atmosphere of theological mystique permeates speculative capital. A hint of this mystique can be gleaned in Startup School's framing of entrepreneurship as a calling. In his lecture on 'Why to Start a Startup', Facebook co-founder Dustin Moskovitz thus described entrepreneurism as a kind of possession. The 'best reason' to start a startup, he argued, is 'basically you can't not do it'. The world needs it done 'and you're the right person to do it'.

Even so, Altman and his colleagues warn that initial startup ideas generally do not address the kind of mass future need required by growth. In Y Combinator's regular startup 'bootcamps', they explained, they thus require participants to draw themselves ever closer to such elusive ideas by using growth itself as a technique. Y Combinator's partners may tell entrepreneurs that revenue is the best metric to use in measuring growth. They recognize, however, that to attract a critical mass of initial users, and as a historical legacy of the form's 'new economy' origins (see Slater, 2000), most internet startups do not charge for products in their early life cycle. Y Combinator thus allows startups to measure growth on the basis of monthly users, or any other 'reasonable proxy' for the revenue they will generate 'whenever [they do] start trying to make money' (Graham, 2012). Startups 'live on growth,' according to Altman, not because growth (in revenue) directly funds startup development, but in the sense that growth is the best 'indicator of a great product'.[6] As Graham elaborated in his 2012 blog, if a startup's initial idea is 'fairly good', it is often 'adjacent' to even better ideas. By 'optimizing for growth,' entrepreneurs can explore this extended ideational space, following 'the imagination of growth' to 'discover' startup ideas. Constantly modifying a startup's idea 'as necessary to keep hitting, say, 10% weekly growth', Graham wrote, will produce 'a quite different company than you meant to start. But anything that grows consistently at 10% a week is almost certainly a better idea than you started with'.

In its pragmatic form, growth operates as a divinatory key to the future, imposing an economy of attention and effort on entrepreneurs. As one might expect, this encompasses the new economy demand that entrepreneurs pursue goals on a passionate, 24/7 basis (see Thrift, 2001). But it also conditions the acceptable objects of entrepreneurial devotion during the different stages of startup development. In Startup School, Altman repeatedly addressed the optimal allocation of entrepreneurial time. Young entrepreneurs, he chided, frequently make the mistake of 'imitating all the outward forms of starting a startup'. They will 'rent a nice office in SoMa [South of Market]', network at conferences, and argue on social media. Meanwhile, they neglect 'the one thing that is actually essential, which is to make something people want'. Y Combinator thus instructs founders 'to work on their product, talk to users, exercise, eat and sleep, and very little else'.

'Investor storytime'

Thus far I have shown that privacy engineers recently converged on a novel explanation for privacy's decline, which centres on the business model, a potent new cultural figure attributed exceptional, if semi-naturalized, charismatic and causal powers. I then showed, however, that when tech entrepreneurs and investors discuss their vocation, business models largely recede from view. Instead, something of the devotional aura elsewhere attributed to the internet's business model (and business models generally) touches down on exponential growth. As just demonstrated, in its operation as ethics, episteme, and techne (Bear, 2016; 2020), growth conditions entrepreneurial being-in and orientation towards time. Through the stories of growth told by institutional authorities in symbolically potent settings like Startup School and Y Combinator bootcamps, entrepreneurs become attuned to the future as the seat of economic and social value. Under venture capitalists' tutelage in speculation, they train themselves to imaginatively access and realize the future by identifying and 'riding' technological and market 'waves', while deferring all tasks perceived to implicate the mere trappings of the startup form.

As should be clear, investors like Altman include the questions of a startup's business model, and of revenue in general, among such properly deferred distractions. Entrepreneurs who demonstrate revenue too soon risk being dismissed for wasting effort properly spent gobbling up market share. Through its role in organizing entrepreneurs' action in time, growth thus projects a temporal logic on startups. By authorizing, and indeed demanding, deferral of revenue until after a great product has been discovered, growth determines when in a startup's lifecycle the internet's business model becomes salient as an internal institutional concern, and when entrepreneurs must initiate the changes to a startup's systems, processes, and modes of user engagement required to 'turn the model on'. Conversely, the model's amenability to growth's temporal dictates, the perceived ease with which it can be institutionally, legally, and materially appended to a startup according to growth's time-reckoning (Munn, 1992), grounds its persistence as the internet's default. The model's temporal alignment to growth is thus as fundamental to its sociological presence and operation, as is the logic by which it extracts surplus value by surveilling human behaviour.

In this section, I pursue this analysis further, demonstrating that growth laminates onto the internet's business model the totalizing drive, which compels startups' continuous intensification of user surveillance. To this end, I propose we analyse Startup School's stories of growth as defining the contours of a sociotechnical imaginary, a 'collectively held, institutionally stabilized, and publicly performed vision … of desirable futures' (Jasanoff, 2015). Conceptually, sociotechnical imaginaries supplement the national imaginaries theorized by Charles Taylor and others by foregrounding the central roles of science and technology in enabling and sustaining idealized forms of social life. Under the sociotechnical imaginary rehearsed in Startup School, the future is, at once, a storehouse of deferred-yet-realizable value, a perpetually receding horizon of new consumer needs, and, per Graham, a resource to be imaginatively probed for insight into needs' fulfilment. Technology here enables new practical solutions to existing problems. As Aaron Levie described in Lecture 12, though, it also continually emerges from opportunistic entrepreneurial attempts to fill the gaps that technological disruptions open between 'between how things are done and how they can be done'. Startups figure as the 'way of the future,' per Altman, not just because of their proliferation circa 2014, but in the sense of being themselves a technology for actualizing the future in the present. If startups are indeed the optimal social technology for this purpose, it is because venture capital grants them temporal dispensation to cultivate the passionate user love from which mass markets are understood to emerge.

Analysing Startup School's stories of growth as constitutive performances of a sociotechnical imaginary addresses a gap in technologists' theory of the internet's business model. It suggests that for the prospect of a business practice predicated on surveilling users to exert, per Zuboff, a palpable magnetism over technology entrepreneurs, imaginative work must enmesh it in a situated vision of the collective good (see Jasanoff, 2015, pp 5–8). To access the ethical vision implicated here, let us shift focus from the stories of self-identified Silicon Valley insiders to those of its insider critics. Consider first David Heinemeier Hansson, a Danish programmer and entrepreneur who co-founded the project management company, Basecamp. Hansson is one of a handful of programmer-entrepreneurs to develop a sustained public critique of Silicon Valley's idealization of exponential growth. In a blog post from 2017, he hypothesized that Silicon Valley's valorization of the future over the present justifies the recurrent social 'absolution' granted to internet corporations for their social harms. So long as they continue to demonstrate growth, he wrote, everything they do – every existing form of time-fullness they 'disrupt' – is *ipso facto* right: 'Mistakes may have been made, but tomorrow is an entirely new day, divorced from any of the days that went before it.'

In tidy recursive logic, Hansson traces growth's normative force to venture capital's own business model. Because most startups fail (Beckert, 2016, pp 132–3), this logic holds, venture capital investment funds only produce windfall returns if they include at least one blockbuster success (Graham, 2012; see Zuboff, 2019, p 73). To ensure this outcome, venture capitalists pressure all entrepreneurs to single-mindedly pursue growth regardless of its toll on self-respect, solidarity, or any other civic reason for collective enterprise.[7] Thus described, the felt necessity to pursue growth participates in an ethos of high-stakes gambling, but follows from the 'temporalizing' practices (Munn, 1992), which venture capitalists deploy to symbolically ground the institutionally recognized markers of startup success in the rhythms of venture capital's circulation.

If such temporalization acts as a disciplinary stick, Hansson suggests, it is accompanied by a moral carrot. In his 2017 blog, Hansson documented his decision to reject growth's path. He reports that when he decided to pursue mere profitability rather than growth and trimmed his startup's product portfolio, he was met with 'incredulity, or even anger'. Silicon Valley peers told him that if the eliminated businesses had financial promise, he was 'crazy to turn down growth'. Hansson interprets this response as reflecting the perception that entrepreneurs who refuse growth fail in a moral obligation to the startup community itself, or more precisely, to its collective affective and financial investment in 'all potential, all the time'. More generously, we might observe, the pragmatic use of growth taught in Startup School carries its own positive moral charge. Used as a proxy for a product's ability to fulfil consumer needs, growth appears to entrepreneurs and investors as a good in-itself. Nonetheless, by mobilizing the intellectual tradition, which represents corporate growth as coextensive with human progress (Buck-Morss, 1995; Fourcade and Healy, 2007), growth forecloses scrutiny of the substantive social interests it ultimately serves. It displaces the speculative intensity, or winner-takes-all ethos, of venture capital with the spectacle of growth itself.

Through the ways they frame the future and link it to the past, sociotechnical imaginaries enable certain ways of thinking about possible worlds while restricting others (Jasanoff, 2015). Consider Maciej Ceglowski, founder of a popular digital archiving service. In a series of presentations at web development conferences since 2013, Ceglowski shared his own experience turning down growth, and established himself as one of Silicon Valley's most prominent critics of the internet's business model. In a 2014 keynote, Ceglowski took aim at the continual failure of this business model to deliver on its own limited promise. By 2014, Ceglowski estimated, the major internet companies had accumulated roughly a decade's worth of data on his browsing, search, and email habits. And yet the ads 'purchased with all this surveillance' remained 'shocking[ly] useless'. Websites continued to regularly target Ceglowski with ads for products that he already owned, or that were obviously intended for women, not men. Pointing to the constant proliferation of increasingly intrusive ad forms, Ceglowski rejected the industry claim that internet users in fact love targeted advertising. Each new historical ad form, he observed, from the banner ad, to pop-ups, and auto-playing videos, 'turn[s] out to be like poison ivy'. People 'click them once' and learn never to touch them again. Maintaining advertising's future promise thus forces it to constantly mutate, 'like the flu'.

In identifying this viral mutation, Ceglowski foregrounds the tension that exists between speculation's infinite promises and the always-inadequate capabilities of present material conditions (see Sunder Rajan, 2007, p 126). Ceglowski insists, however, that this tension, as manifested in targeted advertising's ongoing 'crappiness', does not undermine but rather sustains the internet's business model. Advertising, he explained, involves paying someone to convince a product's users that 'they'll be happy' if they buy it. What sustains startups, though, is not advertising, but a promissory form Ceglowski calls 'investor storytime'. In investor storytime, investors pay entrepreneurs to convince them how rich they will be when their startups finally start selling ads. It works by convincing investors 'that advertising in the future is going to be lucrative in ways it just isn't today'. Under its logic, any failure of advertising is simply grist for more convincing stories: 'It means there's vast room for improvement. So many stories to tell the investors.' To paraphrase Ceglowski: consumers may hate ads now but wait until we have more data to improve our targeting. When targeting does work, just imagine how much more valuable our ads would be if we could only secure more granular data. Silicon Valley chases personal data, from this perspective, 'Not because it's effective now, but because we need it to tell better stories'.

With his depiction of investor storytime, Ceglowski (2014) suggests that the relentlessly intensifying surveillance characteristic of Silicon Valley's internet companies follows not from the internet's business model so much as from how stories of growth take the model up, wedding it to a temporal logic, which renders the speculative promise at its core effectively irrefutable. Investor storytime, in this respect, bears productive comparison to the 'nearly perfect paranoid system' (Masco, 2014, p 20) under which US counterterror experts conjure endless images of existential future danger to justify ever-expanding security capacities.

Doing 'things that don't scale'

In 1998, while still PhD students, Google founders Sergey Brin and Larry Page published 'The Anatomy of a Large-Scale Hypertextual Web Search Engine', an ur-document of Silicon Valley. Anticipating both the web's rapid growth and the technical and institutional challenges this would entail, Brin and Page carefully described the features and applications of what would become Google search. In an appendix notable for its shift in topic and polemical tone, Brin and Page warned that the goals of advertising are irreconcilable with those of providing high-quality search results. They concluded, in a historical irony, that to prevent advertising from introducing inevitable bias into search results, search engines must never become subsumed into the corporate form.

During Startup School, when Y Combinator's lecturers addressed the internet's business model, they treated it as a *fait accompli*. For a professional class trained to build things they perceive to be missing from the world, this sense of inevitability likely contributes to the model's muted Silicon Valley presence. When Michael Seibel discussed business models, however, he suggested that something about the internet's business model specifically embarrasses entrepreneurs, causing them to dissemble and 'run away'. Indeed, many Silicon Valley programmer-entrepreneurs in addition to Brin and Page have historically opposed advertising as inherently hostile to the user experience and thus antithetical to engineering ideals. The list of startups founded by entrepreneurs explicitly opposed to surveillance-based advertising extends beyond Google to companies like Tumblr, WhatsApp, and Instagram. WhatsApp founder Jan Koum, who attributes his support for privacy to his childhood under Soviet surveillance, reportedly kept a handwritten note taped to his desk reading, 'No Ads! No Games! No Gimmicks!'. Nonetheless, under pressure from their new corporate owners, by 2018, each of these companies had implemented the internet's business model, suddenly turning on surveillance-driven revenue and betraying their founding commitments.

In this concluding section, I mobilize growth's imaginary once more to draw out a characteristic subjective experience of the modern commercial internet, and show how it emerges from venture capitalists' temporalizing practices (see Bear, 2014, p 15). We have already seen how in training entrepreneurs to achieve exponential growth, venture capitalists engage in various forms of time-work (see also Kusk, Chapter 4, this volume), attuning entrepreneurs to the sometimes contradictory rhythms of technology, consumer markets, and venture capital itself. Here, by foregrounding investors' insistence that to build great products entrepreneurs must forge deeply attentive, mutually sympathetic relationships with initial users, I identify a further entanglement in this mix.

Despite Silicon Valley's popular association with efficiency and rationalization, when Startup School's lecturers described how to build a great product, they frequently used language closer to that of courtship than engineering. In the first class, for example, when Sam Altman stressed that entrepreneurs must devote their time to building a great product, he specified that it is better to start with a product a small number of people love than one that inspires moderate enthusiasm from a larger audience. As Startup School progressed, Altman and his guests insisted that to 'make [users] love what you're doing' entrepreneurs must, per Y Combinator's famous mantra, 'do things that don't scale'.

In Silicon Valley, 'scaling' refers to the process of building out a startup's institutional and technical capabilities as its users rapidly explode in number. Scaling involves a dual movement of material and institutional expansion – hiring technical, support, and managerial staff; securing more server capacity – followed by efficiency-achieving rationalization and automation. By contrast, doing things that don't scale means doing things 'by hand', person-to-person. When an entrepreneur stands on Palo Alto's streets, flagging down and convincing individual passers-by to download and try her new app, she is doing something that does not scale. Similarly, when an entrepreneur manually performs a service, which her new product purports to provide through yet-to-be-developed software, she is doing something that does not scale.

Doing things that don't scale may sound simply like doing business, but Silicon Valley abhors perceived inefficiencies as 'unscalable' blockages between entrepreneurs and the market. Individually persuading strangers may be a highly effective means of recruiting users, but one too time-consuming and labour-intensive to sustain exponential growth. Manually setting up webpages may cultivate customer trust, but is no way to tap the mass market demanded by growth's imagination.

Nonetheless, in a lecture on product development, Kevin Hale, a Y Combinator partner, attributed his first startup's success to building a product 'that people wanted to have a relationship with'. Based on this experience, Hale recommended approaching each moment of potential user–product interaction as an opportunity to 'seduce'. It is important to observe that such seduction, and the non-scalable activities it exemplifies, are exercises in presence and patience, in attempting to enter into a 'mutuality of being' with initial users – a shared intersubjectivity under which what users experience also happens to the entrepreneur – reminiscent of Sahlins' (2013, p 2) definition of kinship. As Hale and his colleagues argued, to cultivate love, entrepreneurs must – for a limited time, but as long as possible – personally seek out initial users and get extremely close to them. Ideally, entrepreneurs should work in users' offices or homes. Barring such access, they should talk to users constantly, send countless emails, and give highly personalized product help. To ensure entrepreneurs remain 'directly exposed to users … and interacting with them in somewhat real time', Hale recommended taking personal responsibility for customer support. As he described it, routing customer calls directly to those building a technology aligns their respective temporal rhythms, forcing entrepreneurs to experience and react to customers' pain as their own. Such vigilant, labour-intensive care – care in the mode of Big Mother, as the editors of this volume might put it – enables entrepreneurs to test the worldly hypothesis represented by their startup idea against the product roadmap in users' minds, thereby refining their product into something a small number of users passionately love.

In doing things that don't scale, entrepreneurs seek to 'cultivate love' by showing a love above-and-beyond that generally thought possible from a corporation. In so doing, entrepreneurs enact startups as the kind of social actor capable of sympathetic fellow feeling, of exhibiting the moral concern and self-restraint otherwise attributed only to individual persons. As Graham acknowledges, this performative cultivation of love works primarily by implicit contrast to the dismal, opaque interactions that characterize the customer service of most 'mature' American companies. According to Graham (2013), Y Combinator has to teach entrepreneurs the importance of engaging on such intimate terms because, 'They've never experienced such attention themselves'. Their understanding of customer service is informed by the anonymous, bureaucratized misery that cable companies, airlines, and insurance companies, for example, routinely inflict on consumers. Against this backdrop, a startup's ability to speak to users through an entrepreneur's human voice carries a kind of magic, which Graham insists confers competitive advantage.

It is in the context of the intimate, temporally attuned relationships which entrepreneurs cultivate in pursuit of growth that the internet's business model ultimately intervenes. For startups that grow, the period of intimate courtship inevitably gives way to the imperatives of scale. As sincere as some entrepreneurs' disinterest in revenue may be, if they avail themselves of venture capital financing to amplify their technology's impact on the world, investors will inevitably demand they 'turn on' the revenue streams specified in their business model. That the potential represented by a rapidly growing user base, accrued under venture capital's auspices, must inevitably be realized is an open secret of Silicon Valley, one obscured and disavowed by the mythological foregrounding of entrepreneurial curiosity and drive.

The rationalization and automation of person-to-person relations that follow when internet startups scale their operations, and turn on their business model, of course cannot fully purge user–corporate relations of intimacy. Forms of intimacy no doubt persist in the care and concern users exhibit towards internet services, and are powerfully present in the loyalties mediated by internet brands (Foster, 2007; Nakassis, 2013). The open secret of revenue, however, reveals the form of intimacy established by doing things that do not scale to be a cruel one. It is cruel in the sense that it enacts an optimistic vision of the world (Berlant, 2011), in which corporations treat customers as ends in themselves, but it does so under structural conditions which corporate actors know can never persist. It is cruel when cultivated in specific service to the internet's business model because unscalable interactions bind users to a speculative system, which in the course of normal operation will necessarily undermine their privacy, exposing them to targeted advertising's visceral intrusions and systematic attempts at behavioural manipulation.

Notes

[1] For decades, manufacturers suppressed public knowledge of cigarettes' role in millions of annual lung cancer-related deaths without attracting blame to 'the cigarette business model'. As illustrated by Enron's 2001 collapse and the 2015 Volkswagen emissions scandal, public opprobrium for corporate deception has more commonly centred on perceived moral and institutional pathologies, like personal greed and autocratic corporate culture.

[2] Examples include eBay's customer-to-customer auction and Priceline's reverse auction.

[3] Here I adapt for the startup context, Kelty's (2008) term for engineers' tendency to document and analyse their own roles in developing the internet.

[4] In this respect, growth derives social legitimacy and force by implicitly drawing upon the inexorable leaps in computing power that technologists attribute to Moore's Law (see Otsuki, 2016; Bear, 2020). Defined by Intel cofounder Gordon E. Moore in 1965, Moore's Law predicts, based on the regular increase in the number of transistors that can be placed on an integrated circuit, that the speed and capacity of computer CPUs will double every 18 months.

[5] Transhumanists similarly valorize the exponential for its perceived ability to transcend human finitude (Otsuki, 2016).

[6] Growth in these respects can be considered a form of techno-social manifest destiny that unfurls along material, institutional, symbolic, and economic dimensions. For startups that achieve traction, growth as measured in a core metric like monthly users – and as spectacularly staged for investors, using technologies of the imagination (Bear, 2020) like pitch decks and growth charts – necessarily stimulates growth of other kinds: in the numbers of a startup's employees, bureaucratic processes, and technological infrastructures; in its valuation; in the ambition and abstraction of its core idea; and so on.

[7] As Ho (2009) demonstrates, until the 1980s, approximately, US corporations were widely understood to be social institutions with obligations to multiple constituencies (beyond shareholders) and roots in local communities.

References

Altman, S. (2014) 'Stupid Apps and Changing the World', Sam Altman blog post, 7 August. Available from: https://blog.samaltman.com/stupid-apps-and-changing-the-world (Accessed: 25 October 2024).

Bear, L. (2014) 'Doubt, Conflict, Mediation: The Anthropology of Modern Time', *Journal of the Royal Anthropological Institute*, 20(S1): 3–30.

Bear, L. (2016) 'Time as technique', *Annual Review of Anthropology*, 45: 487–502.

Bear, L. (2020) 'Speculations on Infrastructure: From Colonial Public Works to a Post-Colonial Global Asset Class on the Indian Railways 1840–2017', *Economy and Society*, 49(1): 45–70.

Beckert, J. (2016) *Imagined Futures: Fictional Expectations and Capitalist Dynamics*. Cambridge, MA: Harvard University Press.

Berlant, L. (2011) *Cruel Optimism*. Durham, NC: Duke University Press.

Berners-Lee, T., Dertouzos, M., and Fischetti, M. (1999) *Weaving the Web: The Original Design and Ultimate Destiny of the World Wide Web By Its Inventor*. San Francisco, CA: HarperSanFrancisco.

Boellstorff, T. (2008) *Coming of Age in Second Life: An Anthropologist Explores the Virtually Human*. Princeton, NJ: Princeton University Press.

boyd, D. (2014) *It's Complicated: The Social Lives of Networked Teens*. New Haven: Yale University Press.

Brin, D. (1998) *The Transparent Society: Will Technology Force us to Choose Between Privacy and Freedom?* New York: Basic Books.

Browne, S. (2015) *Dark Matters: On the Surveillance of Blackness*. Durham, NC: Duke University Press.

Buck-Morss, S. (1995) 'Envisioning Capital: Political Economy on Display', *Critical Inquiry*, 21(2): 434–67.

Ceglowski, M. (2014) 'Web Design – The First 100 Years', Lecture presented at the HOW Interactive Design Conference, Washington, DC, September. Available from: https://idlewords.com/talks/ web_design_first_100_years. htm (Accessed: 25 February 2024).

Feldman, A. (2023) 'Next Billion Dollar Startups 2023', *Forbes*, 15 August. Available from: https://www.forbes.com/sites/amyfeldman/2023/08/15/next-billion-dollar-startups-2023/?sh=555d1c4c6c4a (Accessed: 25 February 2024).

Fielt, E. (2013) 'Conceptualising Business Models: Definitions, Frameworks and Classifications', *Journal of Business Models*, 1: 85–105.

Fortun, M. (2001) 'Mediated Speculations in the Genomics Futures Market', *New Genetics and Society*, 20(2): 139–56.

Foster, R. (2007) 'The Work of the New Economy: Consumers, Brands, and Value Creation', *Cultural Anthropology*, 22(4): 707–31.

Fourcade, M. and Healy, K. (2007) 'Moral Views of Market Society', *Annual Review of Sociology*, 33(1): 285–311.

Graham, P. (2012) 'Startup = Growth', PaulGraham.Com, September. Available from: https://paulgraham.com/growth.html (Accessed: 25 February 2024).

Graham, P. (2013) 'Do Things That Don't Scale', PaulGraham.Com, July. Available from: https://paulgraham.com/ds.html (Accessed: 25 February 2024).

Heinemeier Hansson, D. (2017) 'Exponential Growth Devours and Corrupts', Signal v. Noise (blog). 27 February. Available from: https://signalvno ise.com/svn3/exponential-growth-devours-and-corrupts/ (Accessed: 25 February 2024).

Ho, K. (2009) *Liquidated: An Ethnography of Wall Street*. Durham, NC: Duke University Press.

Jasanoff, S. (2015) 'Future Imperfect: Science, Technology and the Imagination of Modernity', in S. Jasanoff and S-H Kim (eds) *Dreamscapes of Modernity: Sociotechnical Imaginaries and the Fabrication of Power*. Chicago, IL: University of Chicago Press, pp 1–33.

Kelty, C. (2008) *Two Bits: The Cultural Significance of Free Software*. Durham, NC: Duke University Press.

Lewis, M. (2000) *The New New Thing: A Silicon Valley Story*. New York: WW Norton.

Livingston, J. (2017) 'What's Different about "Unicorns"', Lecture presented to Female Founders Conference 2017, San Francisco, CA. Available from: https://www.youtube.com/watch?v=Ygr3rx4hSsc (Accessed: 25 February 2024).

Magretta, J. (2002) 'Why Business Models Matter', *Harvard Business Review*, 80: 86–92.

Masco, J. (2014) *The Theater of Operations: National Security Affect from the Cold War to the War on Terror*. Durham, NC: Duke University Press.

Masco, J. (2017) '"Boundless Informant": Insecurity in the Age of ubiquitous Surveillance', *Anthropological Theory*, 17(3): 382–403.

McGrath, R. (2010) 'Business Models: A Discovery Driven Approach', *Long Range Planning*, 43(2–3): 247–61.

Munn, N. (1992) 'The Cultural Anthropology of Time: A Critical Essay', *Annual Review of Anthropology*, 21: 93–123.

Nakassis, C. (2013) 'Brands and Their Surfeits', *Cultural Anthropology*, 28(1): 111–26.

Nelson, D. (2002) *Pursuing Privacy in Cold War America*. New York: Columbia University Press.

Nissenbaum, H. (2010) *Privacy in Context: Technology, Policy, and the Integrity of Social Life*. Stanford, CA: Stanford Law Books.

Otsuki, G. (2016) 'Hope Springs Exponential: The Figure of the Exponential in North America', *Rekishi Jinrui (History and Anthropology)*, 45: 23–42.

Porter, M. (2001) 'Strategy and the Internet', *Harvard Business Review*, 79: 62–78.

Sahlins, M. (2013) *What Kinship Is – And Is Not.* Chicago, IL: University of Chicago Press.

Schneier, B. (2013) 'Surveillance as a Business Model', *Schneier on Security*, 25 November. Available from: https://www.schneier.com/blog/archives/2013/11/surveillance_as_1.html (Accessed: 25 February 2024).

Seibel, M. (2016) 'How to Pitch Your Company: Fundraising', *YC Startup Library*. Available from: https://www.ycombinator.com/library/4b-how-to-pitch-your-company (Accessed: 25 February 2024).

Slater, D. (2000) 'Consumption Without Scarcity: Exchange and Normativity in an Internet Setting', in P. Jackson, M. Lowe, D. Miller, and F. Mort (eds) *Commercial Cultures: Economies, Practices, Places.* Oxford: Berg, pp 132–42.

Smith, M.R. (1994) 'Technological Determinism in American Culture', in M.R. Smith and L. Marx (eds) *Does Technology Drive History? The Dilemma of Technological Determinism.* Cambridge, MA: MIT Press.

Sunder Rajan, K. (2007) *Biocapital: The Constitution of Postgenomic Life.* Durham, NC: Duke University Press.

Thrift, N. (2001) '"It's the Romance, Not the Finance, That Makes the Business Worth Pursuing": Disclosing a New Market Culture', *Economy and Society*, 30(4): 412–32.

Warren, S. and Brandeis, L. (1890) 'The Right to Privacy', *Harvard Law Review*, 4(5): 193–220.

Zuboff, S. (2019) *The Age of Surveillance Capitalism: The Fight for a Human Future at the New Frontier of Power.* New York: PublicAffairs.

Zuckerman, E. (2014) 'The Internet's Original Sin', *The Atlantic*, 14 August. Available from: https://www.theatlantic.com/technology/archive/2014/08/advertising-is-the-internets-original-sin/376041/ (Accessed: 25 February 2024).

Afterword: Watching, Waiting, Speculating

Sun-ha Hong

Time has long been a reliable accomplice for technological control. In much of the Global North, human beings are deemed productive, and unproductive, in a discrete and atomizing matrix of labour time that is a relatively recent historical invention (Gregg, 2018). Diverse computational media – productivity dashboards, sleep trackers, border security algorithms for 'suspicious travellers' – shape temporality not merely as data but as moralizing demands (Thompson, 1967): to be punctual like a program, consistent like a perpetual motion machine, long-lasting like a battery. When modern statistical methods began to tether human beings to statistical models, from Adolphe Quetelet's *l'homme moyen* [the average man] (Desrosieres, 1998) to the rise of actuarial paradigms (Harcourt, 2007), this also provoked broader efforts to rationalize human behaviour and social phenomena into more calculable notions, from destiny to risk, luck to probability (Lears, 2003). The shape of technological time corresponds to the shapes into which human bodies are bent and broken, a process we call *efficient* – emblematized not only by the disciplinary factory (Foucault, 1995), but the transatlantic slave ship (Browne, 2015).

These logics divide human beings into unequal categories, those logics themselves being unevenly distributed across space and time. Technology does not temporalize global populations in a unified shift. Instead, it is instrumentalized for existing interests and power struggles. Yet such variation is exactly why critique must identify connections and resonances between these diverse contexts. Technologies of monitoring and judgement are often iterated on historically vulnerable groups before being rolled out into the wider public (Eubanks, 2018). The poor are often compelled to datafy themselves, using the same kind of machines that the more affluent accept voluntarily as luxury items (Gilliard and Golumbia, 2021). A focus on the everyday experience of surveillance and data – for Nepali migrant delivery workers in Malta (Kusk, Chapter 4, this volume), or for care workers and their elderly patients (Meyer et al, Chapter 3, this volume) – reminds us that we must intersect critical analysis of how especially marginalized groups encounter 'AI' or 'algorithms' not as tools or design features, but as a restaging of existing social inequities and violence (Singh and Guzmán, 2022).

This efficiency does not manifest in the perfect synchronicity fantasized by tech utopias or dystopias, but in recursions and repetitions, delays and buffers, where the technical trips over the thick of the social. Just-in-time supply chains enact volatile rashes of waiting and rushing, hiring and firing, everywhere from manufactories to app delivery drivers (Kusk, Chapter 4, this volume). The business of selling crime data has incentivized decades of real-time security theatre, infecting the public with pervasive states of alarm and anxiety (McAlpine-Riddell, Chapter 5, this volume). The datafication of time does not result in more accurate behavioural predictions or an accelerated pace of labour, but cultivates subjects towards particular *rhythms* of clicking, reading, checking, responding (see Berry, 2011). Such cultivation is rarely as smooth as promised, even when the technology is 'successfully' rolled out across whole nations and industries. American truck drivers struggle, not only to meet the brutal pace of work enforced by new electronic monitoring technologies, but in daily efforts to overturn, sabotage, or bypass the myriad ways in these systems fail at their most basic functions (Levy, 2022). Pakistani national identification projects try to render Pakistan's citizens more legible, by standardizing away the deep historical complexities of citizenship and national identity in the region, thus producing new incidents of misrecognition and injustice (Hashimi, 2022). Gig workers and other precarious labourers around the world, are collectively organizing ways to reverse-engineer, deceive, and sabotage the software and its temporal logics imposed on them (cf. Iazzolino, 2023; Williams, 2023). It is precisely because these technologies are so fallible, that they are often accompanied by moralizing rhetoric that exhorts the measured to build affective attachments with the conditions of their measurement – to praise the hypnotic regularity of the factory robot, or to take pride and joy in the shape of self-tracked exercise data visualization (Bruun, Chapter 1, this volume).

To move and live to rhythm is therefore to take it on as *habit* – that puzzling passageway between choice and compulsion, discrete action and background condition. Habit, in the Deleuzian tradition, is socially 'contracted', but operated through the body (Bennett et al, 2013, p 8), which is crucial for hosting the repetition of action into habitual form (Lefebvre, 2004). In other words, it is an interface for configuring patterns of, say, alertness or attention over the longer term. Rhythm, as Vita Peacock (Introduction, this volume) observes through Lefebvre's rhythmanalysis, intersects space and time. It binds people to modes of being and living precisely by targeting the ambiguity between affect and cognition – which scholars of biometrics and biohacking technologies have explored in terms of 'somatic surveillance' (see Berson, 2015; Hayles, 2017). In many of the monitoring technologies discussed in this volume, new practices of vigilance and surveillance take effect, not so much through singular moments of decision (which might perhaps be more easily noticed, theorized, negotiated), but through a creeping habituation of trivial or provisional arrangements into semi-permanent dispositions.

A rhythmic view of data and technology affords a certain elasticity in the relationship between humans and machines: spaces where intensified real-time monitoring is subject to some degree of user control, and integrated into human relations of care and cohabitation. Parental monitoring of children's movement data does not always lead to obsessive tracking, but new ways of coordinating timescapes between family members (Dungey, Chapter 2, this volume). Movement detection systems track people with dementia via live image feeds, reconfiguring expectations of a 'timely response' to falls and other incidents (Meyer et al, Chapter 3, this volume). The accepted/acceptable window of timely response or real-time feedback becomes a threshold for moral and legal responsibility (Stoiber, Chapter 6, this volume).

Yet, more often than not, this elasticity is obfuscated and disavowed through a broader, more mythological scale of technological time: a self-serving fiction of progress and prediction. Here, time moves as an arrow of teleology, in which newer machines supersede inferior ones (including those of flesh), and each and every social domain is progressively quantified into more rational forms of governance. Bodies are destined to be monitored and recorded with ever greater accuracy and frequency, while more distant and detailed future events become increasingly predictable through data – pulling and compressing distant futures into a present made to buzz with anticipatory zeal.

The mechanisms of justification and belief enabling this vision are, however, highly speculative and recursive. From policing and counter-terrorism to workplace surveillance, and from labour productivity metrics to self-tracking practices, systems of datafication regularly depend on the undertheorized hope that we can quantify future events and outcomes (see Molotch, 2012; Hong and Szpunar, 2019; Amoore, 2020) or, at least, that we will have such capabilities in the 'proximate future' just around the corner (Bowker, 2006; Dourish and Bell, 2011). Since its nineteenth-century reconceptualization as a broader force of historical progress, rather than craftwork or individual machinery (Marx, 2010), technology has increasingly loaned credibility and plausibility from speculative futures to justify investments and (mal) functionalities in the present.

Indeed, Silicon Valley's well known petri dish of startups, incubators, and seed rounds essentially functions as artisanal workshops for producing such futures, and hosting ritualized confidence games (Shapin, 2008; Kampmann, 2024), through which those futures may be valued and sold

(Polan, Chapter 10, this volume). Such startups then pitch narratives of fear and anxiety to clients like police departments or schools, arguing that they will be left behind by the inevitable advancement of technology – and that they must commit to ever more complex data collection infrastructures to keep up with the future terrorist, school shooter, or deviant (see, for example, Amoore, 2020). Yet many such systems run on fundamentally unproven conjectures: that facial features can be used to predict crime, or that young students' social media input can foretell depression (see Agüera y Arcas, et al, 2017; Stark and Hutson, 2022). Whole industries bloom within this temporality, in which action is always pre-emptive, proof is always deferred, and uncertainty is never quite dispelled.

The continued social dominance of teleological technofutures functions as what religious studies calls *cosmograms*: a tapestry of loose, backgrounded beliefs and attitudes beneath the wax and wane of individual heroes and stories (Hong, 2022). Even as Big Tech struggles to present new technological innovations, and entrepreneurs who talk big and wear turtlenecks are jailed for fraud, a broader sentiment endures that technology is ever condemned to 'progress', which we too are condemned to chase in its wake. Today, the renewed fantasies around artificial intelligence as a skeleton key to all social problems refreshes these narratives, for another temporary period of felt novelty. Luke Stark (2023) has shown how current-generation machine-learning applications are essentially bound to highly *conjectural* forms of reasoning – abductive, undertheorized, 'good-enough' connections between seemingly superficial indicators to build inferences. In many cases, the result is not truly radically new forms of knowledge, but an amnesiac resuscitation of never truly buried skeletons in the closet of the sciences – the eugenics of Francis Galton, the phrenology of Cesare Lombroso. The time of scientific or epistemic progress, in other words, is not secured by techno-optimist teleologies, but rather is subject to recursive loops of amnesia and relapse. We might recall Derrida's point that the archive conserves a past, but only by placing it in a future: 'If we want to know what it would have meant, we shall know only in the time to come' (1998, p x).

In this context, rhythm provides a quantifiable register for encoding bodies into legible data, even as it relies on countless human acts of anticipation, alignment, fudging, and stretching to maintain its apparent regularity. Writing about drum machines, musicianship, and automation, Jack Stilgoe (2023) writes, 'Rhythm is based on expectations. Rather than reacting to beats, we anticipate them.' Technological time takes on its oppressive quality not by eliminating human irregularity and qualitative complexity, but by overwriting those dimensions with the smooth fiction of total regularization: no blues, only the metronome.

Consider the emblematic case of the motion study, pioneered by Frank and Lilian Gilbreth in the early twentieth century – a story masterfully told in Harry Braverman's (1998) history of labour and automation. Occasional collaborators with and rivals to their more hucksterish contemporary, Frederick Taylor, the Gilbreths sought to subdivide every piece of motion in the workplace into atomic, microsecond units called 'therbligs': a fantasy of human body and movement as a discrete sum of normalizable, interchangeable fragments (Braverman, 1998, pp 120–21). The swing of the arm towards the file cabinet, the two-and-a-half steps from conveyor belt to the pulley, was to be exhaustively recorded such that the average time taken could be calculated and, inevitably, optimized. The production of average time as a unit is rarely innocent, and often coupled with a moralization of the right amount of time one *should* take; the disciplining of motion into machine-readable, algorithmically predictable beats is often ideologized as a virtue. Frederick Taylor famously insisted that his numbers for how fast steelworkers should work were a scientific measure of a 'fair day's work' – never mind that less than 10 per cent of the experienced workers at the site could reach this rate (Braverman, 1998, p 71). Today, these principles are kept alive by dutiful corporate heirs like Amazon, which is exploring algorithmic systems to rotate workers to different tasks just before incurring muscular injury (Hong, 2023). The body is bent and broken until, one way or another, a semblance of regularity at the production line is maintained.

Today, we are caught amid new forms of temporalization that seek to regulate and moralize fleshly subjects. For instance, smart devices and wearables enable new times and spaces of surveillance: Swedish prisons deploy not only movement-tracking systems, but self-care apps promising cognitive therapy towards inmates' rehabilitation into society (Kaun and Stiernstedt, 2020). Some migrants to the US are required by Immigration and Customs Enforcement (ICE) to equip SmartLINK ankle monitors; wearers report having to 'bolt out of their seats' with each sound of the alarm, sweating and scrambling to scan their face in time (Shoichet et al, 2022; Ketter and Byler, no date).

Theories abound regarding these changing configurations of technology and bodies, although it is not always clear what is the symptom and what is the principle. Jonathan Crary (2013) suggests that late capitalism entails the end of sleep, a refusal to allow any time exempt from logics of calculative optimization. Han Byung-chul (2010) put the pulse on fatigue as the manifestation of unbounded productivity, in which the body is caught in an incessant activeness. The Classical Greeks abhorred empty space in their vases, filling them with patterns, tiny human characters, and phalluses, calling it *horror vacui*. Fatigue, in this sense, is late capitalism's temporal equivalent – a drive to fill every spare moment with action and output. Technological change plays its part in these waves of retemporalization. Many of the major focal points for investment and marketing hype in the last decade have involved seeding the physical world with a glut of cheap sensors for ambient data collection (smart cities and homes), and building energy-guzzling infrastructures for massively scaled data collection and recombinatory analysis (the 'big data' revolution, now rebranded as the AI revolution).

The general effect of these efforts is not, again, to actually enact all-seeing eyes of objective and hyperrational control over bodies and time. That would require these technologies actually working as intended, and to the fullest extent of their solutionist promises, which is equivalent to forecasting a politician's historical impact based on their campaign advertisements. Rather than such smooth consistency, what we often find in these technologically retemporalized domains is greater *volatility*, lived forms of uncertainty and speculation for the affected populations. To return to earlier examples, the more granulated and 'optimized' algorithmic systems for delivery drivers become, the more difficult it becomes for the workers themselves to theorize and plan their own work and life (Chen and Ping, 2020; Shapiro, 2020). As data-driven surveillance systems move downstream, from state and enterprise clients to everyday homeowners and citizens, apps like Ring and Citizen essentially leverage their data to incite a pervasive nervousness about real-time crime (Bridges, 2021).

Such volatility – that is, irregularity of rhythm (see Lefebvre, 2004, pp 67–68) and its attendant pressures on ordinary life – demonstrates that the very effort to use data to render factories, schools, or cities more *predictable* to the manager often renders those same spaces more *unpredictable* to those who live and work in them. The subject is forced to adapt, not only by optimizing themselves to the rhythms of production quotas or automated notifications, but by constantly *speculating* about what these systems want from them. Thus, in the Amazon warehouse, the contemporary heir to Taylor's steelworks, the workers suffer not only from the punishingly high pace of work, but a pervasive and basic form of ignorance: 'You couldn't really tell, based on size, whether a box was going to be heavy or not when you went to pick it up. Your body and your mind never knew what to expect' (MacGillis, 2021, p 4). At the same microsecond scale at which the Gilbreths sought to measure and normalize worker movement, Amazon employees find that algorithmic systems are *depriving* them of this information. Rather than the gradual culmination of a hyperrational system, datafication constantly produces new temporal horizons of uncertainty and speculation, in which the citizen must toil to once again become legible to be eligible.

References

Agüera y Arcas, B., Mitchell, M., and Todorov, A. (2017) 'Physiognomy's New Clothes', Medium. Available from: https://medium.com/@blaisea/physiognomys-new-clothes-f2d4b59fdd6a (Accessed: 1 January 2018).

Amoore, L. (2020) *Cloud Ethics: Algorithms and the Attributes of Ourselves and Others*. Pittsburgh, PN: Duke University Press.

Bennett, T., Dodsworth, F., Noble, G., Poovey, M., and Watkins, M. (2013) 'Habit and Habituation: Governance and the Social', *Body & Society*, 19(2–3): 3–29.

Berry, D.M. (2011) *The Philosophy of Software: Code and Mediation in the Digital Age*. Basingstoke: Palgrave Macmillan.

Berson, J. (2015) *Computable Bodies: Instrumented Life and the Human Somatic Niche*. London: Bloomsbury Academic.

Bowker, G.C. (2006) *Memory Practices in the Sciences*. Cambridge, MA: MIT Press.

Braverman, H. (1998) *Labor and Monopoly Capital: The Degradation of Work in the Twentieth Century*. New York: Monthly Review Press.

Bridges, L. (2021) 'Infrastructural Obfuscation: Unpacking the Carceral Logics of the Ring Surveillant Assemblage', *Information, Communication & Society*, 24(6): 830–49.

Browne, S. (2015) *Dark Matters: On the Surveillance of Blackness*. Pittsburgh, PN: Duke University Press.

Chen, J.Y. and Ping, S. (2020) 'Temporal Arbitrage, Fragmented Rush, and Opportunistic Behaviors: The Labor Politics of Time in the Platform Economy', *New Media & Society*, 22(9): 1561–79.

Crary, J. (2013) *24/7: Late Capitalism and the Ends of Sleep*. London: Verso.

Derrida, J. (1998) *Archive Fever: A Freudian Impression*. Chicago, IL: University of Chicago Press.

Desrosieres, A. (1998) *The Politics of Large Numbers: A History of Statistical Reasoning*. Cambridge, MA: Harvard University Press.

Dourish, P. and Bell, G. (2011) *Divining a Digital Future: Mess and Mythology in Ubiquitous Computing*. Cambridge, MA: MIT Press.

Eubanks, V. (2018) *Automating Inequality: How High-Tech Tools Profile, Police, and Punish the Poor*. New York: St Martin's Press.

Foucault, M. (1995) *Discipline and Punish: The Birth of the Prison*. Translated by A. Sheridan. New York: Vintage Books.

Gilliard, C. and Golumbia, D. (2021) 'Luxury Surveillance', Real Life. Available from: https://reallifemag.com/luxury-surveillance/ (Accessed: 16 July 2022).

Gregg, M. (2018) *Counterproductive: Time Management in the Knowledge Economy*. Durham, NC: Duke University Press.

Han, B.-C. (2010) *Müdigkeitsgesellschaft*. Berlin: Matthes & Seitz.

Harcourt, B. (2007) *Against Prediction – Profiling, Policing, and Punishing in an Actuarial Age*. Chicago, IL: Chicago University Press.

Hashimi, Z. (2022) 'Identification and Misrecognition in an Identity Database', in R. Singh, R.L. Guzmán, and P. Davison (eds) *Parables of AI in/from the Majority World*. New York: Data & Society Research Institute, pp 101–10.

Hayles, K.N. (2017) *Unthought: The Power of the Cognitive Nonconscious*. Chicago, IL: University of Chicago Press.

Hong, S. (2022) 'Predictions Without Futures', *History and Theory*, 61(3): 371–90.

Hong, S. (2023) 'Prediction as Extraction of Discretion', *Big Data & Society*, 10(1): 1–11.

Hong, S. and Szpunar, P.M. (2019) 'The Futures of Anticipatory Reason: Contingency and Speculation in the Sting Operation', *Security Dialogue*, 50(4): 314–30.

Iazzolino, G. (2023) '"Going Karura": Colliding Subjectivities and Labour Struggle in Nairobi's Gig Economy', *Environment and Planning A: Economy and Space*, 55(5): 1114–30.

Kampmann, D. (2024) 'Venture Capital, the Fetish of Artificial Intelligence, and the Contradictions of Making Intangible Assets', *Economy and Society*, 53(1): 39–66.

Kaun, A. and Stiernstedt, F. (2020) 'Doing Time, the Smart Way? Temporalities of the Smart Prison', *New Media & Society*, 22(9): 1580–99.

Ketter, K. and Byler, D. (no date) 'Code Red: Population Sorting Technologies as Infrastructures of Feeling in the United States, China and Israel'. Working Paper.

Lears, J. (2003) *Something for Nothing: Luck in America*. New York: Viking.

Lefebvre, H. (2004) *Rhythmanalysis: Space, Time, and Everyday Life*. London: Continuum.

Levy, K. (2022) *Data Driven: Truckers, Technology, and the New Workplace Surveillance*. Princeton, NJ: Princeton University Press.

MacGillis, A. (2021) *Fulfillment: Winning and Losing in One-Click America*. New York: Farrar, Straus and Giroux.

Marx, L. (2010) 'Technology: The Emergence of a Hazardous Concept', *Technology and Culture*, 51(3): 561–77.

Molotch, H.L. (2012) *Against Security: How We Go Wrong at Airports, Subways, and Other Sites of Ambiguous Danger*. Princeton, NJ: Princeton University Press.

Shapin, S. (2008) *The Scientific Life: A Moral History of a Late Modern Vocation*. Chicago, IL: University of Chicago Press.

Shapiro, A. (2020) *Design, Control, Predict: Logistical Governance in the Smart City*. Minneapolis, MN: University of Minnesota Press.

Shoichet, C., Flores, R., and Nieves, R. (2022) *These Cell Phones Can't Make Calls or Access the Internet. ICE is Using Them to Track Migrants, CNN*. Available from: https://www.cnn.com/2022/06/05/us/border-migrants-cell-phones-cec/index.html (Accessed: 9 April 2024).

Singh, R. and Guzmán, R.L. (2022) 'Prologue', in R. Singh, R.L. Guzmán, and P. Davison (eds) *Parables of AI in/from the Majority World*. New York: Data & Society Research Institute, pp 1–15.

Stark, L. (2023) 'Artificial Intelligence and the Conjectural Sciences', *BJHS Themes*, 1–15.

Stark, L. and Hutson, J. (2022) 'Physiognomic Artificial Intelligence', *Fordham Intellectual Property, Media & Entertainment Law Journal*, 32(4): 922–978.

Stilgoe, J. (2023) *What Drum Machines Can Teach Us About Artificial Intelligence, Aeon*. Available from: https://aeon.co/essays/what-drum-machines-can-teach-us-about-artificial-intelligence (Accessed: 12 March 2024).

Thompson, E.P. (1967) 'Time, Work-Discipline, and Industrial Capitalism', *Past and Present*, 38: 56–97.

Williams, A. (2023) *Surveillance Nation: The Real Cost of Amazon's Customer Obsession, Distributed AI Research Institute*. Available from: https://videos.trom.tf/w/dqiwjCySFk9FeoiGw6GJzU (Accessed: 10 April 2024).

Index

References to figures appear in *italic* type. References to endnotes
show both the page number and the note number (58n14).

Printed and bound by CPI Group (UK) Ltd, Croydon, CR0 4YY

07/07/2026

14916220-0003